Bell and Whistles

More Speculative Realism

Bell and Whistles

More Speculative Realism

Graham Harman

Winchester, UK
Washington, USA

First published by Zero Books, 2013
Zero Books is an imprint of John Hunt Publishing Ltd., Laurel House, Station Approach,
Alresford, Hants, SO24 9JH, UK
office1@jhpbooks.net
www.johnhuntpublishing.com
www.zero-books.net

For distributor details and how to order please visit the 'Ordering' section on our website.

Text copyright: Graham Harman 2013

ISBN: 978 1 78279 038 9

A CIP catalogue record for this book is available from the British Library.

Design: Stuart Davies

Printed and bound by CPI Group (UK) Ltd, Croydon, CR0 4YY

We operate a distinctive and ethical publishing philosophy in all
areas of our business, from our global network of authors to
production and worldwide distribution.

CONTENTS

Preface

Late in 2010, Zero Books published my collection *Towards Speculative Realism: Essays and Lectures*.[1] The chapters in that work consisted of material arranged chronologically from 1997 through 2009: from my latter years as a doctoral student at DePaul University through the earliest years of the Speculative Realism movement. *Towards Speculative Realism* proved to be a greater success than anticipated. Whatever inherent philosophical interest the book may have had was clearly augmented by its *Bildungsroman* structure, with the struggling graduate student of the early chapters replaced by an internationally visible author in the final pages of just a dozen years later. The chronological feel of the book was further enhanced by an italicized introductory paragraph at the head of each chapter, often referring to failures or human dramas of the sort that most authors suppress during triumphant recaps of their careers. This structure was meant to encourage the legions of depressed and demoralized graduate students in our midst, as if to say: "your current invisibility, your enfeebled productivity, your rejection by conferences and publishers, and your struggles with tyrannical advisors could well mean nothing a decade from now." Judging from the often poignant quality of reader mail since 2010, the book has had considerable benefit in healing the wounded.

Bells and Whistles is a book in much the same vein as *Towards Speculative Realism*, but it covers the period from 2010 through early 2013: a time of public battles rather than obscure student futility. By the last two chapters of the book, we were entering a period of significant change. The Speculative Realism and Object-Oriented Ontology movements had fragmented, their original members busied with mutual articulation of disagreements. Tristan Garcia, a young French thinker of great promise (see Chapter 10 below), was on the verge of appearing in English and shaking up the battle lines among Speculative Realists. Other significant changes in my work environment were afoot.

Since the chapters in this book were written as standalone pieces and not as organic parts of an integrated book, the reader can expect a certain amount of repetition: Heidegger's tool-analysis continues to appear frequently, as does Husserl's transformation of Twardowski, the distinction between "undermining" and "overmining" assaults on objects, and lingering complaints about Bruno Latour's 1999 assertion that entities are no more than whatever they transform, modify, perturb, or create. Quentin Meillassoux is a frequent target of disagreement; Levi Bryant a bit less so. And since many of the chapters of *Bells and Whistles* were either oral presentations, interviews, or blog posts, an informal style permeates the whole. In my 2011 book on Meillassoux, I proclaimed the benefits of studying a living philosopher in the midst of public emergence.[2] *Bells and Whistles*, much like *Towards Speculative Realism*, allows readers an inside look at my own recent career, with continued glimpses of success, failure, and conflict. In this way they will be able to see each of these chapters as embedded in a wider human life, and perhaps will come to appreciate the obstacles in their own lives as elements of an intellectual drama rather than as biographical distractions from antiseptic theory.

With age it becomes much easier to write (though somewhat harder to find the time to read). The calming rhythm of routine, the natural decrease of youthful anxiety, the waning nervous energies of middle age with their newfound indifference to imaginary threats, the fresh flood of invitations for lectures and written work, concrete professional incentives, a more settled personal and financial life, and growing self-confidence in one's own intellectual footing– all these factors can add up to a staggering productivity. The Derridas and the Žižeks with their multiple books per year are not thirty times more energetic than you are, but simply three times as old and ten times more welcomed. Avoid affectation, scorn the transient pressures of your era, stay close to what you care about most, and someday you may find your thoughts ripe and in demand.

In order to pre-empt any trollish queries as to which of these chapters are the bells and which are the whistles, we can agree to use the term "whistle" for the brief Chapters 1, 5, 9, and 14: a blog post, an unpublished fragment, and a pair of interviews. The other chapters are lectures or essays of a more traditional sort, and here the metaphor of "bells" can be replaced at will by the figures of pipe organs, tom-toms, bassoons, or any heavier instrument of the reader's choosing.

1. Brief SR/OOO Tutorial (2010)[3]

Along with traditional print media, the blogosphere has become increasingly important in the dissemination of Speculative Realism and Object-Oriented Ontology. If the online philosophy world often resembles the Wild West with all its shootouts, marshals, and cattle rustlers, it also offers frontier justice and scattered nuggets of gold. In January 2009 I launched my own blog, "Object-Oriented Philosophy," under the nickname Doctor Zamalek (a reference to the Cairo island neighborhood where I live). After a brief shutdown in March 2009, the blog was relaunched at a slightly different address.[4] The following post, from July 23, 2010, is the one most often cited in standard academic publications, and thus it seems useful to place it in the present collection. Its topic is the difference between two philosophical movements with which I am closely involved: Speculative Realism [SR] and Object-Oriented Ontology [OOO], which partially overlap but do not coincide. Due to increased public confusion of the two phrases by the summer of 2010, it seemed wise to state their differences explicitly. I have made no attempt to smooth out the typically improvised and shoot-from-the-hip style so common to the blogosphere, but I have made some minor changes in punctuation and paragraphing, while adding a few explanatory footnotes concerning related material.

An increased amount of email has started to pour in over the past few weeks, much of it quite gratifying. One thing I've noticed from a lot of the mail is that SR and OOO have started to bleed together in many people's minds. For example, [Quentin] Meillassoux is sometimes being referred to as an "object-oriented philosopher," which isn't true. So, for those who are new to this part of the blogosphere, here is a renewed summary of what the different terms mean.

"Speculative Realism"

This term was a Ray Brassier coinage. It was his idea, in 2006, to assemble the two of us along with Meillassoux and Iain Hamilton Grant for a single event, which then happened in April 2007.[5]

Initially we had a very hard time coming up with a good term for that group of people. At first I was prepared to cave in and let it be called "speculative materialism," Meillassoux's term for his own philosophy, even though I am an *anti*-materialist myself. But at some point a few months before the event, Brassier came up with "speculative realism" instead, and I loved it. He and Meillassoux both eventually soured on the term, for different reasons, but I'm still quite fond of it.

"Speculative realism" is an extremely broad term. All it takes to be a speculative realist is to be opposed to "correlationism," Meillassoux's term for the sort of philosophy (still dominant today) that bases all philosophy on the mutual interplay of human and world.

Please note that the speculative realists *don't even agree about what is wrong with correlationism*! For example, what Meillassoux hates about correlationism is its commitment to "finitude," the notion that absolute knowledge of any sort is impossible. But he *doesn't mind* the correlationist view that "we can't think an X outside of thought without thinking it, and thereby we cannot escape the circle of thought." (He simply wants to radicalize this predicament and extract absolute knowledge from it. Meillassoux *is not* a traditional realist; German Idealism is his true homeland, just as it is for Žižek and to a slightly lesser extent Badiou.)[6]

By contrast, I see the problem with correlationism as the exact opposite. I don't mind the finitude part, which seems inevitable to me. What I hate instead is the idea that the correlational circle ("can't think an unthought X without turning it into an X that is thought") is valid. I see it as flimsy.

In any case, speculative realism survives as a useful umbrella term for many different kinds of new realist-feeling philosophies that work in a generally continental idiom, but the original group of four will have no repeat meetings. The intellectual divergences are now simply too great.

"Object-Oriented Philosophy"

This term is my own coinage, dating to 1999. (If anyone used the phrase earlier than that, I was unaware of it but would be happy to credit them if it is brought to my attention.)

None of the other original speculative realists do object-oriented philosophy. In fact, they are all rather *anti*-object, each in his own way. (Even Grant, whose position is much closer to mine than those of Brassier or Meillassoux, does not think the world is made up primarily of individual entities. These arise for him through obstructions or retardations of a more primal global energy.)

Object-oriented philosophy can be viewed as a subspecies of speculative realism (even though it's seven or eight years older). To be a speculative realist, all you have to do is reject correlationism for whatever reason you please. To be an object-oriented philosopher, what you need to do is hold that individual entities of various different scales are the ultimate stuff of the cosmos. Note that this includes both [Bruno] Latour and [Alfred North] Whitehead as well; I define the term in such a way that Latour's actors and Whitehead's actual entities (and possibly even societies) also count as "objects" in the widest sense.

But then I criticize both Whitehead and Latour for reducing these individual entities to their relations.[7] And I continue to maintain this point despite an increasing number of claims that Whitehead and Latour do no such thing. I'm willing to keep fighting this battle, but I really don't see how the point can be avoided. Both of them not only reduce entities to their relations, but do so quite proudly and explicitly. Indeed, both of them consider this to be among their own major innovations.

In short, object-oriented philosophy involves a fairly general set of minimal standards that leaves a good bit of room for personal variation. You can agree with Whitehead rather than me and still be an object-oriented philosopher. My own version has not just one, but *two* basic principles:

1. Individual entities of various different scales (not just tiny quarks and electrons) are the ultimate stuff of the cosmos.
2. These entities are never exhausted by any of their relations or even by their sum of all possible relations. Objects withdraw from relation.

The rest of my philosophy follows from these two points, I think. As for the related term "Object-Oriented Ontology," this was coined by Levi Bryant in July 2009. Levi, Ian Bogost, and I, along with Steven Shaviro and Barbara Stafford (more as friendly in-house critics, the latter two) kicked off the OOO movement in April 2010 at Georgia Tech in Atlanta.

I hope that helps clarify the difference between the two terms.

Yes, I consider myself both a speculative realist and an object-oriented philosopher, just as I consider myself both a U.S. citizen and a permanent resident of Iowa. OOO can be seen as one of the "states" within a larger Speculative Realist union.

2. The Return to Metaphysics (2011)

This lecture was delivered on April 9, 2011, as the keynote address at the 16ᵗʰ Annual Philosophy Conference at Villanova University, located in the Philadelphia suburbs. The lecture criticizes several "reductionist" and "immanentist" approaches to objects (which elsewhere I have called "undermining" and "overmining" approaches). On the basis of this critique, my fourfold model of objects is then sketched, a few months prior to the English publication of The Quadruple Object *by Zero Books. On a personal level, it was a moment when things felt like they had come full circle. In October 1990 I had come to Villanova for the first time, as a newbie graduate student attending my first academic conference: the annual meeting of the Society for Phenomenology and Existential Philosophy (SPEP). I remember feeling not quite at home at that 1990 conference, where I had functioned mainly as a chauffeur for faculty and older graduate students in a Penn State University car. Just over two decades later, on my first visit to Villanova ever since, I found myself giving a keynote address directly across the street from where the 1990 conference was held. The intervening twenty years of difficult work flashed constantly through my mind. After the conference I drove to my undergraduate alma mater, St. John's College in Annapolis, also for the first time in twenty years. In the library at St. John's, I found my old crudely penciled marginal notes (from 1988) in the English translation of Heidegger's* Vom Wesen des Grundes, *and was both charmed and exasperated by the primitive efforts of those notes. None of my old teachers at St. John's recognized me on sight, and some of them clearly did not remember me even following detailed reminiscence in their presence. The effect of this amnesia on their part was strangely liberating, rather than insulting. Why be bothered any longer by things that no one else can even remember? I should also add that the passport officials at the Philadelphia Airport were extremely rude upon my arrival. After more than a decade spent in Egypt, I was finally being treated as a foreigner in my own country, despite the laughable*

"Welcome home!" that followed their absurdly sarcastic interrogation and snarky luggage inspection. The GPS device in my rental car then led me in circles through the Philadelphia suburbs for two hours before finally taking me to my city center hotel.

Almost from the beginning, "metaphysics" has been an unpopular word in continental philosophy, with a small number of prominent exceptions: the positive use of the term by Emmanuel Levinas comes to mind.[8] But the case of Levinas is the exception that proves the rule, since he is often denounced for the apparent theological bias of this turn to metaphysics. The related term "ontology" has been treated more favorably, as for instance in the early Heidegger.[9] Yet even "ontology" is not one of the major slogans of post-Heideggerian continental thought. In fact, the two terms date from very different historical periods. The word "metaphysics" is famously ascribed to the editors of Aristotle, with *ta meta ta physika* (the writings "after" the *Physics*) reinterpreted to mean what lies *beyond* the physical. The origin of "ontology" is less widely known among those well-versed in philosophy, but it seems to have arisen as late as the seventeenth century. But there is little use getting wrapped up in etymologies, since the two terms have continually been redefined by thinkers with differing agendas. Nonetheless, in connection with recent continental thought, the meaning of the term "metaphysics" is relatively clear. Let me start by describing some of the ways in which "metaphysics" is used in our circles, and also by briefly stating how I would support or reject the various usages.

First, there is the critique of metaphysics in the sense of ontotheology, as defined by Heidegger and pursued by Derrida.[10] The complaint here is that metaphysics has always been a metaphysics of *presence*. One specific kind of being has been elevated to the level of being itself, set down as the foundation for all others. Whether it be water, air, atoms, or the boundless *apeiron* among the pre-Socratics, the Platonic forms, the primary substances of Aristotle, the God of medieval philosophy, matter for Giordano Bruno, the Cartesian substances, Leibnizian monads, the impressions and ideas of empiricism, the Kantian categories, the idealist subject or spirit that followed Kant, Schopenhauer's will, Nietzschean power, Husserlian phenomena, or Bergson's *élan vital*, some entity internal to the world has been taken for the root of the world itself. That privileged entity is always described as directly present to the mind, or at least to the world. This means that in principle it can be described by a known list of features, and all else that exists is explained in terms of this chosen God of each philosophy. In my view, the critique of ontotheology is the greatest forward step of twentieth century philosophy, and should be endorsed and even expanded. I will do so tonight, while also defending my own concept of *objects* as remaining untouched by the critique, and even as the best extension of it.

Second, the critique of metaphysics as onto-theology is often mistaken for a critique of *realism*. This is somewhat paradoxical. After all, the critique of onto-theology requires that something always *escapes* presence in every new model of the most important entity in the world, taken as the root of all others. For example, the engine of Heidegger's philosophy is his critique of the presence of Husserl's phenomena in consciousness.[11] The excess of reality beyond phenomenal presence seems to entail realism, the doctrine of a mind-independent reality. But even Heidegger has often been interpreted as an anti-realist (as in Lee Braver's otherwise excellent book[12]), and Derrida is *in fact* an anti-realist despite an increasingly vocal minority who claim he was a realist all along.[13] As I see it, this claim immediately fails when we look at a piece such as the "White Mythology" essay.[14] Here Derrida jumps from Aristotle's insistence that there must be a univocal *being* of a thing behind any multiplicity of descriptions of it, to the less justified assertion that Aristotle thinks there must be univocal *meanings* for terms, though this is surely refuted in advance by Aristotle's appreciative treatment of poets and metaphor.[15] To be a realist does not entail that one is also an onto-theologian. On the contrary, I hold that *only* realism, *only* a model of individuals with real constitutions outside our interactions with them, can defeat onto-theology. The return to metaphysics that I advocate is a return to realism, which as far as I know was never defended by name in continental circles until the early twenty-first century.[16] Yet we should not advocate a return to onto-theology, which Heidegger is right in viewing as disastrous. While onto-theology and realism are often viewed as twin brothers, I see them as mortal enemies. Only a reality irreducible to any encounter with it, whether by humans or by anything else, provides guarantees against the onto-theology that claims to deliver the root of the universe in person.

On a related note, the word "metaphysics" is sometimes uttered with contempt by those who work in a more scientistic tradition. For them, metaphysics means mere conceptual speculation done in an armchair, devoid of contact with empirical fact. To give an example, my own distinction between the real and the sensual, meaning the real and the phenomenal, has sometimes been dismissed as a "metaphysical" distinction in this pejorative sense.[17] For this sort of philosophy (which is devoted less to science per se than to epistemology) we confront a set of images, and what we need are *criteria* to distinguish good scientific images from bad manifest "folk" images. Yet this standpoint is already not just metaphysics, but a metaphysics in the bad sense of ontotheology. It holds that everything can, in principle, be made adequately present to us (even if in practice this can only take the form of an asymptotic approach), and that it is merely a question of using epistemologically valid techniques to sift the wheat from the chaff. Rather than water, atoms, Platonic forms, God, or Cartesian substance, we now have *good images* as the root of the world.

But as long as we are stuck on the level of images, even if we decree some of them to be scientific and others as worthy only of the naive folk, then this is not genuine realism. It may see itself as the most hardheaded realism imaginable, since it fights so ardently to destroy all illusions and bring us face-to-face with an utterly minimal remnant of the real. Yet this real is no reality at all, since it is completely isomorphic with the possible knowledge we might have of it. Realism is not realism if the reality it describes can be translated without energy loss into human knowledge, or indeed into any sort of relation at all. That will be another of my claims tonight, a thesis I have often defended in print but which still has numerous skeptics: *realism requires an absolute gulf between reality and relation.* No human epistemologist can drain reality to the dregs, and for the very same reason no inanimate thing can exhaust any other simply by bumping into it. Realism does not just mean a world of images verified by science. Nor does it mean merely that some dark, haunting residue lies beyond the grasp of humans alone. Instead, it also means that even inanimate causation does not exhaust the entities that are engaged in it. Human knowledge deals with simulacra or phantoms, and so does human practical action, but so do billiard balls when they smack each other and roll across a green felt phantom. We can develop this theory further in an armchair, a library, a waterbed, or a casino, but waiting for empirical results will never settle the issue, since all such results will be grasped through a prior metaphysical decision: an onto-theological model in which good images are the epistemological foundation of the real.

So far, the return to metaphysics argued for here is a return to realism and a continued rejection of ontotheology, including the rejection of any scientistic claim that the natural sciences should have a monopoly on themes such as space and time, substance, the mind, and the contours of the universe.[18] But we should also consider the rejection of metaphysics found in the writings of

Quentin Meillassoux, one of the freshest and most challenging new philosophers today. In *After Finitude*,[19] Meillassoux champions what he calls speculative thought, while rejecting what he calls metaphysics. As he sees it, metaphysics means a commitment to the existence of a necessary entity, and since he finds himself obliged to champion radical contingency, no necessary entity is possible. While this may sound like a repeat of the critique of ontotheology, it is actually a more specific claim. First of all, Meillassoux holds that metaphysics culminates in the ontological proof of the existence of God, in which God is not only taken to be the root of the cosmos, but is also thought to be necessary by virtue of a "prodigious predicate." As Meillassoux puts it: "Although one may maintain that a perfect being should possess existence, one cannot maintain that our conceiving it as perfect entails its existence."[20] In his view, to reject the existence of a necessary entity goes hand-in-hand with rejecting the principle of sufficient reason. For if everything has a reason, and that reason has a reason, and so on, this series must end in some final reason that is also the reason for itself, under pain of an infinite regress. Meillassoux's claim is that to believe in a reason for anything at all automatically requires belief in a necessary being somewhere down the line. And since this violates the radical contingency that he thinks he has demonstrated, the principle of sufficient reason must be rejected. Things happen for no reason at all. (Or rather, the laws of nature can change for no reason at all; within the scope of these laws, things do have a reason for happening in lawlike fashion, but this is an inconsistency that need not concern us here.)[21] My response to these claims is mixed. On the one hand, I would agree with Meillassoux that a "prodigious predicate" is a bad idea, and would also agree that no necessary being exists (among other things, an entity with no reason other than itself would fail the onto-theology test). But it does not follow that we should abandon the principle of sufficient reason. Quite the contrary, this principle is so important that we must uphold it even under the pain of infinite regress.

For our purposes, then, the return to metaphysics means as follows. We must defend the realist conception of a reality never present to human thought or to anything else. We must also defend the principle of sufficient reason. At the same time, we should preserve the critique of all forms of ontotheology (*including* scientism) and more generally the idea that thought is ever able to grasp its topic directly. But to defend sufficient reason *and* to oppose the ontotheology of an ultimate layer of reality does in fact require that we defend an infinite regress of beings: or "objects," as I call them.

1. The Real is Never Present

First, we should consider what the critique of onto-theology does and does not attack. Despite the occurrence of the word "theology" in this phrase, not all theology is necessarily ontotheological. The belief in a single almighty entity that created the sky and the earth, that judges human souls and assigns them to heaven or hell, and sends a redeemer for the sins of our species may be attacked for other reasons, but it does not *automatically* fail the ontotheology test. It could well be that the universe was created by God, or by a physical singularity at the Big Bang, just as everything real could well be made of subatomic particles. The critique of ontotheology simply means a critique of *presence*, and theories of presence can take one of two basic forms. As a first option, they can hold that true reality exists at the foundation of the cosmos, so that everything else is merely an aggregate built out of this foundation. We can call such theories *reductionist*, since they hold that what really exists is some deep fundamental layer compared with which the higher layers have no reality in their own right. As a second option, they might hold that there is nothing deep and hidden behind what is present to the mind, and that reality can be found entirely in its presence to us, or perhaps in its presence to other entities in the form of networks or events. We can call these theories *immanentist*, since they deny that anything exists besides what is already immanent in the mind, or at least what is immanent in an extended sense of the world that includes inanimate entities.

Let's start with philosophies of immanence. The one that bothers Heidegger is his own starting point, phenomenology. For Husserl, not only must we *start* with what is present to consciousness, we also must finish there, since he holds that even if some things may be hidden from a human observer right now, it is nonsensical to claim that anything might exist that would *in principle* be inaccessible to consciousness. Even if some things are not present to anyone at all in this very moment, all we need to do is find some way to turn our attention to them, and they will become present. For Husserl, this is the being of things: their actual or potential occurrence in the phenomenal sphere. For Heidegger from 1919 onward, this is no longer the case.[22] In his famous tool-analysis, which is probably the greatest moment of twentieth century philosophy, Heidegger contends that our primary way of dealing with things is *absence*. While our conscious efforts are always focused on some explicit purpose, they rely on a hidden infrastructure of hammers, streets, grammatical structures, atmospheric oxygen, and bodily organs— none of them visible as long as they are functioning smoothly, but all of them silently relied upon in our explicit dealings. Since I have given lengthy interpretations of this tool-being on many occasions, there is no point doing it again here.[23] Instead, let's focus on just a few key points. First, my use of oxygen or a hammer do not exhaust these entities. I can be surprised at any moment by the failure of such objects, which indicates that there is a hidden surplus in them that is never mastered by my conscious awareness. This is sometimes explained by saying that for Heidegger all theory is grounded in praxis, in a practical background where things are simply used rather than observed. But this reading does not go deep enough. Notice that praxis is just as stupid as theory in its encounter with things in the world. If my conscious awareness of a hacksaw or chair does not exhaust their being, then neither does my use of these items.

What the tool-analysis shows is that the world is filled with objects as inscrutable and dangerous as hidden bombs that could explode at any moment without our expecting it. The tool-analysis is not just about tools functioning smoothly and vanishing into efficient praxis; it is also about the possibility of *broken* tools, and these are possible only because tools are more than our current use of them. Objects are not immanent, because they lie deeper than any theory and any praxis to an equal degree. Whereas some people say that theory is just a more lucid form of praxis, we could also say that praxis is just a cloudier form of theory. Objects elude the grasp of both. Objects are essentially non-relational. They do come into relations, of course, but insofar as these relations never fully grasp or deploy their terms, how relations are possible is a problem still to be solved, given the inherent autonomy or hidden reserve in the heart of all things. And finally, these objects are deeper than their relations with *each other* as well. Our failure to grasp the depths of the hammer is not due to some special feature of human or animal psychology, but comes from the simple fact that no entity is capable of fully registering the depths of another. The chair does not use all features of the floor any more than you or I do, or any more than a falling piece of paper does. Relationality is the realm of translation and caricature, not of direct contact with the real. This means that the real is never immanent in relations, and this presents a challenge to numerous philosophies of immanence: whether it be immanence in consciousness as found in phenomenology, or the immanence of actual entities in their prehensions as for Whitehead, or the immanence of actors in what they modify, transform, perturb, or create in the admirable philosophy of Bruno Latour.[24]

We might also consider one of the classic philosophies of immanence: the theory of images in Bergson's *Matter and Memory*.[25] Here, there is supposed to be no difference between things in the real world and things as they appear to us. Everything is an image. This is Bergson's frontal assault on the Kantian doctrine of a separation between things-in-themselves and appearances. If there is any difference between things and our knowledge of them, it cannot be a distortion but only a *subtraction* in which we limit the features of objects according to the biases of our practical action.[26] In a different but related vein we have a recent admirer of Bergson, Quentin Meillassoux, for whom the thing-in-itself counts as "in-itself" only because it is capable of outlasting the human lifespan. For as long as humans still exist and think, there is no difference between the in-itself and what we are in principle able to know of it. The primary qualities of things are not hidden in some shadowy underworld, but are precisely those qualities that can be *mathematized*, which etymologically means those qualities that can be learned.

In such cases, the results of Heidegger's tool-analysis might not seem to be as powerful an objection, since they could make counter-arguments against Heidegger. From a Bergsonian point of view, it could be said that the hammer itself is an image, and the hammers of praxis and of perception are simply impoverished versions of this richer hammer-image that remains immanent nonetheless. Meanwhile, from Meillassoux's outpost, at least two objections are possible. First, he would say that when the hammer breaks it still breaks *for us*, so that we remain inside the correlational circle and no deduction of anything outside the circle is possible. Second, Meillassoux might say it is false that the hammer found in use could be dependent on some causal interaction between me and a real hammer lying out of view; given the absolute contingency of everything, there should be no such connection between any two realities at all. Experience passes from my efficient use of the hammer to the sudden shock of a broken hammer, not as the causal result of a hidden surplus but as a purely contingent event or bolt from the blue not rooted in any hidden reality. As for the scientistic position, it might claim (and does claim, in the so-called theory of "real patterns,"[27] or of functionalism more generally) that what we call a hammer exists only at a level of observational scale pertinent to humans, and that there is nothing called hammers in the world itself. The hammer is a kind of epistemological froth in consciousness, not a hidden real causal agent. With each of these objections, the primacy of images appears to be sustained.

But here I would like to introduce a new principle: let's call it the Feeble Image Principle. Consider the following case. Let's imagine that at some point biology thinks it has obtained perfect knowledge of frogs. Every known genetic, anatomical, and behavorial feature of frogs has been exhaustively catalogued. A few years later, as the earth is increasingly bombarded with radiation, frogs become extinct. Our knowledge of these extinct creatures lives on in immaculate biological texts that tell us everything that can be known; yet even if we master these texts, frogs do not return from the dead. Now imagine that some melancholic and daydreaming child mourns the extinction of frogs, and consoles herself by dreaming up the concept of a radiation-resistant frog. This creature seems so real to the child that she imagines she hears them resounding in ponds by night, immune to further danger from the sun. But only a highly imaginative child, or a psychotic, would think that to imagine these super-frogs is the same thing as to create them.

The point is this: images are feeble with respect to what they indicate, and being a kind of image, knowledge is also feeble. Between a frog itself and the knowledge of a frog there is a vast difference in kind, no matter how excellent that knowledge may be. It will be objected that no one but full-blown Berkeleyan idealists deny this trivial truth, and hence that it is not worth mentioning. I answer as follows. If we all agree that the image of a frog does not live, breathe, eat, and reproduce like a real frog, then philosophy *needs to account for the difference between them*. And any philosophy that believes in the direct translation between thing and image automatically fails to do so. A philosophy can insist as much as it likes that there must be "structural" features in common between frogs and knowledge of frogs if knowledge is to be possible. But then it faces the burden of accounting for the *non*-structural element in real frogs that *is not* carried over into the structure of knowledge. It will not suffice to appeal vaguely to some theory of matter in which the structure appears, because then we are back in the most traditional sort of metaphysics: that of frog-forms inhering in shapeless physical matter. In this way correlationism collapses into idealism, but so does that sort of realism which thinks not only that a real world exists, but that the mind is able to copy it. In short, we *must choose* between outright solipsism and a metaphysics in which the gap between object and image is absolute, in such manner that translation or distortion from one to the other must always occur. To conclude, philosophy cannot be concerned with immanence, but only with counter-immanence: not with a wisdom about knowledge, but with a *love* of wisdom about what lies *outside* knowledge. The real cannot be made present without ceasing to be real.

We now turn to reduction. In immanence, we saw that everything was supposed to lie at the surface of the world, whether in consciousness or in a world of concrete events. This failed (as seen from Heidegger's tool-analysis) for the simple reason that immanence is unable to explain change; if everything simply is what it is here and now without anything lying hidden in it, there is no reason why everything would not simply just go on being what it already is. Immanence is a mockery of depth. By contrast, reduction is a mockery of the surface. What seems to us to be real is said to be just a byproduct of something deeper and more real that underlies our gullible illusions. The ultimate form of this doctrine says that "All is One," and that specific entities are somehow produced at the level of mind or of functional uses, with the human psyche arbitrarily breaking distinct chunks of reality away from a unified being (as seen in radical form in the early Levinas).[28] But these days, few people will go quite that far. The more popular version of this theory says that there is a "pre-individual"[29] that is neither entirely one nor already articulated into individual units. The problem with this theory is that it tries to have things both ways. If we view it as one, then there is no reason why it should ever turn into multiple things: not even for a conscious subject, since this subject should merely be part of the One in such a theory. But if we view the pre-individual as many, then it is already broken into pieces that we cannot avoid calling "objects," and we have already seen that objects must be non-relational if they are to have any autonomous identity at all.

So, let's look instead at a more plausible version of reduction, in which objects such as hammers would be no more than the components of which they are built. We have already opposed the attempt to reduce hammers upward into immanence, whether for the mind or for anything else. The hammer cannot be reducible to its effects in this moment, because it is capable of many different effects, and is equally capable of surprising us by failing utterly in its function and thereby giving a glimpse into its unexpressed underside. We must also now oppose the attempt to reduce it downward– to make the hammer vanish into its component pieces rather than into its external effects. And the reason for opposing it is similar to the previous one. Just as the hammer can have multiple shifting effects while not being a different hammer (which would merely fall into the immanentist trap of being unable to explain change) so too the hammer can have multiple changing components within certain limits without losing its identity. To remove a few atoms from the hammer, or even a few thousand atoms, does not change it into something different. The idea that nothing exists but trillions of tiny particles, and that the so-called hammer emerges only through its functional hammer-effects, fails to notice that the hammer is never immanent in any given effect. Nor does the hammer need to be having *any hammer-effects at all* in this moment: a hammer sitting on a shelf is still a hammer even when no one is looking at it or using it.

In sum, objects are not immanent in their current presence to the mind nor immanent in the world, and objects are also not reducible to that of which they are made. Like any object, the hammer occupies a mezzanine level midway between the domestic relations of its pieces and the foreign relations of its outward effects. In traditional terminology, the hammer is not matter or effect, but a form. And it is not an accidental form viewed by some observer, but a *substantial* form that is what it is quite apart from its current relations, and indeed apart from any relations at all. This form cannot possibly be reduced to anything smaller, because it has autonomy from its smaller components just as it does from the larger assemblages in which it becomes involved.

2. Quadruple Objects

It is one of the interesting features of Husserl's phenomenology that while he is certainly an idealist, he *feels* like a realist anyway. Let's begin by emphasizing that despite all the talk of consciousness always already being outside itself by intending various things, Husserl's idealism should be beyond dispute. The starting point of phenomenology is to bracket all theories of the natural world and retreat to a description of how things appear in the phenomenal arena. This is not merely a starting point like that of Descartes, in which we retreat to the isolated *cogito* only to prove the independence of other things a bit later. Instead, it marks a phenomenal status of beings from which they never escape. Any notion of things-in-themselves lying forever beyond the grasp of intentionality is treated by Husserl as nonsense, and even the inanimate physical causation described by science is not deduced by starting from the phenomenal sphere, but ends up entirely dissolved into that sphere. Nonetheless, Husserl *feels* like a realist in a way that is never true for thinkers of the high period of German Idealism. His works are filled with the dense carnal textures of chairs, mailboxes, blackbirds, friends named Hans, and battles of centaurs, all of them resisting reduction to one particular set of qualities or profiles. This side of Husserl is pressed even further by gifted successors such as Maurice Merleau-Ponty, for whom entities are so fleshy and inscrutable that they might appear to push us beyond idealism. But this is somewhat misleading. For just as Husserl is an outright idealist, Merleau-Ponty can at best be described as a correlationist: even when he says in *The Visible and the Invisible* that the world looks at me just as I look at it,[30] it always remains a question of human and world standing face-to-face, not of different parts of the world looking at each other. Merleau-Ponty is no realist. Yet both Merleau-Ponty and Husserl display a fascination and respect for individual things that one never finds in Fichte or Hegel. The reason for this, as I see it, has to do with Husserl's model of intentional *objects*.

The concept of intentionality was famously revived in the 1870's by Husserl's teacher Franz Brentano, who remains a good candidate for the most underrated thinker in the history of philosophy. While quite a number of people seem to agree with this assessment, some of them push things too far by implying that Husserl's and even Heidegger's glory was *stolen* from Brentano. This is an exaggeration. Husserl does make significant innovations beyond Brentano, though they are also the source of the idealist vices that were later reversed by Heidegger himself. When Brentano speaks of intentionality in *Psychology from the*

Empirical Standpoint,[31] he does not say that intentionality aims at an object "outside the mind," though this is often wrongly said. Brentano is quite clear that intentionality means "immanent objectivity," in the sense of objects *internal to the mind*. As for what lies outside this immanent sphere, Brentano is somewhat unclear. The issue was taken up seriously by a number of his students, including his brilliant Polish disciple Kasimir Twardowski in his 1894 habilitation thesis *On the Content and Object of Presentations*,[32] available in English for over thirty years. What Twardowski proposed there was a doubling between an "object" outside the mind and a "content" inside the mind.

Though Twardowski was seven years younger than Husserl, the elder colleague was still finding his voice at this stage, and reacted strongly towards Twardowski's thesis, ultimately rejecting it. Husserl opposed his double model of object and content, as exemplified in his famous claim that the real Berlin in the world and the Berlin of which I speak are one and the same, not doubled.[33] Though this may sound like realism, it is a strictly anti-realist thesis, since Husserl rejects Twardowski's notion of an object "deeper" than the contents of knowledge. But surprisingly enough, rather than rejecting Twardowski's model, Husserl simply *imploded* the object/content distinction into the phenomenal sphere. This is both simpler and more interesting than it sounds. One of the most fascinating moments in the *Logical Investigations* is when Husserl critiques Brentano for holding that our experience is of *contents*; instead, Husserl insists, our experience is of *object-giving acts*. The difference is crucial. To use Husserl's own example, my friend Hans is always seen in a specific physical posture, in a certain mood, from a certain angle and distance in a specific degree of sunlight or lamplight. Hans as a *content* of experience is always slightly different each time I see him, since these contents are completely determinate as to detail, and contain the exact position of his arms and legs and every hair on his head. Viewed in this way,

Hans is a "bundle of qualities" in the empiricist sense. In what is perhaps his greatest philosophical innovation, Husserl is probably the first philosopher ever to say that there is a distinction between object and content within the realm of experience itself. Whereas Twardowski imagined a unified object outside the mind and a highly specific presentational content inside the mind, Husserl transfers this dangerous crevice into the heart of lived experience. As my friend Hans changes his posture and lights a cigarette, as emotions shift wildly across his tormented face, I never imagine that there are simply different "bundles of qualities" in each case– multiple deviant Hans-entities linked loosely by some sort of "family resemblance," as the empiricist tradition would have it. Instead, there is a unified Hans within my experience, and his specific qualities merely fluctuate along his surface: they are *Abschattungen* or *adumbrations*, to use Husserl's famous term. The project of phenomenology becomes the attempt to grasp the object in its unity beneath the many fluctuating surfaces, by means of the famous method of eidetic reduction.

The strange thing is that, even if this was Husserl's greatest innovation in philosophy, he never quite realized that he had made it. The reason for this is simple. If we credit Husserl with being the first to describe a rift between object and content *within appearance*, he could never admit this, since he would never candidly admit that his philosophy is confined to appearance in the first place. The reality of intentional objects is the only reality he knows; the realism/idealism dispute remains a pseudo-problem in Husserl's eyes, even though he fully embraces the idealist option. Husserl would no doubt respond to my claims with the usual point of phenomenologists even today: that consciousness is always already outside itself in intending the various objects, and so forth. Indeed, he might even call himself a bit of a realist, because he cannot conceive of a sense of the real more robust than that of intentional objects. But he is wrong about this, for reasons already noted by Heidegger. Namely, my friend Hans as an object of experience may endure through numerous fluctuations of surface qualities, just as the same is true of a hammer present-at-hand in my grasp. In both of these cases, Hans and the hammer do not hide or withdraw in the least. They are there before me in all their plenitude. Even if they show different faces at different times, I do not need to see all or even most of those faces, since Hans and the hammer are there for me in their entirety as soon as I *recognize* them as Hans or a hammer. Intentional objects are fully present from the start, and are simply encrusted with different profiles at different moments. Moreover, there is always the chance that I could be hallucinating. Both Hans and the hammer might have no reality at all once I fall asleep, die, or turn my head in a different direction. There is no autonomy whatsoever for Husserl's intentional objects, and this is what makes him an idealist, even though he is the first object-oriented idealist in the history of philosophy.

We could call the phenomenal arena an intentional realm made up of intentional objects. But there are problems with this word "intentional." In the first place, it is dry and technical, and thus stylistically boring when repeated too often. In the second place, as already mentioned, there is the potential confusion that many people use the phrase "intentional objects" to refer to those objects lying *outside* the mind, which is the exact opposite of what Brentano and Husserl meant. This is why I coined the terms "sensual realm" and "sensual object" to replace Husserl's own terminology.[34] These words are also meant to indicate the way in which such objects belong to a carnal lived experience characterized by the feel of silk, the burning taste of pepper, and the mournful experience of burning churches and violins played at midnight— as described in the beautiful phenomenological prose of Levinas, Merleau-Ponty, and more recently Alphonso Lingis (who may actually be the finest literary stylist in the entire phenomenological tradition).

In any case, we find that this sensual realm cut off from the real world is split into objects and contents. Let's call them objects and qualities instead. Both Hans and the violin emit different qualities in different instants without our ever believing that they are no longer the same. The sensual object is always there in full from the start, encrusted with numerous shifting qualities from moment to moment. But this fluctuation of qualities in fleetingly durable objects is precisely what we mean by *time*, and here I mean not the time on a clock or calendar, but the lived time of conscious experience. The root of time can actually be found in Husserl's rift between sensual objects and sensual qualities. Note that this is not the same thing as Heidegger's concept of time, in which the depth of the world is fully involved as one of the three temporal moments. The time that emerges from Husserl's model of sensual objects is a twofold drama along the surface of experience.

But we now return to the question of *real* objects. From Heidegger's tool-analysis we learned that something exceeds its presence to us. Despite the beautiful interpretations by Levinas in *Existence and Existents*,[35] this something cannot be a rumbling whole or inarticulate lump until consciousness comes along, since otherwise there would not be different breakdowns and surprises from different tools. Instead, the underworld of reality is already articulated into highly specific districts, shattered in advance into a multitude of discrete objects. And as Leibniz already observed in the *Monadology*,[36] different objects must have different qualities or they would all be alike. In this way, we also find a rift between objects and qualities *outside* experience analogous to the one described by Husserl as internal to experience. For this tension between a real object and its real qualities, the tradition has always used the name *essence*, and there should be no problem using it here. The suspicion in recent decades towards the word "essence" is really directed against the *permanence* of essence, and against the *knowability* of these permanent essences: as if statements could be made about the timeless essential properties of Arabs, women, homosexuals, criminal skull types in phrenology, and so forth. But that is not at all what is meant by the notion of essence here. For our purposes, "essence" simply means that any object has real properties that are not exhausted by their current appearance in the mind or their current impact on other entities more generally. It is not stated that the essence must be permanent. And as for knowability, the sort of essence defended here is absolutely *not* knowable, thereby making it impossible to make any sweeping proclamations about the timeless essence of any individual or group. In short, the notion of essence proposed here is politically quite harmless, although it denies the postmodern dogma that our identity is simply the way we perform it in public. But this is merely a digression made necessary by the recent dark connotations of the word "essence" for many continental philosophers. Essence for object-oriented philosophy means nothing more than the tension between a real object and its real properties in a single instant, not some timeless nature that each thing must possess from the dawn of the world.

We now apparently have two tensions, the "time" that unfolds between sensual objects and their sensual qualities, and the "essence" that names the strife between real objects and the real qualities they possess whether anyone looks at them or not. According to this split, humans would seem to be trapped in a sensual dream world of the fluctuations of time, as if locked up in a gigantic novel by Proust, while somewhere beneath us there lies an elusive underworld of things-in-themselves harboring shadowy things with concealed essences that can never be known. This would appear to be the ultimate intellectual deadlock, unless we can establish some way to cross the border freely between sensual and real. And in fact, both Husserl and Heidegger already define the way in which this happens.

Let's begin with the case of Husserl. Here we should notice that there are *two* separate kinds of qualities. First we have the adumbrations: swirling accidental qualities that can be altered freely in experience or in simple thought experiment without destroying the underlying sensual object. But in this method of eidetic variation, as it is known, the thing still has truly pivotal qualities that cannot be subtracted without annihilating the object. Hans and the hammer both have certain bedrock features even *within* our experience— features that, as soon as they vanish, we no longer feel ourselves to be dealing with Hans or the hammer but with something else altogether. These are essential qualities of the object, but since we have already used the term "essence" for something different, let's call them the "eidetic" qualities of the thing instead. Husserl thinks this *eidos* can be known through direct intuition, but we need not follow him here; even Husserl admits that they can only be known through the mind, never through the senses, thereby endorsing a rift between them. The problem is that Husserl thinks eidetic qualities can be made directly present to the mind just as adumbrations are directly present to the senses, and this is where we must disagree. For it is impossible ever to put our fingers on exactly what makes Hans be *Hans*, or what makes the hammer be *this hammer*. Even with our minds we can only approach it indirectly. If Husserl thinks there is a gap between categorial and sensuous intuition, both forms of direct intuition lie on the side of sensual qualities, not real ones, which can only ever be alluded to. Here we have a surprising tension between sensual objects and *real* qualities, which we have called "eidos" to go along with "time" and "essence," two other tensions we encountered. We find that sensual objects also have *real* qualities, because while Hans and the hammer as *sensual objects* are fully present to us from the start, this is not true of their *eidetic or real qualities*, which always evade direct comprehension.

This leaves us with just one blank tension on the map: that

between *real* objects and *sensual* qualities. Physics and chemistry have long known how useful blank spaces in models can be, and the same is true here. For the gap between real objects and sensual qualities is precisely what is described by Heidegger's tool-analysis. The present-at-hand qualities of the hammer turn out to emanate from a unified hammer-object that is never present, but which operates inscrutably in the depths, beyond all hope of contact. And while this tension between depth and surface is what Heidegger calls "time," it actually deserves the name of "space" instead, so that *Being and Space* would have been a more accurate title for his greatest book. Traditionally, the debate over space has been between space viewed as an absolute container (as for Clarke) and space viewed as a system of relations (as for Leibniz).[37] But notice that space is better viewed as a system of relation *and* non-relation. Things can make contact in space, but they do not thereby fuse together through this contact into a single molten lump. Instead, they retain a certain distance from us and from each other as well. John Locke already observed that true space is not present in experience, since everything in experience touches us directly without distance through the mere fact of its being experienced; instead, space must be *inferred* without ever being directly accessible to us, just as babies must gradually learn that the moon cannot be touched with the hand simply because it can be immediately taken in with the eyes.

In this way, starting from the model of two kinds of objects and two kinds of qualities, we reach a quadruple model of time, space, essence, and eidos. Normally time and space are treated as peerless queens of philosophical speculation, and even Kant sets them apart from all of the categories. But by redefining both time and space as generated by rifts between objects and qualities, we find that essence and eidos deserve to be mentioned in the same breath as these two more famous philosophical continua. And just as time, space, essence, and eidos represent tensions between things, there are specific ways in which each of these tensions can be broken. In *The Quadruple Object* (available in English a few months from now), I called them confrontation, allure, causation, and theory. And in fact there are more than just these four tensions, since along with object-quality pairings there are also those of quality-quality and object-object, which in the book I define as "emanations" and "junctions," each displaying its own distinct features. Thus there are ten possible links in the world rather than four. At any rate, it is useful to have a model of this sort, so as to be able to play with permutations and use gaps in the model to predict the existence of still unknown phenomena, just as the periodic table of elements accomplished in chemistry, and just as the standard model has done for physics since the early 1970's. Metaphysics and physics are not in the relation of master and slave, or mistress and handmaid— but more like that of jazz saxophonist and jazz drummer, playing the same clubs on overlapping nights but having mostly *indirect* lessons to learn from one another. Metaphysics is not the handmaid of theology, or science, or Leftism; it is not the handmaid of geometry, phenomenology, or epistemology. It is handmaid of nothing and tyrant of nothing.

3. The Four Most Typical Objections to OOO (2011)

This was a keynote lecture delivered at "OOOIII: The Third Object-Oriented Ontology Symposium," held at the New School in New York on September 15, 2011. In this brief lecture, held before a large and mostly receptive crowd, I tried to answer some of the recurrent objections to the object-oriented approach. It was one of multiple lectures I gave in New York that month, but the only one that took the form of a written text. For some reason I had remembered the Villanova lecture as polemical and this one as mild. But while rereading these texts for publication, I see that the reverse is the case.

Just six weeks ago, I made a blog post entitled "possibly the 4 most typical objections to OOO."[38] Near the end of that post, I wrote as follows: "Maybe a good crisp essay, dealing exclusively with these four objections, would be worth squeezing in during the next few months." This morning's talk is designed as a good crisp *lecture* on those same four complaints about object-oriented ontology. To me they seem indicative of what the *Zeitgeist* wants in philosophy (at least in continental circles), and equally indicative of what OOO is determined to resist and reverse. The four almost automatically predictable wishes of today's continental philosophy *avant-garde* are as follows: 1. Absolute knowledge, to be obtained either through science or speculative philosophy; 2. Materialism; 3. Hyper-dynamism; 4. Holism. Like a cruel and devious genie released from an old Egyptian lamp, I not only deny these four wishes, but will offer a ruthless twenty-minute assault on all of them.

We can rephrase each of these four wishes in terms of complaints about the principles of object-oriented ontology, as our critics have already done for us. The first wish, for humans to be able to have absolute knowledge, means that humans must somehow make *direct* contact with reality. This can be expanded into the wider proposition that *all* entities must make direct contact with each other. In other words, the wish goes something like this: "Human knowledge of reality seems to be possible. *Therefore*, such knowledge must be a *direct* contact with reality. More generally, mutual contact and influence between objects seems to be possible. *Therefore*, it must be *direct* contact."

The basic principle of object-oriented philosophy, derived in my own case from Heidegger's tool-analysis,[39] is that objects withdraw from all theoretical and practical contact alike. The science of geology does not exhaust the being of rocks, which always have a surplus of reality deeper than our most complete *knowledge* of rocks— but our practical *use* of rocks at construction sites and in street brawls also does not exhaust them. Yet this is not the result of some sad limitation on human or animal consciousness. Instead, rocks themselves are not fully deployed or exhausted by *any* of their actions or relations. When a rock smashes a window, these two entities come into contact in only the most minimal fashion, never sounding one another's depths. Direct contact is actually quite impossible. Not only must knowledge be indirect, but causal relations can only be indirect as well. While this may sound strange, it is really just an expanded version of Socrates' defense of *philosophia* (or "love of wisdom") against Meno, who claims with the Sophists that either we already know something or we can never know it at all— a claim that might be expanded once more to include the causal realm by saying: "either objects make complete contact or they make no contact at all." Instead, the true situation is that we only make *indirect* contact, and I would say the same thing about causal interaction even in the most stupefied reaches of the inanimate realm.

Complaints about this model have come primarily from two groups. The first is the relatively new "scientistic epistemology" wing of continental philosophy. Such people complain about bringing inanimate objects into the picture, and constantly assert (not prove, but merely assert) that there must be a difference *in kind* between conscious awareness and sheer causal contact. Here I respond with two points. First, given that such people want to be committed naturalists, it is unclear why they have so much faith in an "ontological catastrophe" that could suddenly have created a mighty power in one kind of natural entity, humans (or perhaps animals more generally), that would allow these creatures to rise above the world and somehow see it "as" it is. Second, I answer that direct knowledge of anything is impossible because to be truly direct, knowledge of a thing would have to be that thing itself. As long as my knowledge of a tree does not actually become a tree, taking root in the soil and bearing fruit, then knowledge about it is obviously not a direct translation without energy loss, because there remains a difference between the tree and knowledge of it. It hardly matters that no one short of Berkeley explicitly *says* that trees and images of trees are the same thing. Rather, the point is that belief in direct knowledge of the world *entails* such a view, and this view is absurd. Finally, such people reply with the crude practical insinuation that if direct knowledge is impossible, then "anything goes," so that all human claims about anything are equally valid. To this I answer that human enlightenment is not primarily a matter of beating up gullible people. If we have succeeded in destroying alchemy and astrology as purported sciences, this has not been on the basis of *direct* knowledge of chemicals and celestial bodies; such knowledge is impossible due to the withdrawal or surplus of entities behind any of their configurations in the mind, and thus no theory of science based on the direct presence of objects or their forms can be correct. The love of science (which I share myself) should not be distorted into a love of the direct presence of reality before the mind– which is not at all necessary for the practice of science, but *is* necessary for the sort of aggressive scientism that glories in knocking others down by adopting a position of self-appointed direct epistemological insight. This widespread but regrettable human impulse is purely *unphilo-sophical*, since it believes it already possesses the key to wisdom and therefore does not need to love it or long for it.

There is also a second group, more sympathetic to OOO, which gets the point about the withdrawal of objects but simply thinks that we push things a bit too far. These people ask: "Why does direct contact with entities have to be impossible? Why can't contact be direct but *partial*?" The motive here seems to be that such people find indirect or vicarious causation too spooky or mystical. But their alternative theory of indirect-but-partial contact cannot work. For one thing, it simply moves the problem elsewhere. Once it is conceded that I am unable to make direct contact with a tree, it is no more possible to make direct contact with its leaves or branches than with the tree as a whole. Nor is it possible to make contact with, let's say, 78% of the tree that is accessible to humans while only dogs and mosquitoes can sense the other 22%. Objects are unities, as Aristotle already knew, and as Leibniz pressed to its logical conclusion. *Direct* contact could only be all or nothing, never partial. What happens instead is indirect contact, whether in the case of human knowledge or sheer inanimate collision.

The second cherished wish of philosophy in our time is materialism. While there are numerous theories that call themselves materialist, what too many of them share is a love of reductionism. The whole point of materialism is its so-called "parsimony," the ability to get rid of the clutter of the world by imposing capital punishment on numerous supposed pseudo-objects. In recent publications I have counter-argued with the following point: if you think individual entities or objects are not worthy of being the fundamental topic of philosophy, there are only two basic ways this case can be made. One is by saying that objects are too shallow to be the truth. "Horses, flowers, and depressive moods are simply constructions of folk ontology, and science will eventually show us that these can be eliminated in favor of tinier particles or deeper mathematical structures or some quasi-unified lump of which reality is genuinely made. The mid-sized horses, flowers, and moods of which you speak are merely vulgar fictions of everyday life, unworthy of philosophical credence." I have called such theories "undermining" philosophies, since they view the mission of philosophy as the demolition of any gullible belief in everyday things. In fact, such people are often a bit shocked and horrified by OOO, because they think we are relapsing into abject naiveté. But a case should be made for naiveté after so many tiresome centuries in which *critique* was always the major professional tool of the intellectual, with the haughty contrarian and the sneer-from-nowhere internet troll being the ultimate decadent outcome of this now exhausted era of critical thinking. The problem with these undermining philosophies is that they are guilty of a dogmatic reductionism, failing to see that mid-sized levels of the world can have their own autonomy, are often partially independent of their tinier constituent pieces, and can affect their own pieces or even generate new ones.

There is also the flip side of materialism, which is generally of a cultural rather than physical sort, and works in reverse. Rather than saying that objects are too shallow to be the truth, they say that objects are *too deep*. "The notion of a unified object enduring through change is a useless fiction. Objects only appear in some social or linguistic context. They are purely relational. Or perhaps they are 'events' that happen very concretely in one time and one place only. There are simply relations, effects, and events, not underlying hidden objects." Beginning in 2009 at the second Speculative Realism workshop in Bristol,[40] I started to call such theories "overmining" philosophies by analogy with the undermining ones. For they reject all talk of hidden depths beneath the human realm, or at least beneath the immanent realm of relational interactions between all beings, such as found in the not-so-anthropocentric philosophies of Whitehead and to some extent Latour. The problem with overmining theories is that they are unable to explain change. If everything that exists were exhaustively deployed in its current state, without surplus or reserve outside their current effects, there would be no reason for anything ever to shift from its current state.

It should also be noted that undermining and overmining theories usually work as a team, reinforcing one another's excesses or covering each other's backs. This began with Parmenides, in his duality between the undermining oneness of Being and the overmining flux of *doxa* or opinion, but is also reflected in contemporary theories such as that of James Ladyman and Don Ross,[41] heroes of continental scientism, who undermine all individual things with deep mathematical structure and *also* claim that real geological and chemical entities exist as so-called "real patterns," though *only* for human observers— a theory they incoherently claim is still a form of realism, even though their real individuals exist only in correlation with human observers. This is one good example of undermining and overmining at the same time. Another is when so-called "process philosophy" (which holds that objects aren't real because they are just encrustations of a deeper flux) is carelessly mixed with philosophies of relation (which hold that objects aren't real because there are only concrete effects or events, and deeper objects beneath these effects are a useless fiction). This double gesture occurs quite often these days, such as when attempts are made to lump Bergson and Deleuze (who are underminers of objects) together with Whitehead and Latour (who are overminers). Put them together and both backs are covered, just as in Ladyman/Ross materialism: or as Iago puts it, we have "the beast with two backs."[42] But less flippantly, the defect shared by all these theories is their suspicion of the midsized and the middle-range: unified objects that withdraw from all human access and all environmental effects, knowable only indirectly, and located midway between their tinier components and their external impact on the world.

The third wish of our times is to emphasize flux over stasis. This can be viewed most plausibly as a reaction against eternal identities and their apparently oppressive role in stereotyping and pigeonholing humans into various unappealing social roles. By contrast, flux seems to liberate us from the tyranny of nature. Since I have just discussed the metaphysical "undermining" role of flux, let me address here instead the unstated political worry about OOO: the worry that a return to realism means a return to rigid identities after so much work has been done to historicize such identities and reframe them as results of a "performative" process that gives us the freedom to shape our own identities. My first point in response is that too often, realism has been confused with what Heidegger and Derrida call "ontotheology." The critique of ontotheology is a critique of the idea that any specific *kind* of being can stand in for being itself, or that any *particular* being can be an exemplary incarnation of its kind, as for example: "all Dasein is Dasein, but the Ancient Greeks and recent Germans are Dasein to an *exceptional* degree." But OOO completely forbids such privileged incarnations of entities. The fact that my personality and talents have some definite character that exceeds the coding of society and even exceeds my own self-understanding does not mean, first, that anyone has sufficient knowledge of these matters to be able to legislate how I must act on the basis of this character and these talents. Nor does it mean, second, that they cannot change over time. OOO's position on relatively enduring objects is that they can last through multiple events and relations, not that they have a *permanent* or even *eternal* identity over time. Yet after several decades of vigilantly insisting upon such reservations, for perfectly understandable reasons, in our time we have become too theoretically paranoid about speaking of anything essential behind the play of appearances. For this reason, it is important that we work to rehabilitate the word "essence" as a good classical term for the reality of things deeper than their current effects, without retaining the traditional sense of essence as a permanent and eternal destiny for individuals and peoples upon which direct political obligations and roles can be inscribed.

The fourth wish is that relations rather than self-contained objects should be primary. The metaphysical side of this wish has already been dealt with in my remarks against overmining. To over-emphasize relations at the expense of the *relata* that compose them is to make all change in the world impossible. Aristotle already saw this lucidly in his famous critique of the Megarians in Chapter 3 of *Metaphysics* Book Theta.[43] The Megarians claimed that no one is a house-builder unless they happen to be building a house right now, to which we can object that a sleeping house-builder is still more of a house-builder than some wide-awake bumbler who has no idea how to build. This serves as the launching pad for Aristotle's theory of potentiality, which I refuse on other grounds though some versions of OOO (such as Levi Bryant's[44]) are more sympathetic to it.

But yet again, there is the political side of the question. The political motive for the focus on relations seems to be that any focus on individuals seems to imply excessive emphasis on *human* individuals at the expense of larger *human* collectives. And moreover, relations sound like a dynamic source of social change, whereas individuals sound frozen and static, which might in turn sound like a recipe for social stasis rather than dynamism. To this, I answer that OOO recognizes objects of all different sizes. When we speak of individuals, this does not just mean individual human voters or consumers free to act as they please in the liberal marketplace. The bodily organs of humans are also objects, and political parties, unions, and perhaps even "the global oppressed" *could* be collective objects (not all conceivable objects are real, of course, but that is a different question). Furthermore, the term "objects" is not opposed to "subjects," so it is not such a bad fate to be an object. To be an object does not mean to be physical material without dignity, but simply to be a unified entity irreducible to its component pieces or to its effects on the surrounding environment.

As for the idea that relations are innately politically dynamic, we can make the same response here as we did to the metaphysical point about relations: if people, classes, or societies are nothing but their relations, then they are already everything they ever can be, and have neither the reason nor the ability to change. The true principle of dynamism, in human society as well as inanimate nature, is that real objects always exceed their contexts, always withdraw from our control, and are always filled with surplus and surprise. I cannot close this talk by saying "Objects of the world, unite!" because that is precisely what we do not want and cannot achieve. Instead, I would say: "Objects of the world, withdraw!" But even this would be pointless, because it is a *fait accompli*. This is what objects have always done, and it is our task simply to make better use of this fact in our theories and our actions.

4. Object-Oriented Philosophy
vs. Radical Empiricism (2011)

In 2010 I had struck up a friendship with the Warsaw-based editors of the journal Kronos— *Marcin Rychter in particular.* Kronos *has trans-lated numerous philosophical essays into Polish for the first time, including quite a number of Speculative Realist writings. Rychter commissioned the present essay especially for* Kronos,[45] *with the understanding that it would be published in English at a later date. He specifically requested an essay on William James's most metaphysical work,* Essays in Radical Empiricism. *While on vacation in Malta in early November 2011, I reread that book and wrote the following article. Although several readers have kindly compared my writing style with that of James, and despite my deep admiration for the witty and eloquent American thinker, there turns out to be considerable incompat-ibility in metaphysical principles between Radical Empiricism and OOO, as this essay explains. In conclusion, I propose an object-oriented method to counter the overly celebrated pragmatic one: unless an object has reality over and above its consequences for thought, then it is not a real object.*

William James (1842-1910) is well established as one of the leading philosophers to emerge from United States, often accom-panied on such lists by Charles Sanders Peirce, John Dewey, and Willard van Orman Quine. As a writer James is clearly superior to these others, and is perhaps rivaled in this respect only by George Santayana. It hardly needs to be mentioned that literary talent ran deep in the James family: William's father Henry Sr. was a prominent theological writer, younger brother Henry Jr. is one of the nation's most celebrated novelists, and younger sister Alice has gained increased attention as a diarist. Though born into wealth and privilege, William James struggled with nervous disorders and procrastinating tendencies. His personality began to stabilize following marriage at the age of thirty-six, yet he was still unable to produce his first book (the landmark *Principles of Psychology*) until he was nearly fifty years old, in an era when fifty verged on old age. Perhaps the chief intellectual merit of James was his complete lack of provincialism. In a period when intellectual life was dominated by Europe, the New York-born James was unnaturally alert to the ideas of such continental European figures as Bergson, Fechner, and Lotze. But far from being merely receptive, James gave Europe much in return: his innovative psychological theories had an impact on such giants as Bergson, Freud, and Husserl. James's strictly philosophical impact on Europe was less pronounced, but has increased in recent years, with Bruno Latour and the younger Deleuzians frequently expressing their admiration for James.[46] While *Pragmatism*[47] is the most widely read of James's philosophy books, his most significant metaphysical work is surely *Essays in Radical Empiricism*,[48] which only appeared posthumously in 1912 despite having been assembled by James himself five years earlier. At the request of the editors of *Kronos*, I have written this essay to summarize my views on James's radical empiricism and contrast his metaphysical views with my own.

1. The Object-Oriented Position

Many different roads can lead to the same city. But since I reached the object-oriented standpoint by way of phenomenology, it seems best to retrace that road here. The following summary will be brief, partly because I have told the story many times before, and partly because our real interest in this article is William James.

The charismatic ex-priest Franz Brentano opened a new chapter in philosophy in 1874, with his revival of the medieval term "intentionality." Unlike physical reality, all mental reality is aimed at some object: to see is to see something; to judge is to judge some object; to love is to love someone or something. But the things at which mental life aims, according to Brentano, are not real objects outside the mind. Instead, intentionality refers to "immanent objectivity," or objects that exist only inside the mind. Clearly I can love centaurs and hate unicorns, make damning judgments about square circles, and hallucinate golden mountains, even though none of these objects exist outside my act of intending them. As for the status of real objects in the real world, Brentano initially left this issue unclarified. It was his great Polish student, Kazimierz Twardowski, who insisted that the problem be addressed by distinguishing between an *object* lying outside the mind and a *content* inside the mind. This was done in Twardowski's brilliant 1894 habilitation thesis, *On the Content and Object of Presentations*.[49]

As I see it, Twardowski's argument was the most immediate impetus for Husserl's development of phenomenology. From scattered references in publications and letters, we can see that Husserl reacted with a mixture of fascination, rejection, and competitiveness in response to the arguments of Twardowski, who was seven years younger but in some ways philosophically more ripe. Ultimately, Husserl's response was to reject the notion of a separate reality outside the mind. The candle I see and the real candle burning in the room are one and the same thing, not two. The mind is capable of direct contact with reality, and there is no reality unobservable in principle by the mind. Eventually this pushed Husserl towards his later full-blown idealism, in which the world contains no dark residue unexhausted by the mind.

While I find Husserl's idealist turn lamentable, it did yield excellent fruits. Precisely because Husserl limited himself so strictly to a sphere of phenomenal appearance, he devoted himself all the more to uncovering more relief and drama than had ever been found within the mental sphere previously. The empiricist view of mental content had always treated it as made up of discrete qualities packed together in a bundle; an object of the senses was nothing more than all of its content combined. Husserl's ingenuity on this point consisted in not simply rejecting Twardowski's distinction between an object outside the mind and a content inside it, but in collapsing *both* terms into the immanent sphere of the mind. No longer was mental life a matter of definite content alone; instead, it was a duel between object and content *within* the mind. This point is so important that it actually forms the backbone of phenomenology. The experienced world is made up of numerous objects at any given moment– apples, sailboats, animals, castles, icebergs, and moons. Each of these objects is seen very concretely in each moment, from a definite angle and distance and under certain specific lighting conditions. All the details of my experience of these objects belong to the *content* of my experience. Yet there is more to any experience than its explicit content. I can take an apple and turn it in my hands, take a bite from it, and then throw it off into the distance. As I do each of these things the "content" of my experience changes, yet it always remains the same *object* in my experience; never do I think the apple is a different apple just because it shows new facets and features from one moment to the next. An intentional object is not a bundle of qualities, as the British Empiricists and even Brentano still held. Instead, the truth is the reverse: the qualities we experience are always qualities *of the object*. Phenomenological analysis does nothing more than sift through the various changing adumbrations of intentional objects in an attempt to reach the qualities that *cannot* be removed from the object, under penalty of its no longer being the same object. Twardowski's duel between object and content survives at the heart of Husserl's system, but is now completely imploded into the immanent zone of intentional consciousness. By refusing to identify an object of experience with its bundle of qualities here and now, Husserl takes a fresh step in the history of philosophy, one that as far as I know was never approached by any earlier thinker. Those who continue to hammer Husserl for his idealism overlook the additional fact that Husserlian idealism is nonetheless object-oriented to the core.

One of the motives for Husserl's idealism was the need to preserve a space for philosophy where the advancing natural sciences could not intrude. In order to prevent philosophy from decaying into a branch of experimental psychology, it was important for Husserl to bracket off the naturalistic conception of the world and treat the mental sphere as fundamental. All scientific theory must be grounded in what lies present before the mind, the ultimate yardstick of reality. This was the point where young Martin Heidegger intervened, rebelling against Husserl just as Husserl rebelled against Brentano and Twardowski. Heidegger noted that for the most part we *do not* deal with objects as directly present to us. Quite the contrary: in our dealings with hammers, buses, chairs, floors, bodily organs, oxygen, grammar, and everything else, we usually do not notice these objects at all unless they malfunction or go missing. Usually, objects are hidden. They "withdraw" (*sich entziehen*), to use Heidegger's term. Whereas objects in consciousness are present-at-hand, the status of most objects at most times is to be ready-to-hand, withdrawn into the shadows of the world.

And here we encounter a point that is crucial for object-oriented philosophy. Husserl's objects never "hide." The blackbirds and sailboats of Husserl's world are not absent from view, but are always immediately there as soon as I acknowledge them. It is true that these objects are always seen only in a certain partial profile at any given moment, but these profiles do not conceal the bus or sailboat as a whole– instead, these profiles are "bonus information" encrusted onto the surface of objects already grasped as the target of our intentional acts. By contrast, Heidegger is interested in the *real* bus or sailboat deeper than any perception of them. These real objects are the ones that withdraw. The bus as an intentional object can be observed but cannot take me anywhere; the bus as a real object can take me anywhere I please, if only it is properly fuelled.

The usual reading of Heidegger is that he teaches us how all explicit theory is grounded in implicit background practices. Before I can develop a geological theory, I must have a pre-theoretical experience of mountains and earthquakes. But this is a misreading, even if one that Heidegger sometimes falls into himself. It is true that all of our best geological theories do not exhaust the dark background of mountains, crevices, fault-blocks, canyons, and sedimentary layers that they attempt to describe. Yet it is equally true that our *practical* dealings with these things do not do exhaust them to their depths, meaning that praxis is ultimately no deeper than theory. We must also push our reading one step further and see that objects fail to exhaust *each other* as well, despite their probable lack of consciousness. A glacier that grinds through rock and soil does not make contact with all the features of these entities any more than our geological theories or practical use of the soil is able to do. In this way real objects turn out to be radically *non-relational*. Admittedly, Heidegger seems to say just the opposite. He tries to convince us that whereas the objects of the mental sphere seem to be discrete individuals cut off from one another, the real objects of the pre-conscious landscape are entirely defined by their mutual interrelations. But if this were true then objects could never break, nor could they surprise us in any way at all. Objects would be entirely defined by their relations with all other objects *hic et nunc*, and there would be no reason for anything ever to change from its current state. There must be some residue or surplus held in reserve behind any current state of the world, in order for the world to able to sway and shift, or to change its state in any manner. But if objects are radically non-relational, we also need to know how they are able to relate at all, a question also posed by the occasionalist philosophers of medieval and modern times.

The basic model of object-oriented philosophy is thus seen to be as follows. The world is crossed by two dualisms. First there is the difference between the real and the intentional (or the "sensual," as I prefer to call it), and second there is the difference between objects and qualities. Husserl shows us that the sensual realm is torn apart between objects and their constantly shifting contents, while it is Leibniz rather than Heidegger who notes that real objects must all have distinct qualities or they would all be interchangeable, as clearly they are not. (At times Heidegger tends to treat the world itself as a single initial lump that is broken into pieces only derivatively.) But these ideas are familiar to anyone who has read my books, and those books can easily be read by anyone who is not yet familiar with the ideas.[50] Our real interest here is the radical empiricism of William James, which in many respects could hardly seem more different from object-oriented philosophy.

2. Radical Empiricism

Object-oriented philosophy is based on two overlapping dualisms: object vs. quality and real vs. sensual. William James shows no awareness of the first of these dualisms, and flatly rejects the second. In a theory reminiscent of Bergson's global doctrine of "images" in the slightly earlier *Matter and Memory*, James proposes a model in which all thoughts and things occupy a single plane of reality.

The first chapter of *Essays in Radical Empiricism* is entitled "Does Consciousness Exist?" James wastes no time in giving us his answer. On the second page of the book, he frankly declares that consciousness "is the name of a nonentity, and has no right to a place among first principles."[51] (2) And further: "for twenty years past I have mistrusted 'consciousness' as an entity; for seven or eight years past I have suggested its non-existence to my students... It seems to me that the hour is ripe for it to be openly and universally discarded." (3) What James wishes to discard is not just the reification of thinking substance. Instead, he is attacking the very dualism between thoughts and things, which is precisely what object-oriented philosophy endorses in its distinction between sensual and real. "There is, I mean, no aboriginal stuff or quality of being, contrasted with that of which material objects are made, out of which our thoughts of them are made..." (3) Instead, thought must be viewed "functionally," in terms of its capacity for knowing. Instead of the dualism between real and sensual, James suggests the apparently more radical thesis that "there is only one primal stuff or material in the world, a stuff of which everything is composed, and if we call that stuff 'pure experience,' then knowing can easily be explained as a particular sort of relation towards one another into which portions of pure experience may enter." (4) The knower and the known are both parts of "pure experience," and enter into a certain relation that establishes their separate roles. In this way, philosophy can oppose the "neo-Kantism" (5) that views the world as inherently dualistic.

James credits Locke and Berkeley with introducing the term "idea" to mean both thing and thought, (10) just as Alfred North Whitehead would do again two decades later. James's "experience" can be viewed "as subjective and objective both at once." (10) Although James initially seems to be far less of an idealist than Husserl, he sounds much like Husserl opposing Twardowski when he says of physical things that "it is just *those self-same things* which his mind, as we say, perceives..." (11) The whole philosophy of perception since ancient Greece seems to amount to "the paradox that what is evidently one reality should be in two places at once, both in outer space and in a person's mind." (11) And here James makes a concession, admitting that philosophies which distinguish between thought and thing seem to be more logically consistent in addressing this paradox. Nonetheless, he shuns this easy consistency for the reason that such theories "violate the reader's sense of life, which knows no intervening mental image but seems to see the room and the book immediately just as they physically exist." (12) Just as a single point can belong to two distinct lines if it is their point of intersection, so too a room can belong to a house but also to my own biography. (12) Much like Bergson, James is deeply committed to the intuition that we have a direct and immediate contact with reality rather than a mediated representational one. We will soon see how steep a price he is willing to pay for this view.

Any experience, he tells us, "is a member of diverse processes that can be followed away from it along entirely different lines. The one self-identical thing has so many relations to the rest of experience that you can take it in disparate systems of association, and treat it as belonging with opposite contexts." (12-13) He holds to this theory even as the difficulties begin to mount. The room in my mind is easy to destroy, he concedes, while the room in the real world needs "an earthquake, or a gang of men, and in any case a certain amount of time, to destroy." (14) The room in the real world cannot be lived in without paying rent, while the room in my mind can be lived in rent-free. Oddly enough, James concludes that "so far, all seems plain sailing," (15) despite the vast differences he himself has already noted between the mental and physical room. The only complication, as he sees it, comes when we stop thinking of the mental side of perceptions and turn instead towards sheer *concepts* devoid of perceptual underpinnings. To deal with this new situation, James cites the psychologist Hugo Münsterberg in defense of a position that here resembles that of Husserl (18-19): even the centaurs and golden mountains of my thought exist not just inside me, but also outside me as objects thought about. (20) We thus arrive at what seems to be a flat ontology in which physical rooms, perceptions of rooms, and concepts of rooms are all on the same footing, all equally "outside" the mind. The reason they all seem so different to us is simply because "some couplings have the curious stubbornness, to borrow Royce's term, of fact; others show the fluidity of fancy– we let them come and go as we please." (21) A house tends to cohere with its town, owner, builder, and market price, "while to other houses, other towns, other owners, etc., it shows no tendency to cohere at all." (22) As a rule we tend to call the stubborn associations "external" realities and the loose associations "internal" ones. The absolute gap between thought and thing turns out to dissolve into a shaded continuum of greater and lesser stubbornness.

James closes the chapter by openly confronting the most obvious objection to his position, which "sounds quite crushing when one hears it first." (27) Namely, if the real burning candle and my thought of a burning candle are of the same order of being, then how can the attributes of the two be so different? The real candle illuminates the room, might set it on fire, cost perhaps three dollars at the time of purchase, and burns out after a certain number of hours. But the candle in my mind has none of these properties; in fact, it ceases to exist as soon as I fall asleep or die. James's first response is to call this objection commonsensical, and to suggest that thought and thing are not quite as different as might be suspected. (28) James does make a number of interesting points in noting that thought and thing both exist in time, both have a part-whole structure, both exist spatially, and other ontological similarities. He also makes the clever observation that if subject and object were so different, it should not be as hard as it normally is to determine what is objective and what is subjective in various situations. (29) James repeats his earlier claim that "the difference between objective and subjective... is one of relation to a context solely," (30) and again the difference turns out to hinge on degrees of relative stubbornness: "in the mind the various [pieces of extension] maintain no necessarily stubborn order relatively to each other, while in the physical world they bound each other stably, and, added together, make the great enveloping Unit which we believe in and call real Space." (30-31) Thus there is no great difference in ontological kind here, but a pragmatic difference to be determined empirically: a real house stubbornly resists my imaginative powers in a way that the mental house does not.

James makes the counterintuitive claim that *thoughts* of hot and wet things are also hot or wet, just as the things themselves are. He also goes on to cite a number of facts as if they were bolstering his case, though in fact they severely undercut it: "as the general chaos of our experience gets sifted, we find that there are some fires that will always burn sticks and always warm our bodies, and that there are some waters that will always put out fires; while there are other fires and waters that will not act at all." (32) The ones that do act are termed "energetic" by James, so that once more everything exists on a flat ontological plane of images, with some of them simply more energetic than others. Despite James's earlier complaints that addition is a better model of how the world is formed than subtraction, the way that the sphere of subjectivity is constructed seems to be through the de-energizing of energetic experiences into paler versions of themselves. "This would be the 'evolution' of the psychical from the bosom of the physical, in which the esthetic, moral and otherwise emotional experiences would represent a halfway stage." (36) But "thoughts in the concrete are made of the same stuff as things are." (37) For James, there is no distinction at all between sensual and real. The former are simply less energetic versions of the latter.

The remaining chapters in James's book serve as further development of this radical equation of thoughts and things as explained in the opening thirty pages. Like other empiricists, James favors individually experienced parts over arbitrarily constructed wholes. But what makes his empiricism "radical," he says, is that the relations between separate things must also form part of experience. The empiricism of Berkeley or Hume treats the parts of experience as intrinsically disconnected, and this merely opens the door for rationalists to introduce "trans-experiential agents of unification, substances, intellectual categories and powers, or Selves..." (43) James fights both of these tendencies by saying that a connection between things does exist, but that it is encountered directly in experience rather than lying somewhere beneath it. James the philosopher echoes James the psychologist in saying that the fundamental fact of reality is "[the] absence of break and [the] absence of continuity in that most intimate of all conjunctive relations." (50) This experience of "one's personal continuum" (50) is the origin of all concepts of continuity and sameness, and hence we can ignore those "over-subtle intellects... [who] have ended by substituting a lot of static objects of conception for the direct personal experiences." (50) Trans-experiential substances or absolutes are mere fictions compared with these more directly experienced realities.

One of the advantages of this standpoint, James holds, is that it frees us from the idea of a gap between subject and object that needs to be bridged. (52) He famously ridicules this notion as that of a *salto mortale* or perilous leap. (67) Instead, the subject-object conjunction is already given in experience. (53) If I mention Memorial Hall at Harvard, the test of whether I know what I am talking about is whether I can lead you there in person and give some information about the history and use of the building: "that percept was what I *meant*..." (56) For James as for Husserl, knowledge reaches its fulfillment in the direct presence of the thing to the mind. This fulfillment is not a perilous leap from a mind-pole to an object-pole, but unrolls gradually and continuously in time, as my vague notion of Memorial Hall is replaced by increasingly nearer approaches to it. "Knowledge of sensible realities thus comes to life inside the tissue of experience. It is *made*; and made by relations that unroll themselves in time." (57) For James this is what knowledge is, and it is foolish to expect anything more: "unions by continuous transition are the only ones we know of..." (59) The supposed mutual otherness of subject and object is a mere illusion. (60) The representations of things in our mind are not epistemological miracles occurring across a fearful gap, but simply result from a process of substitution. (61) The vast majority of our thoughts involve substitutes for nothing actual, and lead only to "wayward fancies, utopias, fictions or mistakes." (64) In these illusions we are all trapped in our individual lives, and fail to make contact with one another's thoughts, which intersect only at scattered nuclei of reality. Applying the "pragmatic method" (72) to this question, James asserts that the model of knowledge as self-transcendence would lead to no practical difference from that of the model he has just proposed, and hence the dispute is merely "a quarrel over words." (72) Under both models of knowledge, we have no choice but to move gradually and contin-uously towards immediate perceptual givenness of whatever we wish to know. In this way, "the universe continually grows in quantity by new experiences that graft themselves upon the older mass…" (90)

Reality for James is primarily a constant flux of experiences. Yet he must also admit that we do not see the world as an unrestricted flux. As he concedes, with typical Jamesian wit: "Only new-born babes, or men in semi-coma from sleep, drugs, illnesses, or blows, may be assumed to have an experience pure in the literal sense of a *that* which is not yet any definite *what* [i.e., a pure experiential flux]…" (93) These experiences exist entirely in the form of relations, which James (as opposed to F.H. Bradley) treats as *external* relations that are not inscribed in the inherent character of each experience. As we have seen, the fact that something is "conscious" does not mean that it has a different mode of reality from a physical thing, "but rather than it stands in certain determinate relations to other portions of experience extraneous to itself." (123) The pen that stores ink and can be picked up and used to write on paper is the physical pen, while the one that comes and goes in my distracted mind is the perceptual pen. Recall that these two are not different in kind for James, but simply stand in different types of relations to other experiences. But even the physical pen is not an en enduring substantial unity through time, but an instantaneous experience that has "successors." When these successors are "energetic," they also earn the right to be called stably existing physical things, (128) whereas the un-energetic successors are not the physical ones. James as a psychologist had made the same point about personal identity through time, which is not that of a durable substance, but only that of later experiences appealing to and building upon earlier ones. But only insofar as the pen is "appropriated" does it become an experience that belongs to me (130), and it is easy to see that a second mind could easily appropriate the same pen in its own way: "a second subsequent experience, collateral and contemporary with the first subsequent one, in which a similar act of appropriation should occur. The two acts would interfere neither with one another nor with the originally pure pen." (131) Whereas "the pen-experience in its original immediacy is not aware of itself [but] simply *is*," (132) the pen in consciousness simply has my being added to it. The pen itself is the one that is intrinsically neither mine nor yours. (133)

As opposed to the usual view of causality as arising from a secret depth in things, James concludes "that real effectual causation as an ultimate nature, as a 'category,' if you like, of reality, is *just what we feel it to be*, just that kind of conjunction which our own activity-series reveals." (185) It would be "healthy" if philosophy were "to leave off grubbing underground" for it (186), and simply "[refuse] to entertain the hypothesis of trans-empirical reality at all." (195) The difference between our idea of an object and the object itself is nothing other than the difference between a less vivid perception and a more vivid one to which it is capable of leading:

To call my present idea of my dog, for example, cognitive of the real dog means that, as the actual tissue of experience is constituted, the idea is capable of leading into a chain of other experiences on my part that go from next to next and terminate at last in vivid sense-perceptions of a jumping, barking, hairy body. Those *are* the real dog, the dog's full presence, for my common sense. (198)

The last four words of this passage should not be taken as any sort of qualifier. For James, it is not just common sense that equates the real dog with a direct perception of the dog. Much more than this, there is no such thing as the "real" over and above the definitive perceptual experience of a thing. As James puts it a bit later, "a conception is reckoned true by common sense when it can be made to lead to a sensation," (202) and here James treats common sense not as a crusty source of dogma in need of subversion, but as an ally that knows the truth better than overly subtle intellectuals do. Truth should never "consist in a relation between our experiences and something archetypal or trans-experiential." (204)

We should close this summary of radical empiricism with a few choice quotations from the final chapter of James's book, which happens to be written in French (it was read in that language at an international conference in Rome). While none of these passages will be surprising after what we have seen so far, they provide a nice summation of James's philosophy. "I believe that consciousness as we commonly represent it to ourselves, whether as an entity, whether as pure activity, but in any case as fluid, unextended, transparent, empty of all proper content... I believe, I say, that this consciousness is a pure chimera..."[52](222) What we call consciousness is "only a series of intermediate experiences perfectly susceptible of being described in concrete terms."[53](231) Subject and object are only *functionally* different, not two utterly opposite terms as in the traditional dualism. They are "made of the same stuff… which might be called the stuff of experience in general."[54](233)

3. Problems with Radical Empiricism

Essays in Radical Empiricism is a wonderfully imaginative book, written as beautifully as nearly everything penned by James. Here James the psychologist translates his discovery of the "stream of consciousness" into ontological terms, while James the philosophical innovator is delighted at the chance to eliminate numerous supposed pseudo-problems inherited from the past. Indeed, he seems thrilled by the possible emergence of a great new philosophical era. Yet I find a certain incoherence in radical empiricism as proposed in this book, and would like to explain why this doctrine should not be adopted. First, there are problems resulting from James's tendency to conflate the distinction between subject and object with that between thought and thing. These distinctions are by no means the same. For it would be one thing to agree with James that the dog as a perception in my mind is not different in kind from the dog as a thing in the world, so that both are nothing but "experiences" of a different degree of "energy" in each case. James has already told us that there is no dog more real than the dog that is finally encountered in direct face-to-face perception. This claim is already radical enough, in the sense that it verges on frank idealism. Yet it is quite another thing to go even further, and say that there is no difference between I who experience the dog and the series of my experiences of it. James is quick to take this second step while pretending that it is no different from the already dubious step of equating thoughts and things. As he puts it in his French lecture at the close of the book, consciousness is "only a series of intermediate experiences perfectly susceptible of being described in concrete terms."[55] (231) In short, there is no "I" doing the experiencing, but only a series of experiences joined together in an appropriative way and having a similar style. The supposed "I" is really just a bundle of experiences.

The first problem with this claim is that I am in fact something quite different from a bundle of experiences, and for at least two reasons. One is that I can also be experienced by others, even though these others have no direct access whatsoever to my series of experiences. You can read surprise in the movement of my eyebrows and the years of forced Gulag labor in the deep creases of my weather-beaten face. But in these cases the text you are reading is me, not my experiences, which are no more directly accessible to you than yours are to me in return. The other reason why I am not just a bundle of experiences is that I am no more just the things that happen to me than a stone is just the things that happen to it. Rather, certain things happen to us as entities only because we are the things that we are. New experiences are possible only because the world is more than how I have experienced it so far, but also because I am more than what the world has seen so far of me. To give a personal example, next week I will visit Morocco for the first time. Note that I am able to do so even though the history of experiences that James would identify with my "self" contains no direct perceptual experiences of Morocco of the sort that James treats as the highest form of both knowledge and reality. Yet there are elements of my self –love of travel, responsiveness to academic duty– that surged forth when summoned, and grasped the fleeting opportunity of Casablanca. The principle through which new experiences emerge does not lie solely on the side of experiences unfolding in a neutral, observer-free space. Instead, there is someone who is undergoing the experiences without being identical to them, and this someone can embrace, reject, and even change the course of whatever happens to unfold in Morocco.

James is also too fond of the *continuum* as his basic model of reality. Despite his concession that only new-born babes and men reduced to semi-coma have anything like pure experience unarticulated into parts, he does tend to view such continua as the primary sort of reality, and treats any landscape carved up into discrete entities as somehow derivative of this primal swirling flux. The problem here is that the supposed continuum of reality is contradicted by James's own views on other topics. When he wonders in his book how two minds can know the same thing, he does not solve the problem with the radical step of saying that all apparently separate minds are part of a primordial world-lump and hence not as different as might be believed. Instead, James takes it for granted that you are one knower and I am another, and even outlines a process by which each of us can appropriate the same port or landscape for ourselves as experiences of our own. And after all, James's extended polemic in the book against F.H. Bradley (omitted from the present article for reasons of space) is based on James's view that *external* relations exist— relations into which a thing can enter or not enter without affecting that thing's internal constitution. I can go to Morocco or cancel the flight one day ahead of time and still be the same person. In short, while James's love of the continuum *within* any given entity's experience might seem partly defensible, it is entirely contradicted by his assumption that there are numerous different zones of experience, numerous different knowers who are in fact distinct from one another and not part of some continuum of knowledge and experience. Many different entities have experiences of their own, and these are communicated only with difficulty. By James's own admission, there is not a single writhing world soul that simultaneously feels all the pleasures and pains of the cosmos.

But once we see that James is in favor of different zones of experience, of knowers partly cut off from another and drifting through private lives of their own, his erosion of the difference between thought and thing immediately becomes dubious. For if the relations between things are external relations, it is not clear how my direct encounter with the dog can be the same as that dog itself. For if that were the case, the dog would be utterly used up by our encounter, exhaustively deployed in being a perception for me or an experience for me here and now. Yet the dog is clearly *not* the same thing as my experience of the dog, as James fully recognizes when discussing other objects such as candles. The dog residing in my perception cannot eat or reproduce, but at best can only *seem* to do these things, without these appearances necessarily having any causal impact. James's assertion that things have causal relations whenever they *seem* to do so, rather than having subterranean causal powers that one must grub for in the depths, is clearly false. The dog in perception is always viewed from a specific angle and distance, while the dog in its own right need not present itself from any particular angle or distance. When combining these observations with the earlier point that I as a series of experiences am not the same thing as the I experienced by others, we will begin to see the impossibility of equating thoughts with things.

In this way it becomes evident that James either rejects or misses both of the cardinal principles of object-oriented philosophy. If James had lived to speak of Heidegger's tool-analysis, for instance, he would probably have said that the breaking of the hammer is something that occurs solely on a plateau where the hammer is *experienced* by someone or something. The realist pretensions of the tool-analysis would then be rejected, and replaced by a sheer phenomenalism of tool-beings. But this claim would be at odds with James's own firm belief in external relations, since the claim would be that reality is nothing more than how it happens to appear to someone or something over time. But the hammer breaks not because a previous *experience* of the hammer already had the future breakdown inscribed within its heart. Instead, what breaks is something in the hammer that was *unexperienced*— a slumbering residue of fragility that had never emerged into the world of experience until now. The hammer was always more than experience took it to be.

So much for James's unjustified rejection of the first axis between real and sensual. But he fails even to notice the second axis, as found in Husserl's ingenious distinction between objects and their contents. For even *within* the realm of experience, experiences are not equivalent to our experiences of them. Or stated differently, experienced objects are always *less* than what experience takes them to be. The donkeys and zebras trotting across the plain are seen with utter specificity of detail at every instant, yet the donkeys and zebras themselves are not that specific, since they are capable of being encountered in numerous different ways. James is too close to the traditional empiricists in viewing objects as bundles of qualities, and too close to idealism in viewing objects as nothing but their manifestations in the world. At least he avoids the traditional pitfall of idealism through his openness to making experience more global than just a matter for humans and animals.

James is often praised for the so-called "pragmatic method," just as Occam is endlessly praised for his widely misunderstood Razor. The public seems especially fond of methods which allow it to be convinced that other people are merely wasting our time with useless subtleties and non-existent entities. Along these same lines, the pragmatic method tells us that unless a proposed intellectual difference would make some actual difference in the world, then it must be nothing more than a dispute over words. But I would propose that we reverse this into an anti-pragmatic or object-oriented method, and say as follows: unless a given a distinction has ontological consequences that might have *no effects at all* in the practical world, then we are locked in a mere dispute over symptoms, and not yet dealing with the things themselves.

5. Seventy-Six Theses on Object-Oriented Philosophy (2011)

The dOCUMENTA(13) art festival was held during the summer of 2012 at its usual site in Kassel, Germany. Festival director Carolyn Christov-Bakargiev kindly invited me to join ninety-nine other contributors (some of them deceased) in a massive catalog of essays. Eventually I contributed an essay entitled "The Third Table,"[56] which criticized A.S. Eddington's famous image of the two tables (the scientific and the practical) in order to propose the existence of a third table— the one that is relevant to the arts.[57] But before hitting upon that notion, I had initially planned to contribute a piece entitled "One Hundred Theses on Object-Oriented Philosophy." After reaching the seventy-sixth thesis, I had a change of heart and started on the Eddington piece instead. What remains of the initial project is a skeletal summary of seventy-six principles of object-oriented thought in the style of Leibniz's Monadology. *In order to maintain a ruthless economy of expression, I strictly limited each point to a maximum length of thirty words. This unfinished piece was composed in late November 2011.*

1. An object is any unified entity, whether it has reality in the world or only in the mind. Philosophy must be broad enough to deal with both types of object.

2. Let the first kind be called a "real object," or a "thing." Real objects are autonomous forces in the world, existing even if all observers sleep or die.

3. Let the second kind be called a "sensual object," or an "image." Sensual objects exist only insofar as some perceiver is occupied with them. These perceivers need not be human.

4. What we encounter is not reality itself. Our perception of things and our practical handling of them does not exhaust the reality of things; each thing is an inexhaustible surplus.

5. This is not some quirk of the human or animal mind. Inanimate objects also fail to exhaust each other. Fire burning cotton or rocks smashing windows oversimplify their victims too.

6. Heidegger saw this irreducibility of objects to any form of presence to the mind or the hand. His mistake was to see this as resulting form a holistic tool-network.

7. All forms of relation are guilty of reducing things to caricatures. Perception and praxis reduce them to their existence for me, causal relations to what they are for each other.

8. For this reason, Heidegger's network of equipment is no escape from presence. He should have seen this, since his tools can break, meaning that something in them can cause surprise.

9. Aristotle also saw something of this. He tells us that his primary substances or individual things cannot be defined, since definitions are always made of universals but things are not.

10. Leibniz also deserves mention, since his windowless monads resemble our inexhaustible objects. But like Aristotle, he was too skeptical about the reality of compound objects such as corporations or machines.

11. The fact that objects withdraw from each other makes us ask how they interact at all. If fire only encounters a caricature of cotton, how does it burn that cotton?

12. The occasionalist philosophers asked the same question. Some of the Muslim theologians said that God is the only causal agent, as did Malebranche in France and others of his era.

13. We must reject this conclusion– not because God is a laughingstock among mainstream Western intellectuals, but because no specific entity at all should be given a monopoly on causal relations.

14. Hume and Kant are equally guilty of monopoly, placing all causation in the customary conjunctions of habit (Hume), or the categories of the mind (Kant). Nobody laughs, though they should.

15. The objects unexhausted by all contact are the ones we call real objects, or things. If all objects were real, there would be no relations. Not even God could help.

16. Real objects are units, but not empty poles of unity, since this would make all things identical (Leibniz). Things also have qualities that belong to them while differing from them.

17. This strife between real things and qualities is called *essence*. The word has a bad reputation due to arrogant claims that essence is knowable. But essence is never directly knowable.

18. Each thing has an essence. A chair is what it is, deeper than all the events and surface effects through which it is manifest. To say otherwise makes change impossible.

19. If there were nothing but real objects and real qualities, there would be no experience and no causal relations at all. Everything would withdraw into private seclusion, devoid of contact.

20. The world of experience has been described by phenomenology as the "intentional" realm. But this term is often used confusingly in opposite ways, and is also boring and sterile.

21. We will speak instead of "sensual objects" and "sensual qualities." A mailbox, zebra, or cylinder can be seen from numerous angles and distances while still remaining the same object.

22. Unlike real objects and qualities, sensual objects and qualities do not withdraw from access. Experience is full of them. We are sincerely occupied with diamonds, radio towers, and Spanish guitars.

23. The Polish philosopher Kazimierz Twardowski distinguished between *objects* outside experience and *content* inside experience. But Husserl imploded both object and content into experience, making their duel internal to consciousness.

24. The downside of phenomenology is its idealism, but the beauty of the movement is its awareness that experience is made of sensual objects in tension with their sensual qualities.

25. This tension is what we mean by the experience of *time*. Sunlight moves across the beach, and the boy and girl grow old. Waves augment or erode the beach.

26. We experience time because sensual objects remain relatively stable from moment to moment. Differing sensual qualities flicker across their surfaces, preceding them rather than made from bundles of them.

27. But the sensual object also has qualities that do not flicker and vary as sensual qualities do. The sensual mailbox, zebra, and cylinder have certain invariant qualities for experience.

28. The process of discovering these invariant qualities is what Husserl calls "eidetic reduction." Thus we can use the term *eidos* for the tension between sensual objects and their real qualities.

29. These real qualities of sensual objects can never be directly encountered, just as the real qualities of real objects ("essence") can never come to view. We know them indirectly, allusively.

30. Phenomenology overlooks this point, since it is too committed to the direct presence of all reality to consciousness. Heidegger freed phenomenology from this dogma of direct contact with the real.

31. We have not yet spoken of the fourth and final tension, between real objects and their sensual qualities. But this is the easiest of all, since Heidegger discussed it clearly.

32. The hammer in its action, or the covered rail platform protecting us from the rain, are deeper than any theoretical or practical access to them. They are real, not sensual.

33. When the hammer breaks, shatters, or malfunctions, sensual qualities are reassigned from the sensual hammer to an unknown yet real hammer, deeper than the one we thought we knew.

34. We were in contact with the sensual hammer, but the real hammer lies at a distance. This tension between the real hammer and its sensual qualities can be called *space*.

35. Clarke and Leibniz (1715-1716) argued over whether space is an empty container for entities or is produced by relations between them. Both were incorrect: space is relational *and* non-relational.

36. Distant stars are not directly before us, but a number of light years away. Yet they are close to us as something we know about, and as possible destinations.

37. Space is the tension between the accessibility of things at any distance, and the deeper core of their reality that can never be approached or exhausted.

38. We now summarize all four tensions once more, to keep them firmly before the mind in the discussion that follows. They are among the keys to object-oriented philosophy.

39. Time is the fissure between sensual objects and their swirling and vacillating sensual qualities.

40. Space is the duel between these sensual qualities and the mysterious real objects that signal from somewhere beneath them, often in cases of surprise and disruption.

41. Essence is the strife between the concealed real objects and the concealed real qualities that make them what they are. This tension lacks any foothold in experience, and happens elsewhere.

42. Eidos is the gulf between the sensual objects of experience and the real qualities that make such objects what they are, beyond all vacillating flux of surface qualities.

43. Instead of the constant pairing of time and space as peerless queens, we add their neglected sisters to a new quadruple dynasty of time, space, essence, and eidos.

44. These are the four tensions between the two kinds of objects and two kinds of qualities. But we might also ask about objects meeting objects and qualities paired with qualities.

45. Qualities are always attached to objects, radiating from them as from a living heart. For this reason, we give the name "radiations" to the way in which qualities belong together.

46. When sensual qualities radiate from sensual objects, we will speak of *emanation*. The orange is not a bundle of flavors, textures, and aromas. Instead, these qualities emanate from the orange.

47. As for the numerous real qualities that belong to the orange, we will speak of *contraction*, since the multiple real qualities of an object are initially compressed together, not articulated.

48. And insofar as both real and sensual qualities belong to the same sensual orange, we speak of *duplicity*. The object conceals its true features behind a carnival of swirling qualities.

49. We have spoken of "tensions" in the case of objects and qualities, and "radiations" as the way that qualities come together. Between objects and objects we will speak of "junctions."

50. The relation between real objects is one of *withdrawal* or mutual seclusion. Real objects make no contact, and require some sort of indirect or vicarious link.

51. The relation between a real object and a sensual object is one of *involvement*, as when a real observer is concerned with a sensual temple, orange, or blackbird.

52. For a real object, numerous sensual objects are simultaneously present. I live not amidst a single orange, but groves of orange trees. These multiple sensual objects are *contiguous*.

53. To summarize, the four tensions are time, space, essence, and eidos. The three radiations are emanation, contraction, and duplicity. And the three junctions are withdrawal, involvement, and contiguity.

54. These are the ten basic bonds between objects and qualities. Through their formation and destruction, the story of the world unfolds. The universe is crossed with fault-lines, wracked with tremors.

55. For each of the ten kinds of bond, there is a specific way that the bond becomes evident, and specific effects belonging to each of these cases.

56. We focus for now solely on disturbances in the four *tensions*, in which a real or sensual object is paired with real or sensual qualities.

57. Any sensual object, whether tree, candle, or dog, cannot exist without both real and sensual qualities simultane-ously– shrouded in extraneous detail, and possessing deeper real qualities as well.

58. Hence the disturbance in the bond between a sensual object and its real or sensual qualities can occur only by splitting a bond that already exists– a kind of *fission*.

59. When the difference between sensual objects and their sensual qualities becomes openly evident, we can speak of *simulation*, since we thereby simulate how a sensual object might generate different effects.[58]

60. When the gap lies instead between sensual objects and their real qualities, we speak of *theory*, since all thought aims at approaching the real properties of sensual objects.

61. Any real object, withdrawing from all access and all relation, must have a certain internal consistency, but not distinctly separable qualities that exist in tension with it.

62. Thus, instead of breaking a pre-existent bond between an object and its qualities, we must produce a tension that did not pre-exist its production. We can call this process *fusion*.

63. When this occurs between a withdrawn real object and its sensual qualities, we can speak of *allure*, since there is something allusive about the way the object signals to us.

64. But when real objects are fused with real qualities allied with it for the first time, we can speak of *causation*, since this is where consequences unfold for the world.

65. To summarize, the disturbances of the four tensions in the world have been named *simulation*, *theory*, *allure*, and *causation*.

66. All of the arts are a way of producing allure. But there are other ways as well. We should describe what makes artworks different from other kinds of allure.

67. All forms of allure come to our attention through surprise or fascination, since we are not entirely sure what we are dealing with, though we witness its qualities.

68. With Heidegger's famous broken hammer it is not the hammer itself that becomes visible. Instead, the hammer's qualities are assigned to the hammer as to some unknown letter X.

69. The fascination of beauty in all its forms is that of some deeper animating principle beyond any particular visible features. Hence, rules cannot be given for making beautiful things.

70. In courage we see allegiance to one's self and its principles, external consequences be damned. The courageous person views safety, career, and popularity as inessential; the coward does the opposite.

71. In pleasant surprises, we encounter some unexpected lively principle in a book, person, or city from which we had expected only serviceable mediocrity. In disappointment, the opposite occurs.

72. This happens in artworks as well, though we cannot identify artworks with the form of allure known as "beauty." Sunsets, bird plumage, and seductive voices are beautiful without being artworks.

73. And furthermore, there might be genuine artworks lacking in what is usually called beauty. If Duchamp's bicycle wheel is not an artwork, lack of beauty is probably not the reason.

74. Heidegger speaks of strife in his lecture "The Origin of the Work of Art."[59] This strife must be a special case in the world, or everything would be an artwork.

75. His strife occurs between earth and world. But although his "earth" is concealed, it is not what we mean by real objects, because Heidegger's earth is a single global lump.

76. What we need to discover is how strife differs from normal situations, and how the strife in the artwork differs from that of the broken hammer, courage, and so forth.

6. Response to Louis Morelle (2012)

Philosophy is still lively in Paris, as I was reminded in early 2012. For a year or more I had been corresponding with Louis Morelle, a likable French graduate student who had used Speculative Realist writings for his Master's thesis at the Sorbonne. During a long stay in Paris in December 2011-January 2012, I was delighted by my first personal meeting with Morelle, who mentioned that he would be giving a lecture to the ATMOC group (Atelier de métaphysique et d'ontologie contemporain) *at the École normale supérieure. This vigorous society, organized chiefly by the student Raphaël Millière, meets regularly in the basement of the ENS to debate metaphysical issues in a mixed continental/analytic idiom.[60] I had already planned to attend the lecture and thus had read Morelle's text in advance, but was surprised by an invitation to respond to Morelle in person. For this purpose I wrote a brief talk in French entitled "Réponse à Louis Morelle," which here I have translated into English myself.[61] A recording of my exchange with Morelle (on January 13, 2012) can be heard on the ATMOC website.[62] At the same event I also had my first meeting with Tristan Garcia, the young French philosopher of objects whose massive work* Forme et objet *we later arranged for publication in the Speculative Realism series at Edinburgh University Press.[63]*

First, I would like to thank Louis Morelle for his well-informed and provocative summary of Speculative Realism. In many respects it is the most skillful comparison I have seen between the four principal species of this philosophical school. As Morelle has already said, "it is possible to discover a non-trivial philosophical core in [Speculative Realism],"[64] even if clear distinctions can be made between the authors who adopt this orientation. I will now try to explain my agreements and disagreements with Morelle concerning his presentation of object-oriented ontology, the philosophical camp to which I myself belong. But it will be primarily a question of agreements, since his analysis strikes me as basically accurate.

Indeed, as Morelle has just said, the birth of Speculative Realism occurred in the context of "continental philosophy" in the Anglo-American world, a world in which it is always far from the center. Anglo-American continental philosophy, usually pursued in America by non-Catholic thinkers in very Catholic universities, claims to inherit the great tradition of the history of philosophy— Greek in its origin, but recently transmitted by Austro-German phenomenology and French postmodernism. In Paris in 2006, Quentin Meillassoux published his book *After Finitude*. This work rapidly galvanized a small group of obscure and energetic thinkers, English-speaking yet "continental," with the key term "correlationism," which is now almost famous. Morelle has cited the most important paragraph of Meillassoux on this concept:

> By 'correlation' we mean the idea according to which we only ever have access to the correlation between thinking and being, and never to either term considered apart from the other. We will henceforth call *correlationism* any current of thought which maintains the unsurpassable character of the correlation so defined.[65]

Four pages later, Morelle adds that "correlationism can be presented as the unifying characteristic of the quasi-totality of what had been coupled with the term 'continental philosophy,' [with] Bergson, Whitehead, and Deleuze, the only notable... exceptions to this unity."[66] In my opinion, this remark of Morelle's is so accurate that the three exceptions he mentions ought not to be called continentals at all. Anglophone continental philosophy (whether Husserlian, Heideggerian, Derridean or Foucauldian) is by definition a correlationist enterprise. From its infancy, this kind of philosophy has mocked the realist/anti-realist controversy as a pseudo-problem and dismissed it as the preoccupation of mediocre thinkers. The situation is quite different in analytic philosophy, in which this problem has always retained a certain prestige, even among those analytic thinkers who have ultimately declared the problem of realism to be insoluble or invalid. Among continental philosophers up until the onset of Speculative Realism, realism was considered unworthy of serious discussion.

But in the end, what is the problem with correlationism according to the new continental realism? Morelle has noted that the understanding of correlationism is completely different in the various cases of speculative realism. As he summarizes:

> For Ray Brassier, the problem of correlationism is found in the dissolution of the barrier between metaphysics and epistemology… In contrast, for Graham Harman, the problem is the reduction of every statement to its epistemological preconditions… the original sin of correlationism is the implicit presupposition of the superiority of the epistemological relation of knowledge over all other relations… Iain Hamilton Grant sees the correlationist error in the confusion between the structure of knowledge (the Kantian transcendental) and its dynamic preconditions, which can be reconstructed from the structure, but are not found within it… Finally, for Quentin Meillassoux, correlationism errs by ignoring the intrinsic possibility of a relation between thought and the absolute, which is revealed to be the absolute character of contingency.[67]

Far from being the symptom of incoherence of an empty pseudo-movement, such diversity indicates a fertile subsoil able to sustain an enormous populace of non-correlationist philosophes. In this spirit, Morelle continues:

just as the rejection of Kantian and Hegelian idealism gave rise to currents as diverse as Peirce's and James's pragmatism, the logical positivism of the Vienna Circle, ordinary language philosophy, and phenomenology; in the same way the rejection of correlationism enables the birth of heterogeneous philosophical currents capable of communicating with one another.[68]

Aristotle tells us in the *Metaphysics* that substance ought to be capable of displaying different qualities at different moments: Socrates is happy, then Socrates is sad; at 7:00 in the morning he runs through the streets, and at midnight he sleeps and dreams. Yet he remains Socrates. Thus, Socrates is a substance. By contrast, blue is always blue and falling is always falling; thus, blue and falling are not among the Aristotelian primary substances. In analogous manner, an idea is perhaps more substantial the more it is capable of the most diverse external forms. The concealed central idea of any historical era perhaps resembles a substance deeper than the often opposite qualities it manifests.

Here I will speak of the deeper hidden idea not of Speculative Realism as a whole, but only of my own version of it: object-oriented philosophy. Morelle translates this phrase as *l'ontologie objectuelle*, Tristan Garcia as *philosophie objet-orientée*,[69] and Olivier Dubouclez as *philosophie centrée sur l'objet*.[70] I have no particular preference for any of these French terms, and Morelle's choice is perfectly satisfactory. But why this word "object"? Why not "substance," as for Aristotle and Leibniz? Why not "thing," as in Heidegger and more recently Garcia? The reason is simple enough: I use the term "object" to mark the origins of my thinking in the school of phenomenology. Discussion of Husserl generally focuses too much on his obvious idealism. Too little is said of his challenge to David Hume and the Humean theory of "bundles of qualities." In Husserl, the intentional object is a rather durable nucleus within experience, not (as for Aristotle) a real substance *outside* of conscious experience. The Husserlian object remains and endures on the interior of experience as *the same* intentional or sensual object, despite constant change in the profiles through which this object is encountered. On this point Morelle writes: "But such a theoretical gesture is not made without raising a number of difficulties."[71] Maybe so. But in my view, the difficulties are far greater in the Humean theory of the "bundle of qualities," which is less faithful to conscious experience than the phenomenological theory of unified objects.

Concerning my concept of the *real* object, conceived following Heidegger as "withdrawal" (*Entzug* in German), Morelle writes: "The concept of withdrawal is directly inherited from Heidegger. But whereas the German philosopher attributed withdrawal to Being alone, denying it to beings 'immediately accessible,' present at hand entities, OOO claims that withdrawal is the essential characteristic of every reality *qua* individual reality."[72] This is almost always true in Heidegger, who loves unified Being more than specific objects. But a Heideggerian could always respond with the remark that in his essay "The Thing," Heidegger speaks openly of the withdrawal of the jug, the bridge, or the Greek temple.[73] Yes, but for Heidegger (just as for Kant with his thing-in-itself) the withdrawal of these things is always a withdrawal *from us*— from human beings (*Dasein*, in Heidegger's German). It is never a question, for Heidegger or for Kant, of the withdrawal of the things themselves *from each other*. This latter theory of the mutual withdrawal of things, Morelle says correctly, leads in certain respects to a theory resembling the old Arab and French occasionalist theories— even if it amounts to an occasionalism without God, a secular occasionalism. Even Whitehead did not succeed in secularizing it, and Bruno Latour only in part.

Another interesting critique by Morelle of object-oriented ontology concerns the specter of the "sophism of projection."[74]

As he puts it:

> the metaphor [of "flat ontology"] is here quite meaningful: by "flattening" the ontological terrain, and as a result forcing the rethinking of every type of existence and relation "on the same level," the problem immediately arises of knowing *which* level this is, how to succeed in determining its essence, and above all, whether it constitutes a form more or less disguised by projection in the way we just introduced.[75]

Object-oriented philosophy tries to establish a perfectly flat plane, thereby reversing into the danger of the projection of specific human characteristics even into dark, stupid, and mindless matter. And thus the new risk is that of the famous night in which all cows are black. Yes, I candidly admit it. The specter of a night of black cows is the price one must pay for a flat or democratic ontology in which the human-world relation exists on the same plane as the relations between thing and thing. But the more serious risk, in my view, is the opposite one. Namely, from the apparent difference between humans and inanimate things, one ought not to conclude that there is an absolute ontological canyon or gulf between them, as there is for Descartes. For the Cartesian night is one in which all things are either cows or non-cows, and nothing else.

Morelle also cites Ray Brassier's somewhat aggressive critique of Latour in the anthology *The Speculative Turn*.[76] In my opinion there are numerous errors in this critique, but the important point for us here is that Brassier's critique of Latour does not work at all against object-oriented ontology. To quote Morelle's accurate summary of that critique: "Latour is criticized for the complete dissolution of the limits separating real objects from representation; that is, he is guilty of endorsing the impossibility of every notion of the true and false by way of a collapsing of all things into a neutral monism of 'actants' and their mutual 'trials of strength.'"[77] Yes, this is what Brassier says against Latour. But in my own version of object-oriented ontology, there is no dissolution of the limits between real objects and representations. On the contrary: I always defend a *strict separation* between real and sensual objects (as well as a second strict separation between objects and their qualities, but that is a topic for another time). The true problem is the one that now confronts Brassier himself. Namely, he has reduced the world to a carnival of *images*. In this world, some images are scientific and therefore good, while others are illusory "folk images" and therefore bad and worthy of elimination. This is the consequence of Brassier's rejection of the proposed absolute separation between real and sensual (which is indeed "metaphysical," just as he complains). For me, all images are unreal, since an image cannot be anything more than an inhabitant in the experience of a specific being. But for Brassier, there is no difference at all between the real things of the world and the true scientific representations of this world. In my view, he never explains what the difference is between (for example) a potato and a perfect scientific conception of this potato. Stated differently, why is my idea of the potato inedible, and why does this idea not taste better with salt and butter? The objection is by no means vulgar, but is simply one of the classic rejoinders to every metaphysics of images.[78] Which metaphysics authorizes Brassier to make a general condemnation of the "metaphysics" of real and sensual? It would appear to be a rather weak metaphysics of good images and bad ones— but always of images, and images alone.

7. Discovering Objects is More Important Than Eliminating Them (2012)

On January 20, 2012, exactly a week after the discussion with Morelle in Paris, I was back at Goldsmiths College in London, the birthplace of Speculative Realism. This time I was the guest of Susan Schuppli and Eyal Weizmann in the Research Architecture program. The timing of this return to Goldsmiths was ironic, since the 2007 Speculative Realism workshop had been further memorialized just two days earlier thanks to a Serbian broadcast of the workshop transcript on Radio Belgrade.[79] The 2012 event actually involved two talks: the one printed below, along with a more improvised discussion of the political situation in Egypt, where I had supported the revolution against Mubarak but was uncomfortable with the state of things as of the time of this lecture. The morning talk at Goldsmiths, printed here in full, was a critical discussion of the scientistic-eliminativist camp of Speculative Realism, of which Ray Brassier remains the leading representative.

1. Reductionism and Anti-Reductionism in Latour

The words "eliminate" and "reduce" are the subject of frequent debate in analytic philosophy— is there a difference between eliminating things and reducing them, or are these two actions one and the same? In what follows we will avoid this particular debate, and will use the terms roughly as synonyms, with "eliminate" reserved for those occasions when more sinister overtones are intended.

Let's begin with Bruno Latour, who is perhaps today's most famous defender of non-reductive philosophy. We can start by reviewing the most dramatic moment in Latour's career, as reported in his *Irreductions*: "I taught at Gray in the French provinces for a year. At the end of the winter of 1972, on the road from Dijon to Gray, I was forced to stop, brought to my senses after an overdose of reductionism."[80] Latour realized in that moment that every theorist hopes to triumph by reducing the world to their own favored terms. His list includes Christians, Catholics, astronomers, mathematicians, philosophers, Hegelians, Kantians, engineers, administrators, intellectuals, bourgeoisie, Westerners, writers, painters, semioticians, males, militants, and alchemists. It is a classic "Latour Litany," as they have come to be known.[81] But in 1972, pulled over alongside the road in his Citroën van, the young Latour suddenly decided on a counter-principle to all this reduction:

> I knew nothing, then, of what I am writing now but simply repeated to myself: 'Nothing can be reduced to anything else, nothing can be deduced from anything else, everything may be allied to everything else.' This was like an exorcism that defeated demons one by one. It was a wintry sky, and a very blue. I no longer needed to prop it up with a cosmology, put it in a picture, render it in writing, measure it in a meteorological article, or place it on a Titan to prevent it falling on my head... It and me, them and us, we mutually defined ourselves. And for the first time in my life I saw things unreduced and set free.[82]

These remarks are both inspiring and innovative. Nonetheless, some have asked whether this passage amounts to a so-called "performative contradiction." In other words, since Latour claims that nothing can be reduced to anything else, but also claims that everything in the world is an actor, isn't Latour hypocritically *reducing* the world to actants? I have heard the question asked even by ardent promoters of Latour's philosophy, such as Gerard de Vries in Amsterdam. But the same critique assumes a less friendly guise in a polemical article written by Ray Brassier, who is on record as loathing Latour's philosophy. In Brassier's words:

It is instructive to note how many reductions must be carried out in order for irreductionism to get off the ground: reason, science, knowledge, truth—all must be eliminated. [Note here in passing that even the scientistic Brassier here uses reduction and elimination as synonyms.- g.h.] Of course, Latour has no qualms about reducing reason to arbitration, science to custom, knowledge to manipulation, or truth to force: the veritable object of his irreductionist afflatus is not reduction per se, in which he wantonly indulges, but explanation, and the cognitive privilege accorded to scientific explanation in particular. Once relieved of the constraints of cognitive rationality and the obligation to truth, metaphysics can forego the need for explanation and supplant the latter with a series of allusive metaphors whose cognitive import becomes a function of semantic resonance: "actor," "ally," "force," "power," "strength," "resistance," "network": these are the master-metaphors of Latour's irreductionist metaphysics, the ultimate "actants" encapsulating the operations of every other actor.[83]

Not all of Brassier's remarks here are falsehoods. For one thing, it is indeed true that Latour seeks to dethrone "the cognitive privilege accorded to scientific explanation." But this is precisely the issue under dispute, and for Brassier to treat any philosophy that strips scientific explanation of its purported cognitive privilege as thereby automatically refuted is nothing but a *rhetorical* appeal to the inborn prejudice of his largely scientistic readership. No argument is given for why scientific explanation should have such privilege, unless that argument is to be found in Brassier's assertion that the end of scientific privilege would mean that metaphysics is "relieved of the constraints of cognitive rationality and the obligation to truth," and that it can replace "explanation" with "a series of allusive metaphors whose cognitive import becomes a function of semantic resonance..." In short, Brassier seems to be claiming that if the cognitive privilege of scientific explanation is not retained, then human thought must degenerate into a free-for-all of poetic frivolity. For this reason, as Brassier insinuates with an unstated *reductio* argument, the privilege of scientific elimination must be retained. Equally unargued is Brassier's puritanical assumption, also found among many analytic philosophers, that metaphor has no cognitive role to play, and is merely a sort of dancing pony brought into the theater to distract us from an author's lack of precision. Here I am not especially interested in Brassier's polemic against Latour, which is insufficiently engaged with Latour to convince anyone not already enrolled in the scientistic camp. Even so, as is often the case with adversarial critique, Brassier's remarks are somewhat useful. For there is in fact a genuine defect in Latour's specific way of describing actors.

There are several points to consider here. First, is it true (as Brassier and even some friendly in-house critics assert) that Latour "wantonly indulges" in reduction? Second, even if it is untrue that he indulges "wantonly" in the practice, is Latour's model of actors sufficiently insulated from the defects of reductionism? Third and finally, is avoiding reduction a worthwhile aspiration in the first place?

Let's consider the first question of whether Latour's irreductions are hypocritically reductive despite their ostensible horror of all reduction. And here we need to read a bit further in the book than the 1972 incident with the Citroën van. Note that the call against reduction is a *starting point* for the young Latour, not a result. The treatise is not called *Anti-Reduction* but *Irreduction*, and this new technical term has a specific meaning. What it actually means is that actors are not inherently reducible *or* irreducible to each other. Reductions can always be made, but only if a certain price is paid. It is possible to reduce dreams to their underlying psychoanalytic cause, the apricots of Paris to a specific daily price, or the failure of the Parisian Aramis transportation system to the lesson: "Don't innovate everywhere at once."[84] Latour simply holds that this cannot be done instantly and without remainder by triumphalistic royal knowers who dismiss all gullible illusions while grasping the truth directly. Instead, conclusions are reached by mobilizing various actors and showing how they are translated at each stage, not transferred without residue from one to the next. "There is no transport without transformation," as a famous Latourian maxim puts it.

Despite this point of clarification, the more general question remains valid: is Latour's theory of actants a reductionism in its own right? Any theory must simplify the world, of course. Economics must concentrate on economic facts to the exclusion of aesthetic ones; the natural sciences can accept nothing but relevant physical facts when attempting to explain the behavior of physical entities; the price and smell of two billiard balls are irrelevant when calculating their collisions; histories of World War II omit the nearby activities of birds and mice from their account, and make no mention of planetary motions and supernovae during those grim wartime years. But all of this is simplification, not reduction. Reduction would be the more drastic action of claiming that the behavior of birds, mice, planets, and supernovae can actually be *explained* in terms of the movement of Allied and Axis military forces between 1939 and 1945 (or vice versa), an attempt that would be patently absurd. Viewed in these terms, is Latour's actor-network theory merely a harmless simplification, or is it an outright reduction?

Clearly, it is more than a mere simplification. Latour's own theory of actors and networks is a *metaphysics*, after all; it is an attempt to account for the general structure of reality. Unlike the "simplified" history of World War II just imagined, Latour's metaphysics of actants is not only talking about one special, limited realm called "actors" while leaving mice, birds, planets, and supernovae out of his story for the sake of simplicity. Instead, he tries to incorporate all these biological and astronomical entities *and* the movement of Allied and Axis forces *and* the work of scientists *and* the actions of fictional characters into a general metaphysical theory. In this theory explanation is certainly not abandoned, despite Brassier's claim to the contrary. Rather, the entire cosmos is explained in terms of the linking and delinking of actants of all scales, sizes, and shapes.

In this sense, Latour's theory at the early stage of his career represented by *Irreductions* can be thought of as a form of reductionism. Rather than allowing science to have one set of rules, sports leagues another, and friendships yet another, Latour proclaims that these fields (and all others) result from the interrelations of actors woven together in networks of associations. Admittedly, it is impossible to avoid this sort of global reduction whenever one is doing metaphysics, or providing any theory of reality as a whole. Brassier's scientism is simply a different form of metaphysics: one in which the world is made up not of actants but of *images*, and in which the goal is to establish normative epistemological criteria allowing us to sift good scientific images from bad "folk" images. The only way to avoid even Latour's minimal sort of reduction would be to perform a kind of Dadaist metaphysics, simply living everyday life with no attempt to give a general account of it. Perhaps we could simply raise a finger now and then without comment, like Cratylus as described by Aristotle, in a "subversive" gesture against reduction and non-reduction alike. In this sense the attempt to create a non-reductive theory would be pointless, and in fact Latour makes no such attempt. What his theory really tells us is as follows: everything can be reduced to actants, but *actants cannot be reduced to each other*. It is a textbook case of what we now call "flat ontology," as seen especially in the writings of Manuel DeLanda[85] and the emerging French philosopher Tristan Garcia.

The second question is whether Latour's theory of actants provides a sufficient bulwark against those eliminationist tendencies of the human intellect that he hopes to prevent. Elimination replaces the purported reality of something by tracing it back to the genuine reality of something else, and then disposing of it as merely derivative. If we say that consciousness is nothing more than what happens at a physical level even though it *seems* to have an autonomous existence, or if we say that Popeye and unicorns have no reality even as objects of the mind, this is elimination. Scientistic philosophy tends to regard elimination as the sole task of human intelligence: to think means to annihilate gullible illusions in favor of something more solid and real, which inevitably means something more physical (whatever "physical" is supposed to mean). "To think" supposedly means "to critique." This is the standard modern gesture analyzed by Latour in *We Have Never Been Modern*,[86] a technique through which the natural and the human are cleanly separated or purified from one another. In keeping with this modernist conception, scientism tries to valorize the "nature" side of reality while debunking the "culture" side as if it were merely fabricated by humans. What really exists is a dead physical reality, upon which humans make arbitrary personal and cultural projections. Not that the opposite maneuver is any better— as when we are told that there is no dead physical reality, and that therefore *everything* is a matter of human fabrications and projections. It is well known that Latour completely opposes this nature/culture divide and tries to replace it with a multitude of actors that cannot always be cleanly identified as either natural or cultural. And he does this quite skilfully. However, a case can be made (and I have made it in *Prince of Networks*) that Latour simply gives us an upside-down form of eliminationism. This is not, as Brassier claims, because Latour "reduces science to politics," but because he reduces all entities to their *relational effects* on each other. Actors for Latour are whatever they transform, modify, perturb, or create, as he tells us in *Pandora's Hope*.[87] On this view what makes an actor real is not the tiny physical pieces of which it is built (looking downward), but rather the environmental effects it has on the world (looking upward). Whereas Brassier wants to eliminate actors in favor of their ultimate physical or mathematical underpinnings (with the caveat that these can only be approached as a *telos* and never obtained), we could say that Latour wants to eliminate actors in favor of their effects. In this respect he is the heir of a well-developed recent critique of philosophies of substance: that of Alfred North Whitehead. For Latour, everything is real insofar and *only* insofar as it has an effect on something else. Hence, any substantial existence of autonomous things outside their relational contextures must be eliminated. Our third and final question was whether anti-reductionism or anti-eliminationism (since we are using these terms as synonyms today) is a worthwhile project in the first place. Clearly, it would be dangerous to take a stand against all elimination in principle. The progress of rationality must sometimes allow for the elimination of witches, phlogiston, the commercially constructed four food groups, purported yellowcake uranium sales in Niger, or whatever other entities somehow lose the right to be taken seriously. But we must oppose *eliminativism* as the program which holds that progress in knowledge *always and only* consists in eliminating things by tearing them down to their foundations. This occurs most often in the scientistic form of eliminationism, which loves smashing everything to pieces and turning most everyday objects into empty nullities. Yet as I will now suggest, there is also the danger that the same thing can occur when Latour eliminates objects in favor of their actions. Nonetheless, Latour's position remains closer to the truth than the scientistic model, as will also become apparent in what follows.

2. The Beast with Two Backs

In recent years I have written a great deal about the paired concepts "undermining" and "overmining." It is worth reviewing these concepts here. Historically speaking, Western philosophy began as an undermining operation. The method of the pre-Socratic philosophers was to find some smallest or most basic element from which all other objects were built. What was real was not the familiar mid-sized objects of everyday life, but either some root physical element or some unified mass from which all else emerged. As for the philosophers of physical elements, we find Thales who held that everything was made of water; Anaximenes, who thought the first principle was air; and Heraclitus, who may have meant the same thing with fire, though his famous obscurity makes it difficult to know for sure. Aristotle notes half-jokingly in the *Metaphysics* that only *earth* never had a pre-Socratic philosopher devoted to it as the first principle of everything. But this lacuna was partially filled by Empedocles. Shrewdly noting that if water were really the first principle of everything then its opposite (fire) could never exist, Empedocles made air, earth, fire *and* water the four co-equal principles of the cosmos. While these four are often called the "traditional" Greek elements, this quadruple set seems to have been not some prehistoric Aegean folk myth, but the personal invention of Empedocles himself– at least according to Aristotle. Yet surely the most sophisticated of these early theories of elements was that of the atomists, Leucippus and Democritus, who saw neither air nor earth nor fire nor water as physically basic enough, and posited smaller and supposedly "uncuttable" pieces as the root of all that exists. After a long period of unfashionability, atoms were again vindicated in the nineteenth and twentieth centuries, and in this way the atomists have gained more widespread public dominance in our time than Plato or Aristotle could ever claim in their own. A cosmos made of tiny physical pieces has become the default metaphysical standpoint of the average thinking person worldwide today, to such an extent that many see no alternative to it other than arbitrary religious belief. My point here is that this particular form of pre-Socratic undermining is very much with us today. In 2012, only the insane would argue that everything is made of water, or of four elements mixed by love and hate. But the atomist position (with suitable modifications) is not only still respectable, but in some circles almost obligatory: objects in the world are nothing more than clusters of tiny physical puncta, and can easily be reduced to them.

These theories of physical elements make up one family of pre-Socratic philosophies. The other family includes the theories of the boundless, shapeless *apeiron*. Too primordial and indeterminate to look like water or air or atoms, it might be thought of as a huge indeterminate lump out of which all individual beings are determinately carved. The main disagreement over the *apeiron* is whether its existence lies in the past, present, or future. The first theorist of the *apeiron* seems to have been Anaximander, who saw the *apeiron* as belonging to the future. Over time, all opposites will be destroyed through the work of justice, leading to a final state devoid of opposites. The influence of Anaximander on Karl Marx should be obvious enough in this connection; as is well known, Marx did his doctoral work on these early Greek thinkers. Parmenides renamed the *apeiron* as "being," and held that it exists in the present. Being itself is one, undifferentiated and immobile, and the colorful pageant of swirling particular entities in the world is merely a result of the deceptions of our senses and their despicable stepchild: opinion, *doxa*. Others held that the *apeiron* must have existed in the past, and diverged merely as to how it was destroyed. This group includes thinkers as sophisticated as Pythagoras and Anaxagoras, two of the greatest of the pre-Socratics. For Pythagoras, the *apeiron* was surrounded by the void, and at some point *inhaled* the void, thereby presumably filling itself with bubbles and becoming filled in this way with distinct regions and districts. For Anaxagoras, the *apeiron* began to spin very rapidly due to the action of a colossal thinking Mind (*nous*), and the resulting vibration shattered the *apeiron* into pieces, giving rise to the specific entities surrounding us today— each of them filed with countless tiny pieces of all the others. While these theories of the *apeiron* may sound more quaint than the atomism of Democritus, contemporary philosophy is riddled with such theories. Everywhere, we see traces of the idea that the world itself is one until it is later carved into pieces, usually by the human mind. We see a bit of this in Bergson's idea that the identity of things results from the need of practical action to tame the ceaseless flux of the world. We can see it in Heidegger's tendency (inconsistent but frequent) to view being itself as one, and the experience of human Dasein as the sole place where a multitude of individual beings is found. We find it quite explicitly in the early Levinas, for whom only human consciousness hypostatizes a multitude of entities out of a primal rumbling existence. We find it in the early 1990's in Jean-Luc Nancy, who says that reality itself is simply "whatever"[88] and takes on specific form only when things relate to one another. In my view, we find it in Deleuze and Simondon, for whom real individuals are always suspect when compared with a pre-individual field. I also don't see how we can avoid finding it in Badiou's inconsistent multiple, which is not one and is also not made up of units, because one can only mean the count-as-one. The *apeiron* is a different method of undermining from the kind that leads to atoms, water, or air, but the result is the same– individual objects are broken down into tinier pieces and thereby eliminated. It is safe to say that there is no such thing as autonomous, independent horses, chairs, and trees in pre-Socratic philosophy. Instead, there is nothing but a multitude of tiny particles, or a colossal lump more primary than all specific things. In this way, Western philosophy has an eliminationist legacy in the form of an undermining origin that is difficult to shake.

But elimination does not only happen downward, by saying

that objects are shallow and ought to be broken into tinier subcomponents. As suggested earlier, elimination can also occur upward by referring to objects as empty, useless substrata that need not be posited beneath a more immediate level of reality. This is what I have termed "overmining," by analogy with the actual English word "undermining." If undermining treats objects as too shallow to be the truth, overmining treats them as too *deep* to be the truth. In ancient philosophy, the clearest case of overmining is probably the Sophists with their "man is the measure of all things" and similar sayings, though Plato might also be a candidate, depending on how we interpret his *eidei* or forms. But it is in modern philosophy that overmining really first comes into its own. Maybe everything is treated as phenomenal or sensational; maybe the world is regarded as the product of language, society, or power; maybe events are taken to be more real than objects, or as Wittgenstein puts it: "the world is the totality of facts, not of things."[89] If the undermining personality is most often found among the scientistically inclined, overmining is the vice that has come to dominate the humanities. Objects are dismissed as the fantasy of "essentialism" or so-called "naive realism." Reality is its appearance to us, its effects on other things, or its character as a singular event compared with which objects are merely abstractions– or "vacuous actual-ities," to use Whitehead's term.[90]

Overmining and undermining are not wrong in all cases. Indeed, the reason for their great appeal is that both are perfectly good instruments of enlightenment in many cases. If we show that the morning star and evening star are simply two different appearances of Venus, we have undermined the false distinction between them. If we discover that disease is caused by germs rather than by wretchedness or moral turpitude, then we have undermined the unjust stigmatization of the poor. If someone eventually unifies relativity with quantum theory, their status as perplexing separate wings of modern physics will be undermined, and both theories replaced by a more general one from which they both arise. Overmining is equally useful in many cases. If we discover that there is no such thing as witches or possession by demons, and determine that these are false entities unjustifiably unifying a variety of surface appearances, then this is a case of overmining. If we establish that there are in fact seven different psychological disorders that used to be mixed together under the names "melancholia" or "hysteria," then we have made progress in debunking inadequate older terms. It is often the case that certain objects *should* be eliminated, whether downward or upward. Elimination is certainly part of the arsenal of enlightenment. Yet it is neither exclusive in this role, nor is it even the greater part of enlightenment. The progress of knowledge consists only to a small extent of knocking down trees, pulverizing stones, assaulting gullible pieties, and other instances of crushing baby animals beneath the remorseless heel of elimination. In fact, the growth of human knowledge is primarily an *inflationary* project. Today we do not believe in *less* than shamans and witch doctors, but believe in far more entities than such people could ever dream of encountering. Open a catalog of astronomy, and you will be stunned by the number of stellar entities that have already been discovered. The multitude of beetle and bacteria species on the planet is perhaps uncountable. Enter a warehouse superstore, or browse Wikipedia at random, and you might even find yourself emotionally shaken by the number of objects now in existence. Science has always been a largely inflationary project, just as the demolition of decrepit old buildings plays a minor role in the growth of cities compared with the construction of new ones. The problem with undermining and overmining is not that they eliminate specific entities, but that they want to eliminate entities altogether—except for underminers insofar as they retain all the supposedly ultra-tiniest entities, and overminers insofar as they celebrate a profusion of cultural and linguistic constructs.

As global projects, undermining and overmining fail for separate but related reasons. Undermining cannot account for emergence, in which new entities arise that may be causally dependent on their tinier components but which are not reducible to them. Humans have properties that are not just those of organic chemicals made of carbon, hydrogen, and oxygen. Your body remains the same if any number of cells is replaced or removed, as happens constantly anyway. Humans are able to add and remove body parts through various medical manipulations. This is not true only of humans, but of most other objects at most levels of scale in the cosmos. What undermining misses, in short, is that even if there were some tiniest physical or mathematical layer of cosmic pieces, this layer would not contain the secrets of everything that unfolds at all layers of reality. The fact that thunderstorms might be causally explained in terms of atoms and molecules is ultimately irrelevant to the laws that explain the large-scale formation and movement of thunderstorms as a whole.

Overmining has the rather different problem that it cannot explain change. If reality were nothing more than a concrete and highly specific event, with everything completely determinate and no hidden residue lying behind it, there is no reason why the world would ever shift from its current state. If I were nothing more than my current set of relations in the world, there would be no independent "me" to shift into new relations in the future. If the proletariat were purely the product of its economic relationships there would be no grounds to call for revolution, since in that case the proletariat should simply praise the economy for bringing it into existence in the first place. If you were truly defined by your family and friends, you would be stuck with them forever. In trying to evacuate the world of hidden mysterious substances, overmining removes all principle of change from the world.

It should also be noted that undermining and overmining

never appear in isolation. Although one or the other usually sounds the dominant note, each generally require the parasitical presence of its opposite. This can be seen as early as Parmenides, who initially looks like a great underminer who reduces the world to a single, unchanging Being. Yet he also requires the supplement of a surface world of shifting appearance (which he calls the world of opinion) or else he would have no explanation for the apparent multitude of things. In similar fashion, those who reduce the world to atoms, brain cells, or mathematical structures must also find some explanation for why the world *seems* to be other than this— and hence they must always posit a conscious agent on the top layer of the world, capable of spinning a web of deception for itself. It must explain why there *seem* to be actual colors, smells, and flavors in the world even though undermining teaches differently. In the philosophy of James Ladyman and Don Ross, the phrase "every thing must go" means that all objects are eliminated in favor of an underlying unified mathematical structure. [91] Yet to preserve the meaningfulness of science, they must also preserve the independent reality of geological facts, chemical facts, botanical facts, and even facts about traffic jams (the latter example is their own). Yet ultimately these separate regions of science are allowed to exist only as "real *patterns*," meaning that (despite the presence of the word "real") they exist only when some observer is present.[92] For Peter van Inwagen, one of the arch-eliminators of analytic philosophy, there are tiny physical particles and nothing else– *except* living organisms, so that an overmining layer of perceiving entities is added to supplement the undermining one.[93] Even David Chalmers, who is viewed as the most intransigent defender of first-person consciousness, and who holds that even thermostats are conscious, thinks that everything else *besides* consciousness can be eliminated.[94] For Chalmers there may be conscious thermostats, yet there are no physical tables, chairs, or apples, since all of them can be physically reduced.[95] The same supplemental relationship between undermining and overmining happens in reverse. Bruno Latour, who makes his actors so fully determined by their interrelations that there would seem to be no hidden surplus that could ever allow them to change, ends up having to posit an indeterminate "plasma" lying beneath all actor-networks, a plasma said to be the size of the whole of London while the networks are merely the size of the London Underground by comparison.[96] Whitehead also makes his entities completely determinate through their mutual prehensions or relations, and also senses that they need some residual surplus in order to be able to change, and thus he is forced to inject some notion of impetus into his actual entities (even though this is forbidden by his view of entities as instantaneous occasions). Or else he gives that role to God, who serves as his storehouse of potentiality in the form of so-called "eternal objects." To repeat, neither overmining nor undermining can live without the other. They require each other as supplements, giving us only a top and a bottom of the universe, to such an extent that they might be called "the beast with two backs," as Iago puts it early in *Othello*.

What we must assert in order to defeat the beast in all its forms is the autonomy and reality of all the intermediate layers of the cosmos. There are not just people and a few smart animals on one side and subatomic particles on the other, but countless intermediate layers, each with its own autonomous reality. If most intellectual methods take pride in annihilating these intermediate layers, reducing them downward or upward, I hold that the theme of our time is to combat both forms of mining and develop new techniques for getting at the intermediate entities. What I call "objects" lie in between undermining and overmining. A similar idea can be found in the emerging French philosopher Tristan Garcia, though he thinks that objects are the *difference* between their subcomponents and their outward effects. In my view this leaves their autonomy endangered, since every time a few neutrons leave my body, every time my position in physical space shifts slightly, the "difference" between these will change, and thus I will become a completely different person. Instead of this, we need to assert the existence of the object as an in-itself, which is precisely what Garcia hopes to avoid.[97]

But we have already said that human thought generally *knows* things only by undermining or overmining them. We can understand the equations and particles at the root of the world, and we the sense-impressions in our consciousness. But how do we say anything about the reality of objects without reducing them to our way of saying something about either their tiniest components or their most tangible effects? That is the topic that I want to address briefly in the final section of this paper.

3. Discovering Objects

In a sense, all intellectual methods are reductive. Methods attempt to understand realities either by moving beneath them to discover the components of which they are made, or they look upward to the ultimate effects of the same realities. A good example of the first kind of method would be the analysis of food into its ultimate chemicals, a method now decried by Michael Pollan as "nutritionism."[98] A good example of the second kind would be the so-called pragmatic method, always cited with an air of crushing victory, which runs roughly as follows: "Consider the practical effects of the objects of your conception. Then, your conception of those effects is the whole of your conception of the object." Pragmatism is one of the purest forms of overmining ever invented— our conception of objects is nothing more than our conception of their practical effects.

Yet I have suggested that objects are precisely what cannot be overmined or undermined. They withdraw into depths beneath any perfect comprehension, and also emerge as something over and above their components (not as *more* than the sum of their parts, I would say, but as *less* than the sum of their parts,m but that is a theme for another day). If it is true that intellectual methods work by undermining or overmining, reducing cultural facts downward to economic facts or reducing workers and goods to their relations, then to do justice to objects requires something like a *counter*-method. If we want to get at something that is radically irreducible or ineliminable, as objects are, then we need to invent counter-methods.

Nor is it necessary to develop all these counter-methods from scratch. Since objects have always been with us, so too have the counter-methods needed to deal with them, despite the official ideologies that would have us undermine or overmine them all. And in fact, one of the ways we know things without reducing them or eliminating them is by allusion– *allusion*, which Brassier condemns in the passage cited earlier without explanation or argument, as if allusion were obviously sub-cognitive poetic drivel. But notice that even the hard sciences allude to things. For example, the Higgs boson has to be viewed as a proper name rather than a definite description. We do know some of the properties of this entity, and that is how we would be able to identify it if discovered. But that does not mean that the Higgs is exhausted by these recognizable properties. They are simply the means by which we know them, just as we recognize a friend by specific clothing and facial features. New features could and would be discovered in the Higgs boson in the future. In general, the most powerful and vivid language succeeds in saying things *without* saying them— not out of some inherent love for vague fuzziness, but because things can never be directly grasped or known in their withdrawal from human view. Obliquity and metaphor are better tools for getting at the hidden nature of things than any smug, dismissive, or angrily reductive cataloguing of palpable features. Just as it takes years to get to know a person or author properly, and some minutes even to grasp the peculiarities of a simple bottle of wine, objects can only be known through indirect routes. Knowledge is a kind of seductive innuendo, whereas undermining and overmining want it to be something more like hardcore pornography: a direct presence of the thing itself, without any hiding behind supposedly obscurantist masks or veils of propriety.

At least two possible objections come to mind. The first would be that this is a "worthless" claim, since hidden things-in-themseslves mean nothing unless they can affect us in some way. The call for a counter-method would supposedly lead, at best, to a negative theology in which we can only subtract qualities from what we observe without proclaiming anything positive about it. The second possible objection would be that there is a certain arrogance in treating all past human intellectual methods as instances of undermining or overmining, and in calling for a completely new counter-method to replace them all in the name of some newly cooked-up theory of withdrawn objects.

My answer to the first complaint is that we already know *many* things no more than indirectly. We never directly "see" the character of a person, but only specific actions that he or she undertakes in various situations. Nonetheless, when getting to know a person we are forming models of the unseen character behind their actions; we are not just positivists trying to predict future instances of their behavior based on past behavior. When trying to understand the styles of artists, we are not just summing up all of their past works and trying to pinpoint common recurring features. Instead, we are trying to grasp an unseen *style* behind those works that might have produced still other works, and that in fact might literally still produce them in the case of artists still living. Even in the hard sciences there is the case of black holes, which by definition cannot be observed directly by any means at all. Yet when we say that no information escapes from black holes, no one testily compares this assertion to a "negative theology" or complains that we are merely alluding obliquely and poetically to the existence of black holes. As for the second objection, that it is arrogant to try to invent completely new counter-methods differing from the methods of the past, this objection was answered earlier: we hardly need to *invent* such counter-methods, since they have already long been in use, and we simply need to identify, gather, and concentrate them so that they are no longer so lonely in the world.

Aristotle already told us that one of the key features of substances is that they have different qualities at different times. Though he means this as a way of describing features of substances already known, we can reverse the order and use his principle as a means of *discovering* substances in the world. Namely, in order to identify real objects we can look for things that have different qualities at different times, or which are difficult to pin down by means of definite descriptions. While it is not quite true that anyone who is criticized must be doing something right, what does seem to be true is that anyone who is criticized simultaneously *for opposite reasons* must be doing something right, or at least must be doing something genuinely new that is misunderstood from both directions. In this way, what we are seeking is essences deeper than any essentialism, since essentialism is not the claim that essences exist, but the much more dangerous claim that they can be *known*— and therefore that they can be *used* to govern reality by cleanly separating the essential from the inessential and assigning various people and other entities to the essential categories where they supposedly belong. But this sort of essentialism is completely forbidden by object-oriented philosophy, which holds that essences can never be known, but only approached obliquely.

Consider a field such as literary criticism. In recent decades, it might be said that the conflict was between "formalists" who held that a literary text is a holistic self-contained system designed as a machine that works effects upon the reader, and "materialists" who refuse to let the text be an autonomous thing and inscribed it instead in its surrounding conditions of social production. It should now be easy to see that these are simply the familiar overmining and undermining alternatives. Against them, the literary text should not be reduced to its material productive conditions, since these might have produced other things instead, and since the text can move across time and space and still have an impact elsewhere. And neither should the literary text be treated as a holistic system that requires a specific form, since incidents could be added to or subtracted from Dante or *Moby-Dick* without necessarily changing these works. Just as Husserl invites us to grasp the essence of a blackbird or mailbox through a "free variation" that imagines them from different angles and under different lighting conditions, we might engage in a sort of free variation of literary texts that would allow us to get at the real text that is both deeper than its specific words and more shallow than the material conditions that produced it.[99]

The future is not about reducing objects upward or downward. The future is not about triumphalistic pragmatic tests that smirk at the inflationary tendencies of others. This has been attempted throughout modernity, and all it has given us is reductionist nihilism, a contemptuous view that the arts and humanities are not as rigorous as the natural sciences, and often enough a me-too'ish attempt by philosophy to utilize a deductive method despite Whitehead's eloquent arguments that this is impossible.[100] Throughout the modern era, philosophy scrambled to model itself after the most successful human pursuit of this period: the mathematical natural sciences. We had philosophies attempting to establish unshakeable first principles and then deduce ruthlessly from those principles. Or we had philosophies going on a wild debunking rampage and smashing supposed myths, much like modern medicine ridiculing spontaneous generation and witch doctors. The sciences discover objects just like anything else, but due to their demand for exactitude they have a dangerous tendency to identify objects too closely with their palpably discernible qualities. It thereby invites a confusion of the two, and philosophy has too often accepted that invitation.

But what if, instead of continuing in the attempt to make philosophy more like mathematics or the natural sciences, we were to model it after the arts, which can only work by allusion and obliquity rather than through an exact cataloguing of properties and qualities?[101] What if the next five hundred years saw a philosophy modelled after the arts rather than the sciences? If this sounds un-rigorous, then perhaps rigor is being confused with exactitude. And there is a sense in which exactitude is simply another form of overmining, replacing the elusiveness of objects with a total list of their measurable properties.

8. Everything is Not Connected

This was my February 2, 2012 keynote address at the Transmediale arts festival, held at the Haus der Kulturen der Welt in Berlin. It was the largest crowd to which I had ever lectured, with perhaps one thousand people in attendance. It was also among my most successful lectures in terms of audience and media response. Worthy of note is that while I was able to freely mention the name of the politically tainted Heidegger, my first reference to art critic Clement Greenberg was greeted with hisses by contemporary media artists still resentful of Greenberg's long-ago modernist stranglehold on criticism. Otherwise, Berlin was cold and snowy, and bad things were happening at home in Egypt. On the previous night, as I sat with my friend Michael Allan (University of Oregon) at the Canadian Embassy in Berlin at a lecture by philosopher of technology Andrew Feenberg, dozens of supporters of Cairo football club al-Ahly were massacred following a match in Port Said, through a conspiracy not yet identified or even fully acknowledged. Among the dead was American University in Cairo student Omar Aly Mohsen.

"Everything is connected." If one phrase in present-day intellectual life earns almost unanimous approval, surely it is this: "Everything is connected." We admire nothing more than the ability to see connections between apparently disconnected things. Every event in the contemporary world seems to sing the praises of interconnectivity: globalization, convergence, superpowerful communications media and the new cosmopolitanism, along with the nested feedback loops of climate change. To speak instead of autonomous individual things in isolation from each other now sounds like the crusty old philosophy of fossilized bishops and patriarchs out of touch with the latest trends. This lecture will propose a contrary view. One of the best ideas Ted Nelson ever came up with was the notion of "ideas once but no longer liberating."[102] Ideas like fruits have moments of peak ripeness when they are best consumed, and later moments when their taste is less fresh and wholesome. It is my view that the idea that everything is connected is an idea once but no longer liberating— an idea that has become too easy, like an advertising jingle stuck in the brain. In attempting to convince you of this view, I will be speaking of Marshall McLuhan (though somewhat differently from usual), and of Martin Heidegger (whom you may not have read in great detail). What I will try to show is that media theory quickly turns into metaphysics —the theory of ultimate reality— and that metaphysics is beginning to teach us that *not everything is connected.*

We are still too close to the twentieth century to understand it adequately. But when historians a century or two in the future begin to stabilize our conception of the period from 1901 to 2000, there are a number of key figures who will almost surely be part of the story. It is hard to imagine Einstein and Bohr not looking like key figures in physics, or Picasso in visual art. Though Freud has come under punishing assault by psychiatry and even by other psychoanalysts, it is hard to imagine a future in which Freud's breakthroughs into the human psyche look trivial, even if they are rejected. Perhaps more controversially, my bet is on Heidegger to emerge as the consensus great philosopher of the twentieth century, all political baggage notwithstanding. If I were allowed to add just one additional name to this list, especially if I were discouraged from being cautious, my choice would be Marshall McLuhan. Though McLuhan is not the central topic of this lecture, a few of his major ideas will be important for us tonight.

The most basic idea of McLuhan can easily be summarized as "the medium is the message," a claim that goes much deeper than any of McLuhan's specific remarks about television, or graffiti on atomic bombs.[103] "The medium is the message" tells us that while the human intellect tends to focus on the surface effects of things —on the *content* of good and bad television shows, rather than the transformative effects of television as a *medium*— what is truly important is the unnoticed background medium in which this content unfolds. More generally, at least in the West, the intellect focuses on whatever can be stated or argued in the form of clear verbal propositions rather than on the background assumptions lying behind such statements. What is most important, according to this view of the world, is whatever can be made clear and explicit; the rest is vague and fuzzy nonsense. But the McLuhan standpoint is exactly the opposite— what is important *is not* whatever is clear and explicit at any moment. Instead, what is important is whatever is obscure and tacit. Television, videogames, or the romantic or nihilistic spirit of any age lie in the background of our experience, unquestioned.

In 1988, Eric McLuhan published *Laws of Media*,[104] a work co-authored with his deceased father Marshall. The dominant theme of this book is the *tetrad*: the fourfold structure of all media as enhancement, obsolescence, retrieval, and reversal. Before looking at this quartet of concepts, let's consider how the McLuhans relate the interplay of visible figure and concealed background to the Classical Trivium of grammar, rhetoric, and dialectic. We have seen that the modern Western intellect tries to turn everything into visible figure. The real is the rational; the real is the visible; the real is what can be expressed mathematically; the real is what can be stated in clear articulate propositions rather than vague poetic evasions. The real is the good or bad *content* of a television show, which can be judged as good or bad according to empirical evidence and the laws of logic. For the McLuhans, the real is none of this. The modern focus on the legible surface of things links Western rationality with what the McLuhans call "dialectic." Opposed to this surface-loving procedure is what the McLuhans sometimes call "grammar," but even more frequently "rhetoric." (In fact, the difference between grammar and rhetoric remains somewhat underdetermined by the McLuhans, who often treat the two terms as synonyms.) Since "rhetoric" is the more frequently used of the two, let's stay with this word for a moment. If dialectic is the art of the surface, rhetoric is the art of the background. As early as Aristotle's classic work on the subject, the key concept of rhetoric is the *enthymeme*. The enthymeme is a proof that need not be stated explicitly because it is already tacitly present in the spirit. Aristotle's classic example is that when someone says of a person that he has been crowned three times with a laurel wreath it is unnecessary, when addressing an Ancient Greek audience, to explain that this means the person was a three-time champion in the Olympic Games, since all Greeks knew what this meant. All language contains enthymemes. If I now say "take the U-Bahn to Friedrichstraße and find me an umbrella for fifteen Euros or less," what is explicitly stated is minimal in comparison with all the things that I simply *assume* you already know. For example, you probably know that the U-Bahn is the German term for "subway" or "metro," that this is a reasonably safe method of underground transportation, that the public is free to use it without special membership procedures, that the U-Bahn is relatively cheap, that Friedrichstraßse is a fairly major station, and you may even remember that it used to lie in the former East Berlin. You know that an umbrella is equipment to protect us from the rain, that the Euro is common currency used in many EU countries but not in Britain, Sweden, Denmark, or many of the more recent member states, and that the Euro as a currency now seems to be in some trouble. You also know that 15 Euros may be slightly luxurious, but not *very* luxurious, as the price of an umbrella. Furthermore, since we live in a relatively democratic world, you know that my asking you to do this amounts to a request for a favor from an equal; it is not a command from your feudal lord whose evasion would be punishable by whipping or execution. You know that the fairly minimal threats of the U-Bahn may include pickpockets, the criminally insane, or an accident, but not dangerous wild animals, Somali pirates, or death by drowning. As you can see, even in this simple request to buy an umbrella, so much is left unstated yet implied. Language is riddled with enthymemes, which are the exact opposite of clear propositional statements.

Rhetoric is the art of persuasion by means of these hidden background assumptions rather than explicit argumentation. In recent decades, the word "rhetoric" has been associated with postmodern anti-realist philosophies. For example, if some university professor writes a book on the "rhetoric" of Nicolas Sarkozy or Barack Obama, what the book will probably tell us is that there is no objective truth-value in what these politicians have said, and that they are simply manipulating words to gain unearned power over other humans. Note that this is not at all what Aristotle means by rhetoric. For Aristotle, rhetoric is in fact a persuasion based on a hidden *reality*. It is actually true that someone has won at the Olympic Games three times (or at least true that the audience believes so), and actually true that the Berlin U-Bahn is not especially dangerous. The speaker is simply hinting at these facts rather than stating them openly.

In this sense, McLuhan can be viewed as essentially a rhetorician of technology. What is most important is not the dance of explicit content across the television screen, but the fact that we are watching television at all, as opposed to listening to radio or surfing the worldwide web. The basic conditions of the television medium provide deep structure for human experience in a manner far more important than any of the content it transmits. This is very basic McLuhan, but it is very important McLuhan. The hidden background of any situation is in general more powerful than the visible surface. This opinion is not universally shared, of course. We need only cite Edgar Allan Poe's famous remark in "The Purloined Letter" that "truth is not always in a well. In fact, as regards the more important knowledge, I do believe that she is invariably superficial."[105] But we can deal with this dispute a bit later. For now, the point is that *for McLuhan*, the genuine effect of a medium must be found in its hidden background depth, not in its legible outward features.

And not only for McLuhan. This priority of the hidden depths over the visible surface also reminds us of the chief intellectual contribution of Heidegger, whom I take to be the most important philosopher of the past century, his numerous political and human failings notwithstanding. Despite Heidegger's reputation for formidable obscurity and complexity, his philosophy is not that difficult to summarize. In 1901, one of the emerging great philosophies in Europe was phenomenology, founded by Heidegger's teacher Edmund Husserl. Phenomenology has numerous admirable features and a few deeply unfortunate ones, but there is no need to summarize all of them here. Instead, we can focus on just one feature of phenomenology that has its good side and its bad side. There is a style of philosophy that worships natural science, often called "scientism" even by some of its advocates.[106] For scientism, conscious experience can be explained scientifically. The blue appearance of the sky is due to the greater scattering of blue sunlight than red sunlight, and this in turn can be explained by the behavior of atmospheric molecules. In the late nineteenth century, philosophy was very much under siege from scientism, with some observers at that time believing that philosophy would soon be replaced by exper-imental psychology. In this heavily reductionist atmosphere, Husserl's phenomenology followed the opposite strategy. When considering the blueness of the sky, all this talk of molecules scattering sunlight is just a theory. It may be a very good theory, but it still goes beyond what we directly experience for ourselves. What is primary is direct individual experience, and this is why Husserl would not begin with a scientific theory of why the sky is blue, but would instead describe our human *experience* of the blue in as much detail as possible. If science is an analysis of supposedly real things outside consciousness, phenomenology is supposed to be a patient description of things as they appear to us— of the phenomena present in consciousness.

Heidegger was Husserl's star pupil, and was expected to take over the phenomenological movement from his mentor. But from 1919 through 1927, Heidegger spent the bulk of his time preparing rebellion against his teacher. While Husserl claimed that we must focus on what is present to consciousness, Heidegger noted that most of what we encounter *is not* present to consciousness, but silently relied upon as a tacit background. The link with McLuhan should already be obvious. Heidegger's greatest and most famous passage is his tool-analysis, first published in *Being and Time* in 1927 (though presented to students as early as 1919). For the most part, he says, things in the world are not phenomena flickering in consciousness. Instead, they are *equipment* taken for granted until they malfunction. Only rarely do we notice the floor beneath our feet, the oxygen in the atmosphere, the blood circulating through our bodies, the grammar of our native language, the legal system that ensures smooth social functioning, or the hammer that we reliably use while building something of wood. These things remain veiled or concealed in the background, while we focus consciously on something else instead. From time to time these concealed entities may break down in such a way that we no longer ignore them, and they surge into conscious awareness— as when a hammer shatters in our hands, or when tear gas in the streets of Cairo obstructs our access to oxygen. Heidegger is also famous for asking the question of the meaning of being, which sounds so impossibly obscure. But all he really means with this classical term, "being," is that which hides behind all presence, irreducible to any presence to the mind or to anything else.

In numerous publications I have tried to push Heidegger a bit further than he explicitly ventured, and since these attempts will become relevant later in this lecture, they are worth sketching briefly here.[107] The most common reading of Heidegger is that he is trying to teach us that all theory is grounded in practice. Any viewing of a hammer or theory about hammers comes afterward; what comes first is our *use* of the hammer. First comes practice, then comes theory. I answer that this reading is false, and in a sense my entire career hangs on this single point. There is a simple reason that this interpretation of Heidegger must fail. What Heidegger tells us is that our conscious experience of any object never exhausts that object; it always harbors surprises that can erupt at any moment from the shadowy background of the thing. In other words, our consciousness of things does not exhaust the reality of those things, a point that phenomenology only partly grasped. What Heidegger does not seem to notice is that our *practical use* of things also fails to exhaust them. If staring at a hammer leaves many of its secrets undetected, the same is true when we *use* the hammer. Just consider the vast rainbow of hammer-qualities that dogs, bats, or insects might notice in the hammer, but which lie outside the human perceptual spectrum. The various ultraviolet and electromagnetic disturbances in and near the hammer are no more accessible to human praxis than they are to human theory. In short, there is a hidden background in the things that escapes both theory and practice. Heidegger does not teach us about the relation between human praxis on one side and human theory on the other, but about the relation between the inhuman background reality of things on one side and *both* human praxis and theory on the other.

But I always try to push it one step further than this, in a way that will also be relevant to tonight's lecture. Namely, the reality of objects does not just hide from humans, but from other objects as well. The reason that the hammer's reality is deeper than all access is not because of some freak psychological or neurological quirk of humans and a few smart animals such as dolphins, monkeys, dogs, and ravens. Instead, inanimate objects fail to exhaust each other just as humans and animals fail to exhaust them. In the simplest collision between two stupefied chunks of dirt, only a tiny portion of these chunks is relevant to the collision, while their numerous other features remain concealed and unexpressed. Kant's Copernican Revolution in philosophy, in 1781, allowed for things-in-themselves beyond all human access, and this point we must accept. What we cannot accept in this Revolution is its fixation on the single pair of human and world, which becomes a pampered central relation immeasurably more important than the relations between raindrops and wood, sea and beach, seagull and forest, or cosmic ray and moon. Here we should turn to other philosophers, such as Alfred North Whitehead, who places all relations on the same footing as that between human and world. But Whitehead unfortunately views the world in *relational* terms. To oversimplify just barely, entities for Whitehead are really just the sum total of their relations with other entities, and every entity has some relation with every other entity in the cosmos (the so-called "negative prehensions" are still just a special case of prehensions). In short, for Whitehead everything is connected. But for Heidegger, in whose world entities withdraw beyond all human and inanimate contact, not everything is connected, and there is a sense in which nothing at all is *directly* connected.

I hope the link between Heidegger and McLuhan is now clear. For both thinkers, there is more power in the cryptic background than in the visible surface. While this is already expressed by McLuhan in the slogan that "the medium is the message," it is given much sharper form in *Laws of Media* in the discussion of the tetrad. One pair in the tetrad, enhancement and obsolescence, is concerned entirely with this duality between the background and foreground of things. As the McLuhans describe it, every new medium (and all artifacts count as media) enhances, empowers, or augments some features of reality while obsolescing, degrading, or diminishing others. While this is meant to be the same as the difference between foreground and background, there is the mysterious problem that the McLuhans get the two terms backwards. Namely, they say that to enhance something is to foreground it and to obsolesce something is to push it into the background. But the McLuhans, of all people, should have said precisely the opposite, since it is they who ceaselessly teach us that the background is where the living medium can be found. Whatever radio enhances in the world, these enhanced features must remain quietly backstage, silently dominating the world while radio listeners are mesmerized and beguiled by the *content* of radio programs. Whatever cars enhance, it is certainly not foregrounded; what is foregrounded are the hundreds of thousands of urban horses, carriages, and horse services that have now become useless relics of a dead medium. For this reason, the McLuhans should have identified enhancement with invisibility and obsolescence with obtrusive visibility, rather than the reverse. This remains a relatively small issue, yet it is well worth remembering when reading *Laws of Media*.

As is well known, one of the widespread critiques of McLuhan calls him a "technological determinist." I believe this charge to be utterly false, but it is important to zero in on exactly *why* it is false. The reason McLuhan is called a technological determinist should be obvious enough. Conscious human decision and political action seem to take place at the level of explicit mental content. Hence a theory like McLuhan's, which prioritizes the subliminal background labors of concealed dominant media, might seem to reduce humans to the hopeless puppets of an inhuman background medium. And it is true that for McLuhan the background medium is thoroughly constitutive of its content. But there is a further point that must not be overlooked: no medium lasts forever, and for McLuhan no medium decides what medium will replace it. It is *humans*, those supposedly hopeless marionettes of concealed background media, who help determine what medium comes next.

For McLuhan, there are two ways in which media can change

into new media: retrieval and reversal. These are the other two terms in the tetrad to accompany enhancement and obsolescence. In reversal, a medium overheats and reverses into its opposite. The car begins as a tool for speed and efficiency, but reverses into the gridlock of traffic jams. Democracy begins as a leveling equalizer of all aristocracies, but reverses into the cult of privileged billionaires and celebrities. Antiseptics and antibiotics are meant to enhance a germ-free environment, but reverse into the apocalyptic nightmare of drug-resistant super bacteria. Credit cards begin as consumer mobility and flexibility but reverse into immobilizing consumer debt. It is fascinating to see how frequently this happens, perhaps even how *universally* it happens, since universality is precisely what the McLuhans claim for their media laws. While the mediocre fortune teller simply extrapolates from past trends and predicts ever further movement in the same direction, the McLuhan theory correctly projects a limit point where any trend flips suddenly into its opposite. This might at first seem to feed directly into technological determinism: "show me a new medium, and I will show you how it will eventually overheat."

But this presupposes that the car extends experience in one direction only, and that this direction alone is where the reversal must occur. By "overheating," the McLuhans mean information overload. The content of a medium proliferates to such a degree that the mind cannot process all of it, and is reduced instead to pattern recognition. Individualistic democracy becomes so jam-packed with hundreds of millions of souls that the sociologist and the statistician no longer see individuals, but only "types"– the typical Green, paleo-conservative, soccer mom, limousine liberal, or Scotch-Irish Appalachian nativist. What happens is that some previously concealed *form* of the object becomes repeated in such great numbers that it becomes the new content in its own right. This may happen when individuals are reduced to members of wider demographic groups, or it may happen when the sheer physical bulk of cars (not so important when there were not many of them) becomes the central topic of conversation: as movement slows to a crawl on the super-highways and the historic inner space of cities is gutted to make room for a sprawling wasteland of parking garages. And perhaps such overheating is inevitable, as the McLuhans seem to hold. But it is never the case that an entity has just one concealed dimension that can be overheated. Will the possible collapse of the Euro lead to the breakup of the Union, a harsh centralization in Brussels, the downsizing of the Union as a few insolvent members are kicked out, or even a vast enlargement of the Union in an attempt to spread the risk? Will the novel continue as a dominant literary genre for another two centuries of rich exploitation, or will it reverse into an era of short stories, poetry, or a surprising new epoch of oral bards flourishing in resurgent local cultures? The same questions can be asked of the future of any medium, since it is largely unpredictable which hidden components of any given medium will be heated further. While the McLuhans tend to see overheating and reversal as inevitable for any medium, there are numerous possible routes along which a medium may overheat and flip upside-down. Human intervention and historical accident may play a formidable role in determining the next step after the current one. It is hard to imagine a less deterministic theory than this; in fact, it is the very incarnation of fragile contingency.

We find even less determinism when we turn to retrieval, the other of the two "morphological" terms in the tetrad. Every medium, say the McLuhans, has an older medium as its content. YouTube contains television as a manipulable and surveyable content, while Amazon's Kindle does the same for books, and the iPod for music. But there seems to be a paradox here. For on the one hand, the McLuhans say that *every* medium contains an old medium as its content— as if this were some sort of banal, easy feature of any medium, automatically enacted as soon as that medium is produced. But on the other hand, they treat this as the special task of artists, implying that retrieval is an intermittent event rather than a constant and automatic one. For the McLuhans all retrieval, including art, involves what they call a transition from cliché to archetype.[108] What this means is actually rather clear in terms of McLuhan's thinking. We know that every medium obsolesces something by turning vinyl LP's, landline telephones, or (in the coming decade) paper books into hulking chunks of waste no longer needed. They have become clichés, like last week's newspaper, filled with stale news no longer of interest. Old media are not just turned into content but into boring, empty, cliché content: into something obsolete, not at all retrieved. So then, we might ask what the difference is between obsolescence and retrieval, or between cliché and archetype. The clearest answer here comes not from McLuhan, but from the art critic Clement Greenberg [here there was hissing from the front of the crowd- g.h.], who today remains near the low-water mark of his reputation, but who is still one of the most powerful writers and intellects of the past century. In the year of McLuhan's death (1980), Greenberg gave a lecture in Sydney in which he offered the following definition of "academic art," the very embodiment of artistic cliché: "Academicization isn't a matter of academies– there were academies long before academi- cization and before the nineteenth century. Academicism consists in *the tendency to take the medium of an art too much for granted*. It results in blurring: words become imprecise, color gets muffled, the physical sources of sound become too much dissembled."[109] To repeat, Greenberg warns artists not to take their medium too much for granted, and it is hard to imagine a warning that McLuhan would have loved more than this.

What obsolete clichés and retrieved archetypes have in common is that neither is a hidden background medium; both are visible figures. But whereas clichés (such as those of academic art) take their medium too much for granted, archetypes are visible figures that somehow hint at awareness of their own background conditions. In this way a bridge is built between background and foreground, between depth and surface. In philosophy we saw this happen with Heidegger's broken tools. When the hammer shatters, we can no longer view it as a visible figure present in the conscious mind; that visible figure now hints indirectly at the inaccessible being of the hammer, which is the hidden "medium" (in McLuhan's sense) of all its tangible properties. In language we see this happen with metaphor. To say that stars are nuclear reactors and moons are satellites that orbit planets is merely to explain these objects in terms of the accurate ascription of properties to them; the object is nothing more than the sum total of its correctly enumerated properties. But if we follow Shelley's lines "the stars will awaken / though the moon sleep a full hour later,"[110] we are not psychotics who take these statements literally. What this personification really achieves is to hint at a personal depth to the stars and moon that lies beyond an accurate list of their qualities, just as the hammer is deeper than all we can see or say of it. Against the tendency of deconstruction to erase the difference between literal and figurative language, this difference is every bit as real as experience teaches us. You can either reduce a star to its set of accessible traits (that's the literal star), or allude to the star as a persona whose visible features do no more than obliquely hint at it, just as a black hole is known only through the deformation of light and swirling gases in its vicinity. Something similar happens in language with proper names. As Saul Kripke noted, a name is not an abbreviation for all known properties and past actions of a person.[111] To call out someone's name in the night is not just a shorthand way of pointing to a 375-page list of definite descriptions of them. Instead, to call out a person's name is to appeal to something real in the person that exceeds all that is known of them or can ever be known— a "personality" if you are secular-minded, a "soul" if you are not. For each object, there is a kind of "soul of the thing" lying deeper than any known list of qualities. For Clement Greenberg, the tension between an object and its qualities, or between background and foreground, comes in those rare fertile moments when the content of an artwork also shows some awareness of its medium. In Greenberg's case, the flatness of canvas means that the three-dimensional illusionistic painting dominant from the Italian Renaissance onward reached a point of academic decay in the 1860's, and from then on the real innovators were devoted to the flatness rather than to pictorial illusion, with such innovation peaking in the high cubism of Picasso and Braque. One need not accept this interpretation of modern painting to see that Greenberg is making the same point as in the other examples just given. The content of any medium may be stupid in isolation, and the structure of the medium itself may be hidden or inaccessible. But bring the two into some kind of tension, and something begins to happen. Elsewhere, I have used the term "allure" to describe such cases in which an entity is by no means unaware of its medium, but in which the surface is brought into explicit contrast with its own background conditions.[112]

This is the meaning of retrieval for McLuhan, and this is why it requires artistry. Merely to be a visible figure in consciousness is not the mark of something retrieved. Telephone landlines may still be no more than embarrassing clutter when found in the flats of jaded urban hipsters; their former era of dominance is still too close to us. But vinyl LP's, lava lamps, and hookahs have already enjoyed periods of retrieval. The artist is the one who does not just dredge up dead clichés, but who finds a way to make these ex-clichés work in a new cultural background so different from their original one. Yet there are so many clichés to choose from, so many dead forms of yesteryear surrounding us at every moment, that it is purely contingent which dead forms will be revived. Who knows what the best art of fifty years from now will look like? Which currently dull classical philosopher will be retrieved as the invigorating icon of the next generation? This is almost entirely unpredictable for the simple reason that the labor of individuals will largely be the deciding factors in what dead forms are retrieved. With retrieval, even more than with reversal, there isn't the faintest trace of historical determinism. Rather than accusing McLuhan of determinism, it might be closer to the truth to accuse him of granting too much contingent power to individual artists and visionaries.

There is a general irony at work here. McLuhan begins as the thinker of the depths par excellence, for whom the invisible medium of television is everything but the visible content of television shows is nothing. But the only mechanisms in McLuhan's world through which change can occur are retrieval and reversal, and as we have already seen, retrieval and reversal are creatures of the surface. Artists retrieve by manipulating clichés so that they come into productive contact with hidden background media, while reversal occurs through the overheating of the *explicit content* of a medium rather than heating the medium itself. Background media may be ultra-powerful for McLuhan, but at the end of the day, all they really do is just sit there and dominate the visible realm from behind the curtain. They are incapable of change; what changes them are events along the most superficial layer of the content of the world. Thus, in the end, content is not so stupid after all. If the medium is the message, then only the message determines the next medium. A medium can never reform itself, but relies on humans to do this. In the philosophy of Deleuze there is sometimes talk of the sterility of the surface, so that everything happens in the depth of the virtual. While McLuhan starts off appearing to say the same thing, he ends up as a theorist of the sterility of the depths.

So far I have spoken as if it were always *humans* who decided what comes next. This is probably true for the conversion of clichés into retrieved archetypes, since only humans seem to display the needed level of artistic foresight to pull this off. But as for the reversal that results from overheating, it seems clear enough that much of this happens not only against human intentions (who *wanted* traffic jams, after all?) but even outside human awareness. In one famous case, the number of frogs near Hawaii beach hotels overheated without human planning, causing those hotels to flip from peaceful beach retreats into deafening noise hazards. An unexpected increase in solar flares or tsunamis thanks to cosmic cycles could easily flip telecommunciations or the Japanese coastline into fragile territories. Although the McLuhans overemphasize the *human* dimension of history, saying that the four laws of enhancement, obsolescence, retrieval, and reversal apply only to artifacts made by humans, there is no especial reason that the fight against determinism requires explicit human volition. Any buffer zone of uncertainty between a given medium and the medium that follows makes historical determinism impossible, and this might include chance fluctuation in the activities of earthquakes, volcanoes, icebergs, or monkeys no less than conscious human action. If we assume that nature equals determinism and humans equal arbitrary free choice, we have committed the Taxonomic Fallacy, which consists in the assumption that any distinction between two forms of reality (here, determinism and chance) must be embodied in two specific kinds of entity (here, nature and humans). I take Bruno Latour's refutation of the nature/culture divide in *We Have Never Been Modern* to be definitive, and will not cover the point in detail here.[113]

Quite aside from this question of whether inanimate entities can disrupt determinism as effectively as humans, another feature of the McLuhans' conception of history is clear. Just as their views are incompatible with determinism, they are incompatible with any linear or modern conception of history in which archaic objects and practices are forever replaced by more rational ones. History is a movement of retrievals and reversals, with the dead shapes of the past often rising from their graves to dominate the future. Since merely bringing things back leads only to clichés, the McLuhans are not defending the model of history as a *cycle*, which is unconvincing anyway. Instead, history for them has a *periodic* structure, just as each new row in the periodic table of chemical elements repeats the previous patterns at a new level. When pirates re-emerge at the Horn of Africa or slavery booms worldwide, when English begins to act as a worldwide academic Latin, when corporations take on some of the olden characteristics of feudal lords, and non-national armies —mercenaries and heavily armed African security firms— reappear centuries after their banishment following the Thirty Years' War, or when belief in God, astrology, and alchemy *increases* many centuries after Voltaire, some of these developments may be regrettable, but rarely can they be viewed as mere archaic relapses. Instead, they are more likely to be the retrieval of dead forms in a new shape that is adapted to the new historical situation— for better or worse, and admittedly often for worse.

Stated differently, history is less a linear progression from dark to light (as revolutionaries think), or even from light to dark (as reactionaries think), but a dizzying series of reversals or retrievals that convert dead forms into new and living media. This has the following implication for human knowledge and for all human artefacts. Along with the definite characteristics that belong to telephones, cars, James Joyce, Berlin, Portland, Heidegger, Deleuze, absinthe, iPhones, Sarkozy, Obama, or al-Qaeda, there is also a certain degree of cryptic vitality in each of these entities. I have already quoted Ted Nelson's phrase "ideas once but no longer liberating." There are also "cities once but no longer liberating," as when recently fresh and unexplored urban centers become overheated with gentrifying copycats and profiteers who lack the soul of the original explorers. What is the exact moment when the philosophy of Deleuze or Badiou ceases to be fresh and liberating, and becomes simply the new majority dogma that must be overthrown in turn? What is the right moment, as an artist, to drop Berlin and move to Istanbul, Melbourne, or São Paulo? When has a given period of our lives run its course and become in need of replacement? Usually, we speak of "fashion" in intellectual life only in a spirit of ridicule or moralization. We raise the topic of fashion only to condemn those who follow it, dismissing them as superficial hipsters and trend-seekers more committed to impressing their friends than to making progress in human knowledge. No doubt such people exist in large enough quantities. But the behavior being condemned in such cases is not one of fashion, but of the conformity that comes *after* the real breakthrough in fashion. By contrast, to detect a potential shift in fashion is a rare event and one of profound seriousness, since it indicates a high level of taste equipped to tell the difference between a vital cultural form that is truly well-adapted to the background medium and empty contrarian forms that have already become routinized or drained of life. It happens to every school in philosophy just as it happens to every school in the arts. For this reason, I would like to suggest that a taste for new fashions is not the sign of superficiality, but the greatest possible intellectual gift. It reveals a profound sensitivity to the degeneration of established media into clichés and the need to replace them with something much livelier. It shows a profound resistance to what Greenberg called "academic art," or art reduced to a series of inherited surface gestures, unaware of the background medium from which they must take their nourishment.

At last we return to the title of this lecture: everything is not connected. For many decades, it has been an automatic sign of seriousness to assert the interconnectedness of everything. Art must be connected with its social environment and the material conditions of its production. Politics must be viewed globally, never as locally self-contained, since freedom and prosperity in one place must mean the outsourcing of misery and oppression elsewhere. Individual words, metaphors, and personae in a literary work must be seen as holistically interrelated with one another, even to the extent that they fully determine one another. In philosophy, everything must be defined by its relation to everything else— and perhaps individual things are said to be illusory in the first place, mere abstractions from a deeper unifying and all-embracing whole. All academic disciplines must be fused together in a fiesta of interdisciplinary work, against the artificial cutting-up of knowledge into separate fields. The new human lifestyle is supposed to be one of constant multi-tasking, with no clear boundaries remaining between eating time, working time, resting time, and emailing time. Art should not be sequestered in artificial and anti-septic galleries, but should install itself just about anywhere other than a gallery. The geology of our planet must be integrated into a cosmic history of asteroid and comet collisions, with a new warning every few months about some battleship-sized rock that has a 0.02% chance of hitting us. In physics, according to many interpretations of quantum theory, we must stop regarding nature as objective and isolated from human experience, since even experiment shows that our observation of the world affects it, thereby showing that human and world are deeply intertwined. In medicine, we should not just intervene at moments of illness or accident, but should integrate medical emergencies into a wider and more balanced view of wellness, including diet and emotional satis-faction. These examples will all be familiar enough. What they tell us is that for a long time now, the standard mainstream strategy of intellectual innovation has been to make things more interconnected, breaking down barriers, dissolving previous boundaries between separate areas of the universe, and generally defending a holistic approach against the supposedly oppressive atomism that previously ruled the modern world. And of all the examples just listed, there is no denying that many have been extremely beneficial; like most eras of intellectual history, the holistic era has taught us many new things.

Nonetheless, I want to suggest that this holistic era has run its course, has begun to enter a phase of decadence, and badly needs to be replaced by new intellectual strategies. For one thing, it has simply become too easy to denounce specialization and compartmentalization and disconnected realities; there is an increasingly robotic feel to these efforts. At times it is not even clear who is being attacked, since almost everyone in sight seems to be on board with connecting everything to everything else. I take these to be signs of a dying medium, with the holistic approach to everything now running the risk of self-parody. We sense this not only through some vague emotional feeling that it's time for something new (although vague emotional feelings are badly underrated as a cognitive tool). Instead, certain explicit *arguments* come to mind. In some schools of philosophy explicit argumentation is all that matters, and everything else is dismissed as vague and fuzzy poetry. By citing the McLuhans' ideas on dialectic versus rhetoric, I tried to suggest that this triumphalistic view of the role of explicit argument is not quite justified. Most of any situation is unstated and unstatable, and is best approached by way of hint, allusion, oblique reference, and innuendo, just as we do in everyday language. Hegel wrote somewhere that arguments are a dime a dozen. I take this to mean that there's always an argument available for just about anything you want to say, and that while some might be stronger than others, certain arguments appear generally stronger than others for various reasons at various points in history. Imre Lakatos (among others) made roughly the same point when he observed that scientific paradigms don't need to falsified as Popper claims, because they are always already falsified by counter-evidence.[114] Yet we cling to them anyway. Newton's theory of gravitation persisted for quite awhile despite not being able to explain many anomalies including the aberrant orbit of

Mercury, and quantum theory and relativity both flourish today despite being ultimately incompatible. There are some simple philosophical arguments available against holism, yet they have seldom been discussed, simply because they might have sounded boring and reactionary as long as everyone was in the midst of making everything interconnected.

Let's return to Heidegger's tool-analysis. There can be little doubt that Heidegger himself reads his own analysis in holistic terms. The phenomena present-at-hand in consciousness are disconnected and self-contained, Heidegger complains, while the true situation is that the hidden tool-beings lying beneath the surface of consciousness are all deeply intertwined. The hammer is not an isolated physical lump, but gains meaning only from its context, depending on whether it is used as a hammer for construction or as a Viking battle instrument. If the hammer is used to construct a building then this activity defines what it is, and so too does the type of house (a mansion, an orphanage, or a recording studio) Furthermore, the fact that it's a building for humans rather than a zoo or a doghouse makes it a different kind of hammer than it would be in the latter two cases. Only the surface of the world is broken up into pieces, Heidegger says, while the depths are a holistic tapestry of interrelation. And don't forget that Heidegger, in the opinion of many, is the emerging consensus greatest philosopher of the past century. Yet there can be no doubt that Heidegger gets it backwards, just as some of the great experimental physicists have misinterpreted their own greatest results. How did he get it backwards? It is surprisingly easy to see how he did so, once we abandon the reigning holistic dogma and take a renewed look at his tool-analysis. It may be true that the hammer is assigned to countless other pieces of equipment and that they mutually determine each other's function. In fact, this is most definitely true. But it does not tell the whole story. After all, tools are only one half of Heidegger's story– the other half is *broken* tools. The hammer breaks, and this calls our attention to the hammer's existence for the first time in an explicit way. But how could the hammer break if it were nothing more than its smooth interaction with all other pieces of equipment? The answer is that it could *never* break if that were the case. The fact that the hammer can break shows that the hammer is not identical with its place in the tool-system, but that this system only exploits a small part of the hammer. The hammer itself is a sort of surplus or residue lying *outside* the system. In short, Heidegger's tool-system does not prove holism, but instead proves the exact opposite. A world where tools can break is automatically a world where everything is not connected. And what about the other side of Heidegger's world: the phenomena present in consciousness? He claims that these appearances are self-contained and artificially isolated from everything else.

But here once again, nothing could be further from the truth. When I stare at the image of a hammer before me, this image is not at all isolated, because it exists in relation *to me*. Since all phenomena exist for some observer who encounters them, it is quite obvious that phenomena can never be independent and isolated. Instead, they are dependent and parasitical. But the same is true of tools insofar as they function effectively. Just as the phenomenal image of a hammer is dependent on the one who observes it, so too the hammer in action is a parasite dependent on the boards, nails, recording studios, mansions, and construction workers with which it is involved. Phenomena in consciousness and efficient tools invisibly at work are meant by Heidegger to be exact opposites, yet they now implode into the same kind of being: relational, interconnected being. What is much deeper than such relations is the interior life of objects, which is veiled, hidden, or withdrawn not only behind all human consciousness, but even behind all inanimate relation. Entities withhold their secrets from each other no less than from us. This is also the problem with the otherwise brilliant philosophy of

Whitehead. Though it is refreshing when Whitehead returns to a pre-Kantian universe in which inanimate relations are placed on the same footing as human-world relations, Whitehead also reduces things in the world to their mutual effects on each other. In this way, the world once more becomes a great holistic tapestry, or a game of hot potato, or a Ponzi scheme in which each entity take reality from the others with which it interacts, and these from others, and so on to infinity, with nothing having reality in its own right.

So, even though Heidegger usually looks like one of the great heroes of the holistic era of philosophy, I would claim him instead for the opposite camp. What Heidegger actually shows is a complete *disconnection* between things, never able to touch each other fully, since they withdraw behind all human access and even behind all inanimate contact. I would make the same claim about McLuhan. As a media theorist and champion of the global village and multi-layered acoustic awareness, McLuhan also looks at first like an ultra-holistic thinker. He even sees himself this way, just as Heidegger does, as when he blames the bias of Western rationality for breaking the world into discrete self-contained entities when it is really an inclusive whole. But McLuhan is not a holist for the same reason that he is not a technological determinist: namely, there is no immediate link between the background and the figures inhabiting it, nor between today's medium and the medium to come. Instead there is a buffer zone between any two moments in time, a buffer made of chance, contingency, and sometimes the delay of deliberate human action. There is no immediate connection between the horse/buggy and the car, since some technological visionary had to retrieve an older medium when assembling the first plans for the first car. The retrievals and reversals of McLuhan's world are just as surprising as the broken tools of Heidegger's world, and for the same reason— namely, because they summon an unexploited surplus latent in the background of the world.

Climate science is often taken to be a paradigmatic case of the need for a holistic approach: people and climate are not separate, but interconnected. Yet I believe this holistic lesson is the wrong one to draw from climate change, just as holism is the wrong lesson to draw from Heidegger's tool-analysis. The most frightening lecture I heard in my life, at the time, was surely James Lovelock's April 2009 talk at University College Dublin on the irreversibility of climate change. In Lovelock's grim vision as expressed that day, the earth in 2100 will be reduced to one billion souls clustered near the North Pole, with a few lucky inhabitants on temperate islands such as Ireland and New Zealand having to fight off invading climate migrants with deadly force, as Africa burns to a crisp and North America and Russia turn into colossal dust bowls. In answer to the usual objections about temperature fluctuations between warmer and cooler, Lovelock insisted grimly on what he describes as a linear rise in the sea levels without any fluctuation at all. For Lovelock, the critical point will be reached when three things happen. First, the polar caps melt, thereby destroying one of our greatest reflectors of solar energy and ensuring that the earth will absorb even more solar heat than before. Second, the increased heat kills off the equatorial rain forests, meaning that carbon dioxide levels will rise even more, raising the heat of the planet even further. Third and finally, the heat will melt the permafrost, exposing more decaying biomass and releasing even more carbon dioxide into the atmosphere, creating a proverbial "vicious cycle." Contrarian scientists claim that the process might not only be easy to reverse, but even *too* easy to reverse, in the form of cheap sulfur dioxide emissions that could halt global warming at the cost of severe damage to the ozone layer.[115]

But let's assume that Lovelock's predictions are absolutely accurate, and that a runaway process of this kind is already inevitable. Would such a catastrophe really prove that "everything is connected"? No, it would prove that *three specific processes* are interconnected: the melting of the ice caps, the death of the rain forests, and the melting of the permafrost. If we state wildly that "everything is interconnected," then we simply spare ourselves the trouble of determining which climate processes are truly interconnected. We avoid having to understand the inner nature of the permafrost and the forces of freezing that have so far held CO_2 in check across the millennia. We also weaken our ability to anticipate possible *surprises* to our climate models: perhaps some of these processes will turn out to be less damaging than expected while other, previously unconsidered factors will be the ones to push our planet over the edge— maybe some simple consumer chemical thought to be harmless, or perhaps a gas emitted from dying beetles, turn out to be catastrophic factors in the climate process, just as methane from cattle has turned out to be. Stated more simply, before now there was a sense in which the polar caps, rain forest, and permafrost *were not* connected, and bringing them into connection causes disaster, just as premature connection often causes disaster in intellectual fields.

If the model of holistic interaction has in fact run its course as a general-purpose method, do we now advocate an archaic relapse into the old reactionary concept of substance? Not really, since in McLuhan's terms this would simply replace one cliché with an even older one. The goal is not repetition, but *retrieval*, and retrieval means modifying the old to work plausibly amidst the new. There were many problems with the old model of substance, which took various forms. But one of the major problems was the assumption not only that there is a substance or essence of things, but that these are also *knowable*. Everyday objects were reduced to atoms, and these atoms were identified with distinctly knowable features, meaning that in some sense things were reducible to their mathematizability *for us*. The possible knowledge of a thing replaced the reality of that thing. Meanwhile, the claim that each thing not only has an essence, but that this essence is *knowable* led to numerous political abuses by those who claimed to have such knowledge: racism, sexism, Orientalism, or the diagnosis of various sexual practices as perversions and crimes. These problems are avoided if we recognize that each thing is real, that it is has a surplus reality deeper than whatever it happens to be doing at this moment, that since each thing is different each thing has an essence, but that this essence is never completely knowable since it cannot be exhausted by any form of knowledge.

What would result is a model of a world having reality outside the mind, a world in which some things are connected but not everything, in which things have an essential inner reality but not one that can be known or mastered, and can only be approached obliquely through allusion rather than directly through catalogues of tangible properties. Philosophy would resemble the arts more than the sciences. It would also be a world in which, insofar as things withdraw from contact with each other in their mutual inexhaustibility, the contact between things is a problem to be explained rather than an obvious fact to be presupposed. The title "everything is not connected" is grammatically ambiguous, perhaps even awkward, since it has two possible meanings. It could mean "*not everything* is connected," but could just as well mean "everything is *disconnected*." In fact, both of these senses are intended. We learn from Heidegger's hidden tools and McLuhan's unnoticed background media that what is real cannot be mastered by vision or knowledge, and therefore always remains disconnected from us, and (given that Heidegger's analysis works for inanimate relations no less than human-world relations) all the things of the world remain disconnected from each other as well, withdrawn into their private vacuums of reality. Yet they do not just withdraw. Occasionally they do make contact, in special cases that require explanation. Under very special circumstances, politics and neutrons can be brought together for the first time. Under very special historical circumstances Iran and Venezuela become allies, or Cuba and Angola, or China and Tanzania. Under specific and limited conditions, a hammer can touch an orphanage. Connections take work, and they always involve translations and distortions. This is what proves that not everything is connected.

9. Interview with Gitanjali Dang (2012)

In March 2012 I was contacted by the Bombay-based critic and curator Gitanjali Dang about the possibility of doing an interview for a prominent Indian newspaper. Dang sent her questions by email, and given the presumed tight deadline for press I responded as quickly as I could. Unsurprisingly enough, the resulting interview proved to be too technical for the general readership of the newspaper, and they declined to run it. The interview restates my dislike for scientistic positions, and also express disagreement with the famous claim by Wittgenstein recommending silence. Absent the requirement of sticking to the newspaper's strict word-count limit, I have taken the liberty of expanding some of my answers slightly for the present book.

Gitanjali Dang: From your keynote speech in Berlin in February,[116] as also from your writings elsewhere, it becomes quite apparent that you are fairly disenchanted with scientism.

Graham Harman: I love science but detest *scientism*, the view that all philosophical problems can be solved by the methods of natural science. In recent years I have written, for example, of the cases of Thomas Metzinger[117] and the Broadway-like team of James Ladyman/Don Ross.[118] The scientistic attitude is nicely summarized in one of the most brazen passages from Ladyman and Ross: "Special Relativity ought to dictate the metaphysics of time, quantum physics the metaphysics of substance, and chemistry and evolutionary biology the metaphysics of natural kinds."[119] Please note that not all *scientists* even want this kind of subservient, masochistic, handmaiden's attitude from philosophers. Here are some refreshing words to the contrary from the physicist Carlo Rovelli: "I wish that philosophers who are interested in the scientific conceptions of the world would not confine themselves to commenting [on] and polishing the present fragmentary physical theories, but would take the risk of trying to look ahead."[120]

What can the actions of tiny particles tell us about politics, literature, or even geology? Scientism responds by saying that only physical things exist, and that hence everything must be grounded in the workings of fundamental physical reality. Ladyman and Ross *claim* to allow for a "rainforest" of entities at all different scales, but for them things like mountains, planets, and artworks are generated only as the correlate of some observer; the world itself is not made up of things, hence their book title: *Every Thing Must Go*. What they really think is that only the bedrock level of the universe is there— plus human observers, though it is unclear why such observers would be distinct enough from the bedrock to generate distinct, scientifically treatable entities at higher levels.

Even if we were to agree that only physical things exist, it would not follow that only the smallest layer counts. You can remove or replace a few thousands atoms from Shakespeare's body, the United States Congress, or a volcano without changing these realities at all. Even mid-sized objects are real and have their own laws at each level. These levels are not in some sort of supernatural world, different from the laws of particle physics. But in no way are they exhausted by the bedrock level from which they emerge. Stated more simply, we must oppose all reductionist zealotries. Whereas the sciences each deal with one specific kind of object, philosophy must deal with *all* kinds of objects, including large, artificial, and imaginary ones. I have never understood the debunker's instinct, which strikes me as an arrogant power play against other humans: "How naïve you are! Accept my instruction."

Gitanjali Dang: "These problems are avoided if we recognize that each thing is real, that it is has a surplus reality deeper than whatever it happens to be doing at this moment, that since each thing is different each thing has an essence, but that this essence is never completely knowable since it cannot be exhausted by any form of knowledge."[121] These lines, written by you, are strongly reminiscent of Wittgenstein's declaration: whereof one cannot speak, thereof one must be silent, which has sometimes been viewed as problematic.

Graham Harman: I don't say we must remain silent, I say instead that things are never *directly* knowable. No artwork, indeed nothing that happens in the world, can be paraphrased in a series of clear propositional statements. Any statement is merely an abstract version of what it talks about: or stated differently, a translation. I can write the most detailed book ever written about dogs, yet there will always be something more about dogs that I haven't said. We are often given a false alternative between knowing something directly or not knowing it at all. But philosophy was always supposed to be a third option, at least in the Greek tradition in which Western philosophers work. According to Socrates, gods have total knowledge and animals have none, while humans are somewhere in between. The Greek word *philosophia* means not wisdom, but love of wisdom. Philosophers love wisdom because they don't have it.

Gitanjali Dang: Why do you read the breaking of the tool as a sign of everything not being connected? It could also be that the hammer breaks because it wants to draw attention to itself, a breaking of the hammer as a party trick. To draw a parallel: failed suicide attempts are often just shouts for attention.

Graham Harman: If the hammer wants to break to draw attention to itself, this means it has desires not expressed in its current reality. Unfortunately, the same goes for suicidal people. If they fit so neatly into their current environment, there would be no hidden suffering in them. Returning to the case of hammers, if they were nothing more than their current usefulness, they would be exhausted by their current actions and could never do anything besides what they are doing right now.

Gitanjali Dang: It has been observed, that as of May 26, 2011, 94.5% of all articles in the English Wikipedia lead eventually to the article "Philosophy." The rest lead to an article with no wikilinks, links to pages that do not exist, or get stuck in loops. If this is a metaphor, then being networked is not so bad because all networks lead back to philosophy.

Graham Harman: Really? This is brilliant! All roads lead to philosophy, or they lead nowhere. I can't possibly improve on what this statistic teaches us, so I will remain silent about "that whereof I cannot speak" and let the 94.5% figure speak for itself.

Gitanjali Dang: Heidegger's hidden tools and McLuhan's unnoticed background media tell us that what is real cannot be mastered by vision or knowledge, and therefore always remains disconnected from us. The words "authentic" or "original" could easily replace the term "real" and each of these terms has been variously problematized already. Please comment.

Graham Harman: I wouldn't agree that the concepts "authentic" and "original" have been successfully problematized. Postmodern intellectuals are always trying to problematize everything except their own fundamental bias, which is that everything is produced by society or the play of signifiers and nothing has any inherent reality. I disagree. We might not be able to *know* what is authentic or original, but that doesn't mean that the authentic and original don't exist. We all recognize that there's a big difference between someone who lives a life in keeping with their own genuine talents and commitments, and others who live false lives borrowed from others. What we should resist is the idea that any individual person is *empowered to tell us* what is genuinely Indian, American, or Turkish. That's when big problems arise. But there's nothing at all wrong with my asking, for example: "What does it mean to be American?" I reject the postmodernist smirk that is directed against such questions.

10. Garcia's Jungle

This talk was given on June 22, 2012 in Zagreb, Croatia, as part of an event hosted at the MaMa cultural institute in commemoration of the nineteenth anniversary of Presses universitaires de France (PUF). Because of the PUF-related theme, I decided to speak on one of the most exciting recent books published by that press: Tristan Garcia's Forme et objet. *Shortly after my first meeting with Quentin Meillassoux in July 2006, he had told me to keep an eye out for the 25-year-old Garcia, his former student at the École normale supérieure in Paris. In an uncharacteristically long email, Meillassoux highlighted some of the major features of Garcia's emerging philosophical position. He later told me about Garcia winning the Prix de Flore for his debut novel,[122] and occasionally kept me posted on Garcia's massive philosophical treatise as it worked its way through the publishing pipeline. In November 2011, Garcia's book was finally published in Paris, with its first footnote mentioning my own* Tool-Being *along with Manuel Delanda's* Intensive Science and Virtual Philosophy,[123] *the two 2002 books that launched the new realist trends in continental philosophy. My younger French contacts quickly concluded that Garcia's book was a masterpiece. Such was the curiosity over the new work that internet orders led to impossible delays, and finally I gave up. Only upon arriving in Paris did I manage to purchase a copy of Garcia's book, on December 26, 2011. I studied it closely throughout the month of January, and even had the luxury of two personal meetings with Garcia himself: a charming, thoughtful, and intellectually gifted person.*

In September 2009, Press universitaires de France launched its MétaphysiqueS series with a reprint of Etienne Souriau's long-forgotten *Les différents modes d'existence*, with a long introductory essay by Bruno Latour and Isabelle Stengers. During the nearly three ensuing years, the series has drawn increasing attention.

Through the work of its four energetic editors —Elie During, Patrice Maniglier, Quentin Meillassoux, and David Rabouin— the series has already established itself as one of the anchors of another important period of philosophy in Paris, the city that has dominated continental thought since the Second World War. Another anchor in Paris, not yet as widely known as the series at PUF, is the even younger group of thinkers associated with Raphaël Millière's group ATMOC (Atelier de métaphysique et d'ontologie contemporains) at the Ecole normale supérieure. An English-language mirror site of the ATMOC website will soon be available,[124] and will show Anglophone readers that their repeated calls for a merger of analytic and continental philosophy is almost a *fait accompli* in Paris— perhaps the last city one would expect to serve as the headquarters for such a merger.

Speaking of mergers, which person embodies both the exciting new series at PUF and the fascinating basement seminars of young Millière and his comrades? That person would be Tristan Garcia, born as recently as 1981, but already a force to be reckoned with in European philosophy. His massive book *Forme et objet: Un Traité des choses*, or *Form and Object: A Treatise on Things*, was published last November and has already been the subject of numerous reviews, most of them written in a spirit of admiration. *Forme et objet* has also served as a rallying point for younger French thinkers who admire the author's verve and style. Garcia has followed up on the book with several additional lectures, despite his announced intention of retreating for a year into his parallel life as a writer of fiction. Garcia, who is both intensely prolific and remarkably friendly, seems ready to take his place among the most-discussed philosophers of the decades to come. Everyone connected with European philosophy will want to become familiar with the basic concepts of Garcia's philosophy relatively soon. This should be easier in the Anglophone world once we have an English version of *Form and Object* on the shelves, which could happen within the next two years.

My talk today has a twofold aim. For those who have heard little of Garcia, I want to explain the key points of his ontology. I will begin by covering the first portion of *Forme et objet*. That first half of Garcia's book, entitled "Formally," deals with things *n'importe quoi*, or no-matter-what-they-are. In other words, Garcia begins by establishing what Manuel DeLanda calls a "flat ontology," one that treats all things simply insofar as they are things, rather than according to any sort of hierarchy. This portion of Garcia's book is marked by an abstract technical precision reminiscent of Hegel's *Science of Logic*. The second half of Garcia's book (which I will not discuss today) gives us something more like Hegel's *Phenomenology of Spirit*, as various concrete shapes of reality pass before us: time, culture, economics, gender, generations, and death. Even for those who do not agree with Garcia's basic principles, the second half of the book poses an immediate challenge for contemporary philosophy to move from general technical discussions to a more concrete philosophy of life. Garcia has spent less time procrastinating than those now in the now middle-aged generation of Speculative Realism, all of us in our mid-forties— some of us fairly prolific, but none as quick to deliver encyclopedic philosophical claims as Garcia has already done. Though he is a full generation younger than we are, we suddenly find ourselves in the position of having to catch up with this unexpected sprinter.

In the second part of my talk, I will briefly discuss a recent lecture that Garcia gave at ATMOC in Paris on his similarities and differences from the Austrian philosopher Alexius Meinong, a member (with Twardowski, Husserl, and others) of the so-called Brentano School. Meinong is often treated by the likes of Russell and Quine as a needlessly inflationary ontologist who makes room in the world for non-existent and even contradictory objects. The resulting situation of a rampant multiplication of entities often leads to complaints about what is called

"Meinong's Jungle." Garcia runs in the opposite direction, claiming that Meinong should have been even *more* inflationary, that he betrayed his own principles in serving up an ontology that was insufficiently flat. That is the meaning of my phrase "Garcia's Jungle," which by Garcia's own admission is even thicker (or at least flatter) than Meinong's. Garcia also hints in passing that my own ontology is not as flat as his. On this point Garcia is definitely correct. Object-oriented philosophy, at least in my version of it, has never been entirely flat. My ontology is slightly bumpy, as seen most easily from the fourfold structure of real objects, real qualities, sensual objects, and sensual qualities. The quadruple model of objects is a direct challenge to flatness. For this reason, after summarizing Garcia's points about Meinong, I will say something about my differences from Garcia.

1. Garcia on Things and Objects

"Our time," Garcia begins, "is perhaps one of an epidemic of things."[125] What he seems to have in mind is the flurry of industrially produced objects, of media-generated images, of informational entities in the internet, all joining the still-present tangible physical entities of earlier civilization such as farm animals, herbs and spices, and objects that clutter junkyards. The sheer size of this armada of things makes it difficult at first to put them in any sort of hierarchy. As Garcia continues, still on the first page of his book: "It becomes difficult to forbid anything from being equally 'something,' neither more nor less than another thing. We live in this world of things, where a cutting of acacia, a gene, a computer-generated image, a transplantable hand, a musical sample, a trademarked name, or a sexual service are comparable things." The very spirit of the age encourages a "flat ontology," to use DeLanda's term. Garcia also finds it important that after two centuries of philosophies of human access the pendulum should swing to the other side, so that we should start to speak of things again. But these are merely transient local reasons for focusing on things. The real reason, Garcia argues, is that while a philosophy of things is capable of doing justice to minds as special cases of things, the reverse is not true. Just as geese are "imprinted" by the first living creature they see as a maternal object, philosophers who begin with human thought are imprinted by this gesture and never escape from it, never bring us back to things. In order to do justice to things, our ontology must be completely flat so that nothing at all is left out. Things must be "de-determined" to the point where everything is included. In Garcia's words: "The goal of this de-determination is to have at one's disposal a cross-sectional plane of every container, of every order which maps the relief of the physical, biological, animal, and human universe, of artifacts, of works of art, of economic networks of production, of exchange and consumption, of differences of classes, of genders, of ages."

Garcia invites us to consider three different models of things. The first is the classical model in which predicates or accidents are like tributaries feeding a mighty river of substance, in a purely hierarchical relation where the substance dominates the predicates. Garcia describes this classical model with a contemporary example: "If I become attached to the being of some redness, the texture of denim, and some cut or pattern in the form of an hourglass, I can imagine three arrows carrying the being of red, the being of denim, and the being of the form of an hourglass in the direction of a fourth arrow: a dress which is red, denim, and in the form of an hourglass. And yet the dress is not predicated on anything, while the red, denim, or form of an hourglass are predicated on the dress." The problem here is the hasty hierarchy that does not permit things to be considered in their democratic flatness. But the second model is more contemporary, more hip. In Garcia's words:

The second model consists not in distributing being substantially, but vectorially. One thus conceives trajectories of being, identified with events, facts, powers, intensities, or intentionality. These vectors of being come first, bearing and supporting being, displacing it, but without ever finding a stopping point, a buffer, or an objective consistency. In such a representation that which is in the world is not identity, but difference, trajectory, becoming, a continuous projection of being which never opens onto a compact being, closed upon itself. There is no in-itself. Being is never an arrow whose direction turns around towards its own flight. Nothing is self-contained, sealed. The ontological plane is open and extends by flows, forces, becomings. To give an account of the apparent existence of things, of identifiable and re-identifiable stable entities, this model conceives the possibility of determining figures at the intersection of different trajectories. These figures are sealed, like a triangle whose three sides would be a panache of ephemeral vapors emitted from three aeroplanes scanning the sky... [For this model] a thing is a secondary effect, a construction, or an illusion at the junction of diverse events, of vectors of being.

The problem with this model is that "it tends to dissolve, to disseminate being, and it transforms things into effects, illusions, secondary realities." For Garcia, both models are equally false. For "the first produces a thing which is too much a thing, which is 'compact,' while the second generates a thing which is not thing enough, which is a construction, a volatile projection." After discounting these two models just a dozen pages into his book, Garcia already shares with us the key to his own philosophy. Namely, the thing is neither in-itself nor in-its-effects but is instead the *difference* between these two. The two great philosophical questions for Garcia are these: "what are things made of?" and "what do things make?" What is the basic stuff of the cosmos, and what is the structure of the cosmos? We might even say: what is the small and what is the big? For Garcia, every thing embodies both of these questions, since every thing is the point where these two opposing currents meet. He shares the fine example of a piece of black slate, an example that has already captured the imaginations of several reviewers of the book and deserves to be quoted at some length. As he puts it:

Take, for example, a block of black slate, a random rectangular sample taken from the space of continental collision. Few people will contest that this block is a thing. Obviously, one will be able to point out that it is necessary to have an active subjectivity to divide or distinguish this block of matter, lying on the ground or dusty soil, in order to perceive it as such. But this slice of black slate possesses certain qualities of cohesion and of solidity that allow one to dissociate it from its environment, manipulate it, transport it, and consider it quite simply as 'something.' What is it composed of? It contains quartz, clay-like minerals, mica, some traces of feldspar. And all these components themselves have a certain atomic structure. But in a wider sense, they also enter into the constitution of the rock as "thing": its rectangular form, the irregularities of its surface, the porphyroblasts coated with pyrite, its somber color, its delicate texture, its weight, its fragility –because it is extremely easy to break – and all the primary or secondary qualities by which we can recognize it.

We will say that this is *everything which is in this thing,* every path of being which leads to the constitution of this black slate in my hand. And yet from *everything which is in this slate* is never to be inferred *that in which it is.* Among everything which composes it, I will not find the position of the slate in the world, the relations in which it inscribes itself: the fact that it is now in my hand, the function of a weapon that it can exercise if someone attacks me, but also its place in the landscape, its rank in the series of slices of slate scattered alongside this valley. That which it is, this unique thing which exists in the world, held in my hand, is outside itself. The slate can in fact enter in turn into the composition of the side of a mountain, a roof, or a collection of rocks... it is no longer a question of *that which is in the slate*, but of *that in which this slate is*.

A mass of things are in it, and the slate itself can enter into the composition of a mass of other things. The black slate is thus not in itself. It is not a substance on which various qualities (its weight or its colour) are predicated. But neither is it an ephemeral entity, not existing in itself, constructed by my thought, my senses, and my action, from events and becomings (a certain variation of density of the matter, some effects of geological transformation, the trajectory of luminous rays). No, the black slate is the relation, inscribed in the world, between the being which enters the world and the being which comes out of it, and which enters in turn into another thing (into the soil, the landscape, the classes of other objects, my perception, the world in general).

Everything for Garcia is always torn in two directions, made up of both tendencies: the thing is that which is in it *and* that in which it is. This is Garcia's way of avoiding reductionism in either direction— and Garcia is quite adamant in his anti-reductionism, his quest for the initial democratic flatness of all things, including imaginary and even contradictory things. When a philosophical theory tries to reduce things to substances or events without considering the active *difference* between these two forces in everything, then such theories treat things as "compact," a word that means the same in French as in English (but which the English language owes to the French of the late 1300's, and is ultimately derivable from the Latin *compactus*, meaning "concentrated"). Just as "correlationism" is Meillassoux's key polemical term, *vorhanden* is Heidegger's, and "vacuous actuality" is Whitehead's, so too is "compact" the major polemical term of Garcia's book. He laments as follows about theories of the compact:

> As if one were capable of reducing the black slate to being nothing but a material thing, or a natural thing, or a social thing. As if one then were capable of considering matter, nature, or society as things outside appearances, absolute, remaining in themselves. This specter of the "compact," which will be the adversary of our entire adventure of thought, will only disappear on one condition: for each thing to have a sense, it must have *two* of them. Nature or history as things contain a multitude of things (first sense), but they will in turn be contained by things other than themselves (second sense).

We should also mention Garcia's attitude towards two prominent terms in recent continental thought: realism and materialism. Despite his expressions of gratitude towards Speculative Realists, Garcia himself shies away from the term "realism," apparently because he does not find it sufficiently flat. He wants unreal and contradictory objects to be included in his ontology along with real ones, and seems to worry that realism will grant hierarchical priority to real things over imaginary ones. As for materialism, he is initially even harsher for the very same reason: we cannot privilege one type of thing (solid material/physical entities) over immaterial types. Nonetheless, what Garcia appreciates in the term "materialism" is the idea that all entities should be of just one kind, with no special zone of spiritual or incorporeal entities following rules different from those of physical matter.

"The majority of our life," Garcia writes, "consists not in saying, doing, seeing, or understanding no-matter-what, but rather in establishing differences of importance, that is to say in limiting every thing to a sphere of belonging: the interest in intimate life, familial life, its country, social class, culture, works of art, beauty, love, sexuality, sports, knowledge, certain practices, nature, animals, ideas. Within each of these possible spheres of interest, some things always *matter* more than others, that is to say, they belong in an eminent, exceptional manner to this domain, to this group, or to this 'microcosm.' The majority of existence consists in defining, paying attention to, and defending what matters." Not so for Garcia's flat ontology, whose primary technical term is *n'importe quoi*: the thing "no matter what," "no matter what it is." Nothing that exists could be a "no matter what"; everything we can think of is already something *determinate*. "The no matter what is that which can be indifferently this or something which is not this, or even this *and* something which is not this— nothing prevents no-matter-what from being a contradiction, but nothing constrains it from being contradictory either; it doesn't matter." Nonetheless, the "no-matter-what is not nothing. On the contrary, no matter what —that is to say 'equally this *or* that *or* every other thing'— is something."

One of the chief features of Garcia's attitude towards recent philosophy is that it lives in *fear* of the flattening power of things. As he puts it in one passage: "human thought always conspires to resist a thingly epidemic, which carries in embryonic form the menacing power of the no-matter-what." Garcia identifies a number of different strategies for limiting the scope of thinghood, all of which he rejects. (32-33) First, in such thinkers as Aristotle and Descartes we find the idea that what is *contradictory* cannot be a thing. Second, in Wittgenstein's *Tractatus* there is the attempt to exclude the *unspeakable*. Third, there is the transcendental strategy of largely restricting things to what is *knowable* about them. Fourth, and somewhat amusingly, there is the cultural restriction of *taboos* that exiles certain things from the status of acceptable things. Fifth, there is the concept of the *sacred*, in which certain things are taken to be *more* than things: it would obviously cause outrage in many circles to speak of Jesus or other prophets as being *things* in the same sense as mailboxes, toasters, and grains of dust. In some contexts this is still enough in the year 2012 to earn us death by hanging, beheading, or bombing. The sixth strategy strikes a bit closer to home among today's intellectuals, who pride themselves on breaking cultural taboos and scoffing at sacred entities: this is the moral and political restriction on thinghood. As Garcia puts it so skillfully: "The sixth strategy, *moral and political,* consists in establishing insurmountable differences of nature between things and certain goods, of sensible subjects, of human individuals, of values, of works, or of ideas which must not be reified, lowered to the level of things as other things. This risks the irremediable fall of every value and of every dignity. Marxism, in a critical mode (of alien-ation, of reification), has illustrated this just as well as classical liberalism (in a contractual mode, and in differentiating various types of justice, various possibilities of relation to goods and to persons). Today, universalist humanism as well as animal ethics embody this spirit by distinguishing the human being, or the set of sensible, suffering beings from other things." (32-33) Thus it is not just religious people who exclude certain entities from thinghood. The same holds for portions of the political Left as well, such as with their ongoing complaints that object-oriented philosophies are guilty of "commodity fetishism," even though Marx only claimed that *value* is constituted by social relations of production, not that *reality itself* is thereby produced. In other words, the charge of fetishism cannot arise when someone merely says that trees exist when no one is looking, but only from saying that trees have an inherent *value* even when all humans are absent.

For Garcia, everything which exists, no matter what it is, is *something* rather than an indifferent no-matter-what. Contradictions are always *specific* contradictions. The square circle is not the same thing as the odd number six, since both flout logic in highly distinct ways. The non-white white and the non-city city are different affronts to the logician. The same is even more obviously true of taboos, which are highly specific in each case and often mutate into non-taboos, in which case their objects become explicit subjects of handling— the six-year-old with a horse phobia might someday become the world's leading horse trainer. Even the sacred, which often *creates* its object as an exception to the existing order, worships a God of a specific character, however vaguely this character might be known. The same is true for both the inexpressible and the unknowable. As Garcia puts it in another wonderful extended passage:

> If I walk alongside a property which is forbidden to me, drawing up a plan of its walls, I certainly don't have access to whatever is found in this mysterious place, but I can still map the contour of the estate. I can visualize the form of that which escapes me, the outline of its inclusion in the world. I know therefore *that which* this property *is,* its form, without knowing *that which is* this property, that is to say whatever is found inside the residence. In other words, although I found myself condemned to never enter the manor, I would have known at least that the manor is *something* in the world, whatever it encloses. Even that which I do not know, that is to say that for which the coming and going is judged impossible, that which is between that in which the thing is and that which is in this thing (between the location of the property from the outside and its exploration from the inside once its doors are open), I must know that it is something, in the absence of knowing that which is this something. The surrounding walls of knowledge do not give me access to the manor of transcendence. But they do not prevent me from identifying and from locating that which I do not know – on the contrary, they oblige me to stay there. It is "that which I do not know," thus it is certainly a thing, it is neither all nor nothing nor no matter

what thing.

The same holds even for the supposed exception of humans from the status of thinghood. For we do not take an equal interest in all injustices, nor are we always more interested in all people than in certain inanimate things. For Garcia,

it is necessary to comprehend, in order to be able to respect the human person as a thing like other things, which is no longer a better something than a duck, a pebble, a speck of dust, a chair, a word, or the entire sky. It is always necessary to know at what point no-matter-what is something so that we can perceive and defend objective differences between things. Reification, the reduction of our world to a world of things, is not an evil, a dehumanization, a desensitization, or a disenchantment of the world, but the precondition of a humane comprehension of the differences between things. A system of exception to the world of things is never a system of "moral" or "just" thought. It is a metaphysical system of the determination of inequalities between things, of "more-than-things," which cannot be a part of itself.

Or stated differently: "To know why I do not pay the same attention to another human being, a mosquito, a piece of gravel, a word, and a fourth of a leaf is not a question of principle. It is a question of interest, in the strict sense. What is interesting and what is not interesting? It is the question of knowing that which matters to us, what matters to life and to *human* life, because from the formal point of view of the no matter what everything is equal."

But what is the status of this "no-matter-what"? Is it linguistic, for-us, in-itself, a simple abstraction, or what exactly? For Garcia all of these questions miss the point, since the no-matter-what already encompasses them all: "It concerns the possibility of being *either* real *or* possible, *or* real and possible, *or* neither real nor possible, *either* constructed *or* given, *either* natural *or* artificial, *or* natural and artificial, *either* true *or* illusory, of not being all of these at once, but of indifferently being capable of registering, or not, one of these determinations, whatever it is." To this realm of absolute extensity we can oppose the *intensity* of values, which turns out to be a very important concept later in Garcia's book:

> Yet a value, whatever it is, positive or negative, seems each time a means of forcing a thing to be more what it is than anything else; to valorize a thing is to transform the strictly *extensive* character of every thing into an *intensity*. Thus, a beautiful thing and more beautiful than another is a bit more of a thing than an ugly thing. Thus, a true relation between two things is a bit more of a relation than a false relation. A value is that which affects the being of a thing by fundamentally rendering it intensive: beauty affects the thing, truth the relation between things, the good the relation of a thing to the world. Each time, the importance of the thing is accentuated or attenuated by its own value; that which is beautiful is *more* of something. There is *more* between two things which maintain a relation of truth than between two things whose relation is false. That which is good augments the world *more* than that which is bad.

In the second half of the book, intensity and valorization play an even more important role in allowing Garcia to explore multiple specific topics in the manner of Hegel's *Phenomenology of Spirit*. But in this first half of the book, the portion on which we are focusing today, the discussion of how some things matter and are important sets the table for Garcia's concept of "world," which links up in turn with his conception of "form":

In order for some things to matter more than others, to be either more beautiful (for us or in relation to some idea that we have of them) or more ugly, more true, more false, better or worse, it is necessary that a plane exists on which no thing is more thing or less thing than another. This plane is situated neither beyond nor below our values, from which we could abstract, or that we ought to attack with a hammer, or to fully deconstruct. It is nothing other than the plane of reference of our importances.

The flat world, where no thing is more important than another, supposes neither an abstraction nor a reduction, neither asceticism nor critique, neither genealogy nor deconstruction. The flat world is neither more nor less real than the planes on which the importances are played out, where things are exchanged, where we give to them or receive from them, as so many variable intensities. This is the flat world of the *no-matter-what*.

For Garcia, the twentieth century taught us repeatedly that no-matter-what could be something. Painting, for instance, "set out to represent the red, without any longer representing the table, at the moment of the modern passage to abstraction (in a Rothko canvas, or a Klein monochrome), giving to this color a status of *something* possibly independent, for the same reason that the table or the chair were substances. And everything which seemed, on account of metaphysical arguments, to benefit from a status of more-than-thing was progressively lowered to the level of a mere thing: *something,* not everything and not nothing." Despite this increasing flatness of daily life and aesthetic achievement, modernity also had a tendency to split the world reductively into more-than-things and less-than-things, as when the sciences turned atoms and other tiny particles into super-things while rendering ideas less than things, since they only inhere in matter. And here again, Garcia returns to the basic claim of his ontology of the in-between: "A more-than-thing is that which is in-itself, a less-than-thing is that which is in and by another thing." With this gesture, Garcia tacitly agrees with my own critique of undermining and overmining, with the major difference that he assigns the in-itself to the undermining fallacy, whereas for me the in-itself is what is between the two extremes of composition and relationality.

There are numerous additional riches in the first half of Garcia's book, but for the sake of time we limit ourselves to a few key points. One is that the thing is not only a middle ground between that which is in it and that in which it is. It is also a milieu or middle ground between the no-matter-what and the not-no-matter-what. In Garcia's words: "That which 'enters' into something is no-matter-what; that in which something 'enters' is 'not no-matter-what.' No-matter-what is something and something is not no-matter-what. Each thing is thus a milieu, a fragile link between 'no-matter-what' and 'not-no-matter-what.'" Each thing relies on its relation to something else which is not another thing: namely, the flat world of the no-matter-what. A thing is not necessarily one (since this would be another way of curtailing a purely flat ontology, and for Garcia unity is always relational, since a thing is one only with respect to other things), but it is always *alone* insofar as it is related to the flat world of the no-matter-what. But on the other side of the coin, insofar as it relates to other things it is what Garcia calls an *object*.

Things can communicate only insofar as they are alone in the world: two lovers are always alone, says Garcia in his poignant but also familiar example (since Rilke had already made the point so forcefully). Being simply means to be *contained* by something else, to be present in some environment, which is why for Garcia the question of being is a false problem from the start. There is also and always Garcia's critique of the compact, but we can leave that for the concluding summary. Let's turn now instead to Garcia's interesting lecture on Meinong, delivered on April 13,

2012 at the ATMOC seminar in Paris.[126]

2. Garcia and Meinong

The initial similarities between Garcia and Meinong are obvious enough. Like the earlier thinker, Garcia urges that we not restrict in advance what can or cannot count as a thing. He insists that "*Forme et objet* is not a neo-Meinongian book; [that] it proposes an entirely different theory of the object," Garcia defends what he calls the "weak ontological constraint" in Meinong, or "the wild initial impulse" rather than the eventual mild backtracking of Meinong and his later scholastic followers. From the very start, Garcia sees one problem with Meinong that stems from his legacy in the Brentano School: the fact that consciousness has an intentional structure. This makes consciousness a *special* kind of entity, and it remains unclear whether Meinong regards consciousness itself as an object. At the same time, it is always clear that there cannot be an object that would not be the object of a possible consciousness. As Garcia puts it: "The first consequence of this separation inherited by Meinong is that an object [unlike intentionality] has no object. And the second is that that which has an object is not truly an object. Stated differently, it would make no sense to speak of consciousness as one object in the world among others, as we can already see in Husserl's aversion to any kind of naturalistic model of consciousness. And furthermore, it would make no sense to speak of things-in-themselves that would not be possible objects of conscious awareness, another point easily visible in Husserl no less than in Meinong. The things must be observable by consciousness, or else they are not things. This is the first of several constraints found in Meinong that make Garcia uncomfortable. Meinong begins by trying to be as flat and democratic as possible, but quickly starts to add needless conditions to this flatness; Garcia's aim is to adopt the radical initial insight of Meinong and push it even further, so as to follow the spirit rather than the letter of Meinongian philosophy.

For Russell, Quine, and other opponents of Meinong in analytic philosophy, it is necessary to have what Garcia calls a "strong" ontological constraint. If every possible thing exists, then we will have objects that both exist and non-exist simultaneously, such as unicorns, square circles, and the white non-white non-city city. In other words, there is a pre-eminence of being over the object. The problem that motivates Meinong and his "weak" ontological constraint is precisely the reverse. If there are things that do not count as objects according to the strong constraint, then we are left with a number of sub-objects whose ontological status will be unclear. The non-circle circle must be *something*, since we understand what it means, and if it is not an object then we will face the burden of knowing what it is. Or as Garcia puts it:

> Between the weak ontological constraint and the strong ontological constraint, we witness the birth of a genuine dilemma. Each of the two positions is in fact haunted by a paradox which is the negative of the other. The paradox that haunts the strong ontological constraint is as follows: as soon as we accept that there are objects which are not, we find ourselves with objects which *simultaneously* are and are not. The contradiction here bears upon being. The paradox which haunts the weak ontological constraint is this: if we do not accept that there are objects which do not exist, then we find ourselves with something which will not be something. The paradox here bears upon the entity.

In Meinong's responses to Russell, we get the sense that he wants non-contradiction to be a local or regional principle governing certain kinds of entities and not others, much as Newtonian physics would be preserved as a special case of Einstein's theory for entities that are not too massive and not too close to the speed of light. For the defenders of a strong ontological constraint, the fact that a contradiction can lead to anything whatever means that a contradiction *is* anything whatever. But for Garcia, the decisive argument in favor of a *weak* constraint is that "even a contradiction is not 'no matter what'; it is necessary that determinations be attributed to it," so that a square circle and a non-unicorn unicorn are two different contradictions, not the same one.

But Garcia does not only complain about the likes of Russell and Quine and their strong constraint. He is equally negative towards what he calls the "neo-Meinongian Scholastics" who spend too much energy in *classifying* different types of objects, out of a fear that for Garcia is little different from that of Russell and Quine: the fear of a bloated universe in which everything would be equally real. Thus we find them distinguishing between real objects which have being, ideal objects which have being, non-existent non-contradictory objects, non-existent contradictory objects, incomplete objects such as "the object which is not blue," and other such elaborate categories. The problem with these neo-Meinongian theories is that they try to be both liberal and classificatory at the same time, and rather than the best of both worlds it leads them to the worst. The original wild impulse behind Meinong's theory is tamed and betrayed, rendered mediocre.

The real problem faced by Meinong is internal. There are three competing constraints on things in his philosophy. Let's start with the first: the representational constraint. As Garcia already mentioned, the Brentano School is obsessed with the problem of representations without objects, but leaves no room for the problem of objects without representations (and this is the flaw that later develops into Husserl's full-blown idealism). Stated differently, there is no room in Meinong for object-object relations without the presence of human observers; his theory of objects is implicitly a theory of human *reference* to objects. "And in fact," Garcia asks, "why should I think that the table and the paperweight enter into relation as objects only from the moment when I enter into relation with their relation?" In a manner reminiscent of Meillassoux's "archefossil," Garcia notes that the world existed for billions of years before representing entities appeared. If it is countered that inanimate entities *could* have been represented, Garcia would answer simply that they *were not* represented yet somehow related nonetheless. But Meinong's wish to be as liberal as possible in determining what counts as a thing is fatally undercut by his strong constraint that all things should be representable by consciousness.

Next, we can see that Meinong adds other implicit constraints to his otherwise liberal position on things. One of them concerns temporal identity. Is the table at time T_1 the same as the table at time T_2 and time T_3? One can certainly adopt this standpoint, but it already presupposes a hierarchy in which the fleeting individual moments of a table are ontologically derivative of a deeper table-nucleus that endures through all the various table-instants. The same problem arises in connection with space: "what are the relations between the parts of an objects and the whole? Between table legs, tabletop, and table? Between the atoms and molecules of the table? Are all of them equally objects? Or rather, are they parts of a superior object?" (M12) So, are parts somehow *less* than things? Are there first-class and second-class objects? All these questions indicate that Meinong wants to allow for a liberal flatness of objects and *at the same time* for their classi-fication into higher and lower.

The final problem for Meinong's classificatory scheme is what to do with *events*. His defenders cannot just claim that he only "cares" about objects and not about events, because one cannot be neutral on this question— the twentieth century made every effort to demonstrate that objects are undermined by events and are merely abstractions from these events: "the Heideggerian

Ereignis, Whiteheadian process, Bergsonian becoming, the Badiouian event." In other words, perhaps a Meinongian theory of objects can never be sufficiently flat, since it distinguishes at the outset between things and the transient events in which things might become involved. All three of these problems explain why Garcia considers himself a friend of Meinong but a greater friend of truth, since what he prefers is Meinong's "wild initial impulse" of flatness, sold too cheaply along the road.

Garcia concludes the lecture with an interesting theory of the anxiety of influence. As he writes: "Every book of philosophy that imagines itself to be innovative is built on a disappointed reading of other philosophers: in building for ourselves a deformed image of a great philosopher who preceded us, we imagine that [the philosopher] finished on such or such point by betraying that which we had initially found most precious in [the philosopher.]" And though Garcia once told me that his own intellectual background was primarily in the Frankfurt School, his own closest intellectual ancestor may in fact be Alexius Meinong, the supposedly inflationary object theorist of the Brentano camp. We have seen that what disappoints Garcia most in Meinong is his wavering between three incompatible constraints: the constraint that all objects must be representable, the constraint of being as liberal as possible in deciding what counts as a thing, and the constraint of having to classify different types of realities. In two key passages of the lecture, Garcia generously credits Speculative Realism with destroying the representational constraint, while also claiming his own contribution to a renovation of Meinong. As he puts it:

> The heritage of the contemporary critique of correlationism at work in Speculative Realism is particularly important for the project of *Form and Object* because it allows me to fold the pole of representation, intentionality, or consciousness onto that of objective relations. Inheriting the already rather distinct

conceptions of Graham Harman and Quentin Meillassoux with respect to correlationism, we use them in order to unburden ourselves of the requirement imposed on the object of responding to subjectivity through a correlation that would have systematic primacy over both the subject and the object...

The exit from the 20th century instigated by Speculative Realism liberated me from the intentional constraint; my own philosophical gesture consists in liberating myself from the constraint of classification, by splitting in two the object able to accommodate each thing and the object entering into relations among things.

Let's briefly discuss what Garcia means by this, before ending with some more general reflections on his philosophical position. The first impulse of thought, Garcia says, should be to seek the weakest constraint on what counts as a thing. Philosophy should be able to include everything, no matter what it is. But there cannot be *no constraint at all*. After all, philosophy cannot treat "no-matter-what" as itself a thing, since every individual thing is *determined* in some way, and is never a no-matter-what. In this connection Garcia often uses the unfamiliar term "tinology," which is derived from the Greek word *ti* (or "what") and was coined, as far as I can tell, by Pierre Aubenque. It is important for Garcia to insist against the Russell/Quine axis that contradictions *do* have some minimal determination. In a fascinating analysis, Garcia explains the difference between various contradictions along the following lines. A non-human human has the *possibility* of being a circle, but not the *possibility* of being human or the possibility of being non-human, since it is constrained by definition to be *both* of these. But for a non-circle circle, the situation would be the reverse. The non-circle circle would have the *possibility* of being human (since it is indeterminate with respect to humanity) but is *constrained* to be a circle and also *constrained* to be a non-circle. Thus, the non-human human and the non-circle circle are two different things, not one. To eliminate all constraints and allow for something to be purely indeterminate would be to *compact* the no-matter-what. We will say more about the compact shortly.

Having any determination at all is all it takes to count as a thing. Any further determinations than this will be shared by some things and not others. And this, says Garcia, is what explains the fact that his book has two parts. The first part, entitled "Formally," concerns only things *qua* things, things as having any determination at all rather than specific ones. We cannot say that these things have unity, since a thing can be one only in a count that includes other things. Instead, the things are marked by *solitude*; they are alone in their solitude. In Garcia's strangely beautiful words: "My hand is only something when it is the sole thing, when it is alone in the world. Where my hand is something, nothing else is something: all that which is not my hand is undifferentiated, whether it be my finger, the blue of the sky or the word 'hand.' And where my finger is something, my hand is not."

But insofar as things are not alone in their solitude, they either contain or are contained by other things. We have now left the field of *things*, defined by the first half of the book, and entered that of *objects* (the second half of Garcia's book is entitled "Objectively") which are always greater or lesser, asymmetrical in their relations with one another. Atoms are contained in the coffee mug but the reverse obviously does not hold: the coffee mug is not contained by atoms. The state of being contained is how Garcia defines *being*, which for him is nothing mysterious at all. The opposite of being is not non-being, but *comprehending*, in the sense of *containing* something else. Garcia admits that the targets of these ideas are the concepts of substance and the in-itself, which I will discuss again at the conclusion. Just one key point remains. The concepts of being and comprehending concern the extensive relation between different things. But for Garcia there are also *intensive* relations of things with themselves. A thing can be more or less itself insofar as it comes more or less in relation to itself: a difficult but important concept in his book.

3. Garcia vs. Substance

This has been a quick summary of a long and well-constructed book, but we are now in a position to raise a few questions about Garcia's model of the world. First, there is his observation that we can speak both of that which is in a thing and that in which a thing is. In one sense this means that a machine can be defined both by all the components that are in it and by the environment in which it is situated. In another sense, Garcia also says that a thing is "no-matter-what," rather than any tangible components. But let's leave this possible ambiguity aside for a moment and speak only of the first sense of the claim. The thing is situated between its components and its environment. In my own object-oriented philosophy, this means that the thing is identical *neither* with its components nor with its environment, since we can change a few atoms in the table without changing the table itself, and we can slide the table around on the floor a bit without changing the table itself. The table for me is a thing-in-itself situated between its components and its environment, and not fully accessible to either.

Two things surprise me about Garcia's position here. First, he tends to identify the table-in-itself with that-which-is-in the table, rather than simply identifying the table-in-itself with the table. For why would we ever identify the table-in-itself with table components? The pieces of a table are a physical necessity for the table to exist, but no one who claims that a table-in-itself exists identifies that in-itself with the subcomponents that build the table— other than hardcore materialists who think that the table in-itself is nothing more than physical fields or particles, and such people don't believe in the existence of tables in the first place. Garcia's concept of that-which-is-in-a-thing is also now somewhat cluttered, since it seems to include three things simultaneously: the components of a thing, the thing-in-itself, and the no-matter-what that is shared by all things in its indeterminacy.

But the second point is of more immediate importance. Namely, Garcia defines the thing not as a hidden midpoint between its components and its environment, but as the *difference* between these two. The table is the *difference* between its parts and the environment in which it is positioned. And there are two problems with this. First, it suggests a game of hot potato in which reality is always to be found somewhere else: if the table is the difference between its components and its environment, both of these in turn are things that will be the difference between that which is below and above them, and we will have a world filled with differences but lacking in positive terms from which everything else can differ. But perhaps the bigger problem is that this will turn everything into a gigantic relational ontology. If I am the difference between my bodily reality and my social role, then I will be changing constantly. Whenever I inhale and exhale or lose a few cells, whenever I age by a few minutes, gain or lose readers, when my retirement funds rise or fall on the stock market by a few Euros, or even when my daily environment changes in some minor, petty way, then I will become a different person. Entities are made too hypersensitively dependent on everything that surrounds them. There will be nothing in the things that is protected by firewalls from outside changes, and as I have argued elsewhere, this will mean (as it does for all relational ontologies, including Whitehead's and Latour's) that everything will always be fully deployed in reality at every moment with nothing held in reserve. The sidewalk table five meters from the road is deeply constituted by its being *exactly* five meters from the road; there will be no "table" separate from its location "five meters from the road," and thus it is impossible to see how the table can ever be moved. Garcia has a conscious motivation here, of course. He is so committed to flatness that he does not want "table five meters from the road" to have a lesser ontological status than "table" in its own right. But the price to pay for this sort of flatness is all objects must be fully determined at all times, completely in league with their components and their environment and hyper-sensitive to all changes in both. There can be no objects that would be something over and above their current environmental determinations. For me, what allows new things to happen is the mismatch between objects themselves and their current predica-ments, as previously compressed or hidden forces are unleashed. For Meillassoux this problem is handled through the radical contingency of all things, with anything able to happen at any moment for no reason whatsoever. But where, for Garcia, is the principle of dynamism in things?

11. First OOO Lecture in Russia

From Zagreb I flew directly to Russia to give the following lecture on June 27, 2012 at the Higher Institute of Economics in Perm, located just west of the Ural Mountains. Here I have replaced the generic original title of the lecture with one that better expresses my childlike thrill at travelling for the first time to Russia, an almost unthinkable journey during my Cold War youth. En route to Perm there was time to visit central Moscow for several hours; in Perm itself, there was a visit to an open-air Soviet weapons museum featuring decommissioned intercontinental nuclear missiles. Just as remarkable was the chance to see that Speculative Realism and Object-Oriented Philosophy were forces to reckon with in the intellectual life of Perm, centered in the remarkable Piotrovsky Bookshop. In this early afternoon lecture (packed with young Russian students) I discussed the meaning of metaphysics while discussing the views of Levi Bryant and the joint authorial team of Markus Gabriel and Slavoj Žižek. Ironically, I would meet both Gabriel and Žižek for the first time in Germany just a few days later, at Gabriel's summer school at the University of Bonn. It was there that Gabriel, a kind of prodigy in the German philosophy world, announced a new direction in his thinking: "fields of sense" ontology, which by his own admission has led him to renounce portions of his co-authored book with Žižek.

1. Metaphysics, Epistemology, Ontology

Philosophy moves slowly: unlike the arts and sciences, unlike politics and technology. For philosophy, a century is just long enough to give us three or four major thinkers, and true revolutions cannot be expected more than once in three hundred or four hundred years. While there may be disagreement as to which philosophers represent revolutions or turning points, it will not be especially controversial if I claim that the philosophy of Immanuel Kant is the most recent total revolution in the history of Western philosophy. Since the first publication of the *Critique of Pure Reason* in 1781, philosophy has always looked different than it did before. Thousands of books have been written on Kant, and perhaps millions of things have been said about him. But what is the simplest way to characterize Kant's philosophy in just a few sentences? Perhaps it is this: for Kant, human beings cannot make direct contact with the things-in-themselves, but only with phenomena. As a result, the old style of dogmatic metaphysics is no longer possible, and we must shift into the mode of "critical philosophy," which discusses the conditions of possible human access to the world rather than making direct claims about the world as it is in its own right.

The period following Kant is known, of course, as the age of German Idealism: beginning with Reinhold, Beck, Maimon, and Fichte, and reaching its full maturity in Hegel. In the early twenty-first century, German Idealism is once again greatly in fashion, encouraged by the prominent status of Alain Badiou and especially Slavoj Žižek. In a 2009 book, Žižek and co-author Markus Gabriel discuss the relation between Kant and German Idealism as follows: "German Idealism was designed to effectuate a shift from epistemology to a new ontology without simply regressing to pre-critical metaphysics."[127] This passage makes a definite claim concerning a supposed historical movement (metaphysics to epistemology to ontology) and Gabriel/Žižek claim further that while most contemporary philosophy remains stuck in epistemology, the German Idealists were already on the right track in giving us the basis for a new ontology. As is well known, there is no standard way of distinguishing between "metaphysics" and "ontology." Every author has a different attitude towards these terms: some treat them as interchangeable synonyms, while others make subtle distinctions between them, or even denounce one as the ultimate philosophical evil while using the other as a term of praise. These varying attitudes need not concern us here. Instead, we will simply describe how Gabriel and Žižek use the terms:

1. Metaphysics, or rather, "pre-critical" metaphysics. There is no mention by Gabriel or Žižek of a "post-critical metaphysics," so they seem to be using the phrase "pre-critical metaphysics" in the same emphatic and redundant way as the phrase "sweet sugar." That is to say, the pre-critical kind of metaphysics is not just one kind among others, but rather *all* metaphysics is pre-critical. The term "metaphysics" is henceforth negatively marked. What they mean by metaphysics seems clear enough. They are talking about the sort of dogmatic metaphysics that felt itself able to speak directly about the world without first passing through Kant's critique of the human apparatus of knowing.

2. Epistemology. This seems to be Gabriel and Žižek's term not only for Kantian philosophy, but for any of the philosophies of finitude that have existed since Kant. Heidegger would be a good example. In the eyes of Heidegger, pre-Kantian dogmatic metaphysics would clearly be impossible as well, since for Heidegger human Dasein is always *thrown* into a world that always partially withdraws from explicit presence to us. Absolute knowledge of any sort is impossible for Heidegger, whose conception of truth as a historically rooted form of "unveiling" is proverbial. Neither Kant nor Heidegger allows us direct access to the things-in-themselves, and thus Gabriel and Žižek hold them guilty of an "epistemology" that limits us to reflecting on the conditions of human access to the world, with no hope of absolute knowledge.

3. Ontology. For Gabriel and Žižek, this is the direction that true philosophy must take— the direction pioneered two

centuries ago by German Idealism. It is true, they claim, that we cannot make direct contact with things-in-themselves as pre-Kantian dogmatic metaphysics tried to do. It is equally true, they say, that we should not remain stuck in mere "epistemology," wringing our hands over the human inability to make direct contact with the real. For in fact, there are no inaccessible things-in-themselves. If we think of a mountain outside thought, then by the same stroke we are thinking of it, and this is a so-called "pragmatic contradiction"— sometimes also called a "performative" contradiction. Accordingly, there is nothing that transcends thought. Nothing is unthinkable; there is nothing that cannot eventually be made present to consciousness. The way to get rid of epistemology, according to Gabriel, Žižek, and their German Idealist ancestors, is not to find some trick to allow us to make direct contact with things-in-themselves again. Instead, we should realize that epistemology was always a pseudo-problem from the start. There is no mysterious gulf between us and the things that requires a special theory to explain. The human subject can make contact with the real whenever it pleases, since the subject and the real belong to the same space and do not differ in kind.

Before moving further, let me state for the record that I do not agree at all with this typical German Idealist maneuver. Perhaps a medical analogy will be helpful in showing why. Imagine a patient with terrible pain in his legs due to arthritis (the analogous "pain" for us being the inaccessibility of the things-in-themselves). Pre-critical metaphysics resembles a doctor in denial about the pain in the patient's legs: "Don't worry, there is no problem here. Just walk wherever you want." By contrast, Kantian epistemology realizes that there are severe pains in the legs that will never go away, but offers to manage the pain through exercise, acupuncture, massages, and occasional trips to Black Forest health spas. What Gabriel and Žižek call "ontology," however, is a more radical approach to the problem. They agree that legs without pain will never again be possible. But they are tired of a medicine that spends all its time fussing over delicate procedures for reducing the pain in the legs. The solution for them is obvious: simply amputate the patient's legs. The analogy may sound extreme or unfair, but it is clear that this is precisely what they ask us to do. If "epistemology" consists in expending energy on studying ways to bridge the human-world gap, and if it has already been shown (as Kant showed) that direct passage across the gap is impossible, then there seem to be only two possible solutions. First, we can deny that an autonomous "world" side exists, as the fans of German Idealism recommend. Second, we can deny that a genuine "human" side exists, by reducing it to the same physical laws as the rest of the world, through the detour of neurophilosophy. And it is striking how often these two options go hand in hand in present-day continental thought, with praise for Hegel in one moment and equal praise for the hardcore Thomas Metzinger in the next.[128] If matter is praised on one side and spirit on the other, what both have in common is a monistic outlook in which the knowing human subject has direct access to the real and can use this privileged access to annihilate whatever it happens to regard as mere ideology. What this outlook really hates about Kantian epistemology is the notion that absolute truth is unattainable by humans. Yet this is the *best* part of Kant, and the most important part of his Copernican Revolution. It is also the portion of Kant that is carried further by Heidegger, as we will discuss again shortly. But first, there is something else to be said about the wildly charismatic Žižek.

2. The Spear That Smote You

In his 1993 book *Tarrying with the Negative*,[129] Žižek entitles his fifth chapter "The Wound is Healed Only by the Spear That Smote You," referring to a line in Richard Wagner's *Parsifal*, the final opera of the composer's career. Just two years ago, Levi Bryant blogged wonderfully about this Wagnerian trope:

> Žižek, speaking of Wagner, likes to speak of us as being healed by the spear that smote us and it is in this context, I believe, that [Object-Oriented Ontology] is particularly interesting. When Žižek speaks of the spear that smote us as healing us he is alluding to the way in which the wound, far from being the problem, is, in fact, the *solution*. In a psychoanalytic context, for example, your symptom is not something to be eradicated, but rather, over the course of analysis you undergo a subjective transformation with respect to your symptom, coming to discover that it is the very secret of your desire and source of your *jouissance*, such that the removal of the symptom would amount to the removal of the very principle of your subjectivity. It is not that you continue to live your symptom in the same way —washing your hand three hundred times a day, for example— these sorts of minor symptoms do in fact disappear. Rather, it's that the fissure that generated those "empirical symptoms" is itself trans-formed.[130]

Shifting from psychoanalysis to philosophy, Bryant continues: "Something like this, I think, is at the heart of [Object-Oriented Ontology's] ontological gesture. For the last three hundred or so years we have had variants of *skepticism*. Philosophy has grown to be equated with epistemology *tout court*..." And further: "Kant's move was to restrict knowledge to images on the wall of Plato's cave (appearances) arguing that we can never escape the cave. We are all heirs of this move today. Between Kant and later Wittgenstein, for example, there is not a difference in kind, but a difference in *degree*... That we are restricted to appearances or the 'for-us.' And in all these cases, in this infinite variety of anti-realisms, what is everywhere and always being argued is that presence cannot be attained or established." And finally:

> [Object-Oriented Ontology's] move is not to stubbornly claim that 'no, our representations correspond to things in themselves!,' but rather [it] makes the Wagnerian gesture of healing us on the sphere that smote us. Its thesis is not some new-fangled attempt to attain presence or an *adaequatio rei et intellectus*, it is not an attempt to square the circle purporting to show that relations don't change things. Rather, [Object-Oriented Ontology] challenges the central ontological premise of these epistemic skepticisms: *the thesis that objects are present to themselves or to other objects.*

The interest of this important post by Bryant is that he effectively uses one of Žižek's favorite metaphors for non-Žižekian purposes. Both Žižek and object-oriented philosophy agree on the impossibility of making direct contact with an in-itself outside the mind. And both Žižek and object-oriented philosophy agree on the paralyzing effects of "epistemology," or the notion that philosophy can only concern itself with the technical mechanisms of how humans relate to the world. The crucial disagreement concerns what should be done to avoid both pre-critical metaphysics and epistemology. We have seen that for Žižek the solution lies in realizing that there was never anything outside the mind, and hence that all epistemology is worthless. By contrast, Object-Oriented Ontology holds that epistemology is simply *too limited*, since it treats a basic gap in reality as a special product of tragic cognitive features found in human beings alone. And here once more, I can hardly improve on the formulation of Bryant: "in arguing that objects withdraw from all relations, whether humans or otherwise, [Object-Oriented Ontology] is simultaneously able to integrate the claims of… skepticisms… and turn what appeared as a vice (the impossibility of *knowing* objects) into a virtue (the very being of objects). Where previously the wound was seen as residing in *us* (objects withdraw from us because of the manner in which our cognition actively reworks them), the cut, the withdrawal, is now located in the *things themselves*."

On that note, let's return to the announced title of this lecture: "The Return of Metaphysics in Contemporary Continental Philosophy."[131] We recall the terminology of Gabriel and Žižek. There is metaphysics, which holds that we are able to speak directly of a world outside the mind. There is epistemology, which claims that a world exists outside the mind but that we can never reach it. And finally there is ontology, which denies the existence of a world outside thought and thereby secures the absolute for direct accessibility to thought. This third option is the one recommended by Gabriel and Žižek, and inspired by German Idealism. According to this particular terminology, what Gabriel and Žižek call for is "The Return of *Ontology* in Contemporary Continental Philosophy," meaning a return of the German Idealist doctrine that the things-in-themselves are superfluous. And since the present lecture calls for "The Return of *Metaphysics* in Contemporary Continental Philosophy," for Gabriel and Žižek this could only sound like a return to *pre-critical* metaphysics, pre-Kantian metaphysics, dogmatic metaphysics, in which the human mind gains direct access to a world located outside the mind.

Yet this is not the case, as Bryant argued so effectively in the blog post just cited. But I would like to offer another way of looking at the problem. Consider the position that Gabriel and Žižek call "epistemology," the position that a real world exists outside the mind but cannot be directly known. It is rarely noted by anyone that there are two distinct theses combined in this single position: finitude and anthropocentrism. We can consider these one by one. First, "epistemology" obviously implies finitude. There is a world out there beyond us, but we cannot get to it directly. Instead, our access to that world is mediated by the conditions of our finitude, which for Kant is defined by space, time, and the twelve categories, and for Heidegger by the specific historical conditions of our Dasein. When Gabriel and Žižek (or Quentin Meillassoux) try to overcome epistemology in favor of ontology, it is this *finitude* that they wish to reverse. They realize that this cannot be done by way of pre-critical metaphysics, since we cannot speak of the world-apart-from-us without immediately turning it into a world *for* us, since it is we who are speaking of the world without us. The truth is immanent in the circle of human thought, and therefore perfectly accessible to reason. Philosophy can remain a form of rationalism, since the real is the rational and the rational is the real, just as Hegel told us.

But however boldly such thinkers try to reverse the *finitude* of epistemology, they leave its anthropocentrism intact. After all, epistemology does not only claim that access to the world is finite, they make this claim only for *humans*— or for some distracting expanded variant of humans such as "all rational beings." They are committed to this anthropocentrism due to the faulty argument that they use to escape Kantian epistemology. The reason the things-in-themselves do not exist is because it is we who think them, and therefore they do not exist in themselves, but only as thought by us. For the same reason, it makes no sense to try to move beyond the anthropocentric basis of ontology, which for such thinkers is the only rigorous way to proceed. We cannot ask about what it is like for fire-in-itself to burn cotton-in-itself, or for one stone-in-itself to strike another, because the very existence of an in-itself has already been refuted (or so they believe). For them it makes no sense to ask about the nature of the relation between two non-human things, because simply by asking about it we are thereby relating to it. The relation between fire and cotton or between two stones cannot even be asked about; for them, this would be nonsense. The only relation is the human-world relation, and since there is no world-in-itself apart from humans, that human-world relation is by no means finite. To summarize, the Gabriel/Žižek/Meillassoux "ontologists" defeat the finitude of epistemology at the price of embracing its anthropocentrism.

And this is the crux of the matter, since object-oriented philosophy does exactly the reverse, preserving the *finitude* of Kant's position while renouncing its *anthropocentrism*. As we have seen, the Gabriel/Žižek "ontology" model follows German Idealism in accepting what Meillassoux aptly terms "the correlational circle." We cannot think of objects outside thought, because precisely by doing so, we think of them. This entails that we cannot think of the relation between any two things apart from human thought, because this itself is a thought, and hence all relations are reduced to human relations with the world. Anthropocentrism is guaranteed in advance. And once it is guaranteed, then there is no longer any dark residue in the world outside the reach of humans, and this means that Kant's finitude is impossible. Philosophy becomes both anthropocentric and infinite, just as in Hegel's philosophy.

But if we do not accept the validity of the correlational circle, the results are rather different. If I say that I am thinking of a tree outside thought, the "ontologist" will counter by saying that this is a performative contradiction, since I claim to be doing exactly the opposite of what I am actually doing. But this response by the ontologist is an example of the logical fallacy known in Latin as *petitio principi*, or in English as "begging the question." For when I say "I am thinking of a tree outside thought," I make two claims: (1) I am thinking of a tree, and (2) its existence is something more than my thinking of it. And there is no contradiction here at all. At most, the "ontologist" could claim that there is no evidence for the second point. But what the ontologist *cannot* claim is that point 1 and point 2 are in contradiction. To make this claim is to *presuppose* that if I am thinking of a tree there *cannot* be anything more to its existence than its being thought. All that the "metaphysician" does is think a tree that can be thought but whose being does not consist in its being thought. Admittedly, there are cases when no such thing exists. I may say "I am thinking of a unicorn outside thought," and this turns out to be false— not because it turns a supposedly unthought unicorn into a thought unicorn, thereby leading to a performative contradiction, but simply because of the fact that there are no unicorns existing independently of being thought about. Stated differently, the fact that something can be thought does not entail that it does not exist outside thought. Far from being a devastating argument, the correlational circle is a flimsy basis on which to build a philosophy, one that borders on a mere word trick.

Once the correlational circle is rejected, the situation with "epistemology" looks rather different. Now, its *anthropocentrism* must be rejected. We are perfectly free to ask about the relation between cotton and fire, or between two stones, quite apart from any human access to this relation. And what we find is that finitude is present even in the inanimate realm. When fire burns cotton, it has no contact with the color or smell of the cotton, which are irrelevant to flames that have neither eyes nor noses to detect these properties. With respect to colors and smells, flames are perfectly stupid. Just as human cognition of a cotton ball is finite, governed by space, time, and the twelve categories, so too is the fire-cotton interaction a drastic oversimplification of these two entities by one another. If Kant was in error, it was not through his defense of finitude, but rather through his defense of anthropocentrism. Rather than overthrowing Kant in favor of some form of absolute knowledge, some form of what Gabriel and Žižek call "ontology," what we need is to spread the Kantian vision across the cosmos as a whole. For what Kant actually gave us was not a poignant theory of the special limitations of poor human beings. Instead, he gave us a noumenal/phenomenal distinction that holds for all relations whatsoever. Rocks, fire, cotton, and flowers all exist as things-in-themselves, since they all have reality outside the relations into which they enter. But they also all exist as phenomenal caricatures for the various other entities that confront them. I encounter the cotton ball in one way, the fire encounters it in another, the boll weevil in still another. The cotton ball is not exhausted by any of these relations, or by the sum total of all its real and possible relations. You cannot get a noumenon by adding up an infinite number of phenomena. A real object cannot be built of images. Instead of finitude being a sad limitation on human thought, it becomes the positive character of all entities that exist. This is how object-oriented philosophy aims to return to metaphysics, and not a metaphysics of a "pre-critical" kind. Instead, it can only be a "post-critical metaphysics," and that means one that takes seriously Kant's thesis on finitude, which the model of German Idealist ontology does not. The spear that smote us was not Kant's anthropocentric bias; this is a simple limitation that is easy to overcome, not a major flaw that deserved to give rise to a counter-movement four decades in duration. Instead, the Kantian spear that smote us was the inaccessibility of the things-in-themselves, and the way to be healed by this very same spear is to realize that the wound is not a wound at all, but the positive structure of how things are.

3. Object-Oriented Philosophy and Bryant's Onticology

But not all object-oriented theories are alike. Earlier I quoted Levi Bryant's eloquent defense of how the movement makes progress beyond skepticism and idealism alike. Nonetheless, I cannot agree with all of the principles of Bryant's philosophy, which he terms "onticology."[132] There are perhaps three major disagreements: first, Bryant rejects what I call vicarious or indirect causation; second, he rejects what I call sensual objects; third, he rejects what I call real qualities. But before disagreeing with Bryant, it is necessary to explain what I mean by each of these terms. And that requires a brief explanation of my own philosophical position.

The phenomenology of Edmund Husserl was an attempt to eliminate all hidden entities and turn philosophy towards a rigorous consideration of what appears to consciousness. We cannot follow the sciences in explaining human experience by way of chemicals, sound waves, the laws of optics, or other such entities. After all, these are just theories, however well backed they may be with experimental evidence. Ultimately, the only immediate knowledge we have is our knowledge of phenomena, which Husserl asks us to describe in patient detail rather than explain them away with scientific theories. A slow-motion rebellion in phenomenology began in 1919 at the hands of Martin Heidegger, who had been the heir apparent to Husserl as prince of phenomenologists. As Heidegger noted in his famous tool-analysis, for the most part we *do not* encounter things as present in consciousness. Instead, we rely upon them silently, using oxygen, kidneys, floors, and transportation networks without taking much notice of them at all. It is usually only when they *break* that we take explicit notice of entities. Whereas Husserl's phenomena are always presented in consciousness, Heidegger's tool-beings *never* are, since they forever withdraw from explicit presence into a dark and shadowy underworld. Heidegger's question of the meaning of being is the question of this underworld, a question that Husserl could only view as nonsense. Let's call Heidegger's world of hidden or withdrawn objects the "real" world, since it is there whether we think of it or not. It is roughly the same as Kant's "noumenal" sphere. At the same time, let's call Husserl's world of phenomenally accessible objects the "sensual" sphere. (He calls it the "intentional" sphere instead, but for various reasons it is better to use a different word.) Husserl's "sensual" is a reasonably good, basic equivalent for Kant's "phenomenal" realm.

In this sense, Husserl and Heidegger might at first be read as if each were simply insisting on the rights of one half of Kant's model of reality. Husserl seems to be someone who focuses on the phenomenal while denying the existence of any noumenal sphere, which would seem to place him very close to German Idealism. Heidegger, by contrast, seems to be focusing on an indeterminate noumenal sphere withdrawn from all presence. The main problem with this reading is that it misses what is most important about Husserl. For while it is mostly true that Husserl confines his philosophy to the phenomenal realm, he also describes a fresh tension within this realm that no previous philosopher had noticed. It has often been argued that real objects may exist in the depths, but that humans encounter only specific *qualities* rather than objects. This is basically the position of British Empiricism. According to David Hume, we do not encounter an apple, but only a bundle of apple-qualities; since these qualities seem to appear together with regularity, we form the habit of treating them as a unified "apple."

But here Husserl makes a breakthrough that cuts against the grain of British Empiricism. What he noticed (and this point is the basis of all of phenomenology) is that we primarily encounter *objects*, not qualities. When I see my friend Hans standing in a certain posture, wearing a specific shirt, and having a specific short length of hair after his recent trip to the barber, Hans is not just a "bundle of qualities." The proof of this is that I can circle around Hans and observe him from different angles, watch him change his posture, change his shirt, or even witness his hair growing longer over time. As all of these changes occur, Hans becomes a different "bundle of qualities," but he does not become a different Hans. In short, we look straight through any bundle of qualities towards an underlying object *beneath* these qualities. The qualities themselves are swirling accidents that can shift from one minute to the next, not crucial foundation stones of the thing. And furthermore, the object called Hans is not a *real* object lying outside all experience, since I am in direct contact with Hans as soon as I look at or acknowledge him. Hans is not withdrawn from all access into a hidden underworld of being. Indeed, Hans might not exist at all: for I may be drugged or insane, and Hans may be my imaginary friend, no more real than a centaur or unicorn. What Husserl discovered is the existence of a sensual *object* in tension with its sensual *qualities*. Hence, there is a second axis in the world. Along with the polarized opposition between the hidden or real or noumenal and the visible or sensual or phenomenal, there is also a rift between the sensual object and its sensual qualities. But the same division also occurs in the heart of the real. Real objects must have specific qualities, or they would all be the same, a point already made by Leibniz early in the *Monadology*. Instead of the usual twofold structure of a real world outside the mind and a phenomenal world inside the mind, what we have instead is something more complex and interesting. Namely, we now have a fourfold structure of real objects, real qualities, sensual objects, and sensual qualities, whose various permutations provide the basis for a new metaphysics.

One other point needs to be stressed. Given that objects withdraw not just from us but from each other as well, there is a serious philosophical problem in understanding how objects make contact at all. When I hold an apple, or when fire burns cotton, it makes no sense to say that one object touches another "directly" but "partially," as in the usual objection to my position. We cannot say that one object makes contact with 72% of the other object while allowing the other 28% to be hidden from view. The reason is that objects are units, not just aggregates of pieces. If I make contact with 72% of an apple, then perhaps I would be making contact with seventy-two different *parts* of an apple while failing to make contact with twenty-eight other parts. The apple itself is nowhere to be found in all this piecemeal contact. And moreover, there would simply be an impossible regress, since it would remain just as mysterious how I am able to make contact with the seventy-two parts. For I would also not be in direct contact with each of these seventy-two parts, but only with perhaps 72% of each of these parts, or maybe 10% or 85% of them, and so on to infinity. In the end, contact between one object and another either occurs or fails to occur: "partial" contact is not an option.

On the one hand, since objects withdraw from one another, they seem not to make contact at all. This was the problem identified by occasionalism, which first appeared in early Islamic theology and later became prominent in seventeenth century French philosophy. But while the occasionalists deserve praise for understanding the difficulty of any two entities making direct contact, we cannot adopt their solution of making *God* the universal mediator of all relations, since there is no reason other than piety why God should be able to make direct contact if other entities cannot do this. The only way to solve the problem is locally, in the "secular" fashion pioneered by Bruno Latour.[133] Every entity, not just God, must have the ability to forge links with other entities, despite the paradoxical impossibility of doing so because of the principle that all things withdraw from each other. For reasons explained in my publications, the solution to the problem must go roughly as follows. Two real objects cannot make contact directly, and hence they must be linked a sensual object; likewise, two sensual objects cannot make contact directly, but are linked only by a real object, such as a conscious agent. In this way, the fourfold structure and the problem of indirect causation fit together at the very heart of object-oriented philosophy.

We now return to the major differences between Levi Bryant's philosophy and my own. To repeat, those differences are as follows: first, Bryant rejects what I call vicarious or indirect causation; second, he rejects what I call sensual objects; third, he rejects what I call real qualities.[134]

As for vicarious causation, Bryant is on record as seeing no problem at all with direct relations between entities. In Bryant's case this is somewhat strange, since he is also on record as agreeing that entities always *translate* one another whenever they relate. In other words, Bryant agrees that when an apple is encountered by a human, a raindrop, a pig, or a worm, all of these entities fail to exhaust the reality of the apple, since they simply translate it into human terms, raindrop language, pig phenomena, or worm understanding. Bryant agrees with me that exhaustive knowledge of a thing is never possible. And nonetheless, he does not see any especial problem with how two objects can make direct contact. The problem Bryant faces here is that translation is also a starting point, not just a result. It's not as if fire and cotton make easy direct contact and *only then* does the fire translate the cotton into some caricature or distortion. Instead, the fire and contact only make contact with images or simulacra of each other from the start. And this entails that only vicarious or indirect causation exists, not some direct form of relation. The real cotton and real fire must always be mediated in their link by a sensual object.

I realize that for many people, indirect relation is the strangest aspect of my philosophy, the one they are most willing to abandon even when they agree with other aspects. But just as every galaxy is believed to harbor a black hole at its center, every important new theory has a central paradox at its core. Indirect or vicarious causation clearly serves the role of the central paradox for object-oriented thought, the price one must pay for acknowledging the withdrawal of objects from direct accessibility or contact. Attempting to soften the edges of that problem by treating it as a pseudo-problem is to miss what is most powerful in the object-oriented position, and risks turning into a sort of "Object-Oriented Lite" that is too eager to flatter the dominant postmodernist philosophies of the past twenty years. If you are willing to admit that objects translate each other, you should also be ready to concede that even their *initial* contact is just a translation.

Bryant's other two objections are reducible to a single point of disagreement: his rejection of the fourfold structure of reality. For Bryant's onticology, the key distinction is between "virtual proper being" and "local manifestation," which suitably reflects the Deleuzean flavor of Bryant's prior path of thinking. Imagine once again that I am holding an apple. Numerous different entities encounter the apple in ways that are phenomenally different. For Bryant, these different ways of encounter are all different "local manifestations" of the same underlying apple. But what, exactly, makes each local manifestation different? When reading Bryant's argument here, one has the impression that the local manifestations are simply "bundles of qualities" in the old empiricist sense. If I view the apple from the left and then from behind, the visible qualities of the fruit are different in each moment, and thus each local manifestation seems to be different. In other words, there is no such thing as a "sensual object" for Bryant, who like most Deleuze-inspired philosophers takes little interest in Husserl. Whatever unity there is in the various local manifestations of an apple is not to be found on the surface of perception, where swirling, kaleidoscopic bundles of qualities change from one moment to the next. Instead, the unity of objects for Bryant is entirely anchored in their "virtual proper being," in the real subterranean or virtual realm. There are no sensual *objects* for Bryant, but only sensual *qualities*.

With that point in mind, let's shift our attention from Bryant's sensual to Bryant's real. For me, real objects are withdrawn objects that also have withdrawn real qualities. We can't have direct access to the real qualities of an orange any more than we

great jumps in life more likely arise from our symbiosis with other objects, leading to those ultimately temporary stabilities the paleontologists Niles Eldredge and Stephen Jay Gould termed "punctuated equlibria."[136]

The danger of Bryant's conception is that it leaves us trapped in a model in which the real is too *indeterminate* and the sensual is too *determinate*— a model in which the real apple has no qualities but just capacities, while the sensual apple of experience is overly defined by *all* of its qualities, so that an added fleck of color as I rotate the apple is enough to constitute a brand new local manifestation. The real apple would be undermined (by turning it into a capacity rather than an object) while the sensual apple would be overmined (by turning it into a bundle of qualities). This is one of the primary dangers faced by Bryant's philosophy in the near future, and here I believe his lack of interest in Husserl will make him pay a serious price. For it is only from Husserl that we learn the flaws in the "bundle of qualities" theory of experienced objects.

Bryant does not see the sensual world as containing any *objects*, so there is no internal tension within the sensual realm for him. We also saw that Bryant doesn't think that real objects have *qualities*, meaning that there is no internal tension on that level either. It seems that for Bryant the "real" is entirely made up of objects, while the "sensual" is entirely made of qualities. Rather than a fourfold structure, Bryant gives us a more standard twofold structure. And this misses the brilliance of both Husserl (who splits the sensual world in half) and Leibniz (who split the real world in half). Yet the return to metaphysics requires that we not miss the brilliance of either of these thinkers, who will be badly needed in the years to come.

12. McLuhan as Philosopher (2012)

*In the summer of 2012, Erick Felinto and others organized a travelling
conference in Brazil that assembled numerous authors on media theory:
primarily Americans, Brazilians, and Germans. The cities hosting the
conference were São Paulo, Rio de Janeiro, Salvador, and Fortaleza,
though various participants arrived and departed at different stages of
the trip. (For example, Bruno Latour was with us only in Rio de Janeiro
and Salvador.) In Fortaleza I closed the tour with a separate lecture on
Marcel Duchamp and Clement Greenberg that will be published in the
journal* Speculations[137]. *But the following lecture was given on the
first three stops of the trip: in São Paulo on July 30, Rio de Janeiro on
August 2, and Salvador on August 6. The lecture was my latest attempt
to come to terms with the underrated legacy of McLuhan, who is still
taken seriously by too few intellectuals in our time.*

Marshall McLuhan has been internationally famous for half a
century. For most authors, the danger of fame is that of becoming
a boring known quantity. There is a painful logic at work here: an
obscure author becomes an honored public figure only once that
author is stripped of the ability to surprise us. A standard interpretation of the author's work arises, supported and enforced by
various institutions, and a thinker who was originally daring and
rebellious is now represented on stage by chorus and security
guards. The only solution to this predicament (usually a
posthumous solution) is to fall so far out of fashion that an
ingenious reinterpretation of an author's work becomes
necessary, though probably one that the author would never have
endorsed. Here is the treacherous fate of important intellectual
figures, who triumph for only a few brief years before being trivi-
alized into official versions, and later (if they are lucky) twisted
beyond recognition by their most gifted grandchildren.

It is Marshall McLuhan's good fortune to have avoided this

typical cycle: partly because he is viewed by many as too frivolous to belong in the canon of recognized intellectual heroes, partly because he goes rapidly in and out of fashion with the emergence of each new wave of technology, and partly because he has never been taken seriously as what he really is— a philosopher. Today I want to convince you that McLuhan is a figure of tremendous value for philosophy: not because McLuhan is more than just a media theorist, but because philosophy ultimately may be nothing more than media theory.

McLuhan's most famous phrase is immeasurably more famous than those of Plato, Aristotle, Kant, or Hegel. McLuhan's most famous phrase is: "The medium is the message." What this means for McLuhan is that the explicit *content* of any medium is less important than the presence of that medium itself. The difference between high-quality and low-quality television programming is insignificant when compared with the transformative background effects of television, which differ greatly from those of radio, which differ from those of the newspaper and the town crier. For McLuhan, the unnoticed background conditions of our media overpower all conscious human discrimination and decision. This has led to repeated charges that McLuhan is a "technological determinist"— especially in Britain, where intellectual life is so often dominated by questions of Leftist politics. Later, I will try to explain why the charge of technological determinism misses the point.

But first I would like to note an ambiguity in the concept of "medium" that will serve as the engine of this lecture. We have seen that for McLuhan, the medium is that which hides in the background, silently dominating our awareness even as we remain hypnotized by the surface content of television, telephone, the newspaper, or the e-book. In this respect McLuhan is the clear ally of Martin Heidegger, with his contempt for the visible figures of presence-at-hand and his poetry of Being, which withdraws behind all conscious access.

There is at most a difference of *attitude* here, since McLuhan claims to prefer the vanishing literate culture of explicit visibility to the emerging tribal culture of group inclusion and concealed background effects, while Heidegger openly deplores the culture of presence. Moreover, while Heidegger treats technology as if it reduced all objects to a stockpile of present-at-hand materials, McLuhan sees the new electronic technologies as doing just the opposite, removing the literate-visual culture of presence in favor of something perhaps more challenging. Shortly, I will address the McLuhan-Heidegger relation with respect to their shared attention to the cryptically concealed background and the central role of fourfold structures in their thinking.

But there is a second sense of "medium" that apparently has little to do with hidden backgrounds. This is the medium in the sense of the *mediator*. Two quarreling friends are afraid to approach one another directly, and are invited to lunch by a third who is able to patch up the quarrel. A postal service mediates the written communication between two friends who live in distant parts of the globe. A regent mediates the transfer of power between the dead king and the infant prince. Fleas mediate the transmission of bubonic plague from rats to humans. In these cases, the medium is by no means that which functions as a hidden background; rather, it is the explicit mediator of contact between two other things. In fact, here it is the very opposite of a ground— it is a *figure* that enables the communication between two grounds that would otherwise not be able to communicate. It might seem that there is no such concept in McLuhan, but I will claim the opposite. And here the parallel is not with Heidegger, but with Bruno Latour.

1. The Figure, the Ground, and the Tetrad

In saying "the medium is the message," and in this way denying that the content is the message, McLuhan makes use of a distinction drawn from Gestalt psychology between figure and ground. As he puts it in the posthumously published *Laws of Media*, co-authored with his son Eric:

> All situations comprise an area of attention (figure) and a very much larger area of inattention (ground).... Figures rise out of, and recede back into, ground... For example, at a lecture, attention will shift from the speaker's words to his gestures, to the hum of the lights or to street sounds, to the feel of the chair or to a memory or association or smell. Each new figure in turn displaces the others into ground.[138]

The McLuhans immediately add that

> the study of ground "on its own terms" is virtually impossible; by definition it is at any moment environmental and subliminal. The only possible strategy for such study entails constructing an anti-environment: such is the normal activity of the artist, the only person in our culture whose whole business has been the retraining and updating of sensibility.[139]

We will deal later with the role of the artist in McLuhan's world. For the moment I simply wish to note that Heidegger himself might easily have written the McLuhan passages just quoted. Heidegger too might have said that "figures rise out of, and recede back into, ground," that "attention will shift from the speaker's words to his gestures, to the hum of the lights or to street sounds," and that "the study of ground 'on its own terms' is virtually impossible." Nor would such remarks be peripheral to Heidegger's philosophy. In this way, McLuhan finds himself in close proximity to one of the greatest philosophers of the past century, and indeed probably the greatest.

Heidegger found his original voice by overcoming phenomenology. The entire point of Husserl's phenomenology was to suspend all consideration of a hidden ground of natural, physical causes and to focus only on what is present in consciousness. But Heidegger reversed this insight by noting that normally we *do not* deal with things as present in consciousness. This is a derivative mode, grounded in our unconscious, inattentive dealings with entities. To use McLuhan's example, Heidegger would say that the words of a lecturer are a minimal figure immersed in a vast and tacit background of gestures, lights, street sounds, the tactile feel of the chair, and memories and associations and smells. Heidegger would say that for the most part, things remain in that tacit environmental background, and that only in special cases do they became present, most often in cases of malfunction— the broken hammer, the forgotten word in the midst of a speech, the emergence of smoke and flame from the kitchen, the disappearance of ocean liners at night far out at sea.

This is Heidegger's famous tool-analysis, which I hold to be the most important moment in the past century of philosophy. Its resemblance to McLuhan's foundational insight should already be clear enough: the background is more powerful than what is present; ground is mightier than figure. There are some obvious differences, of course, but all are to McLuhan's credit. What withdraws from presence for Heidegger is being itself, and being tends to be treated as a single shapeless mass with no other role than to undercut human thought and action with its immeasurable depth, much like the *apeiron* of the pre-Socratic philosophers. For McLuhan, by contrast, it is individual entities that withdraw: televisions, telephones, playing cards, kites, and trains. Perhaps the background effects of these media cannot be studied directly, as McLuhan admits, but their specific effects can at least be detected in indirect fashion. And then there is McLuhan's richer conception of history. While Heidegger serves up a linear account of growing presence and growing technological darkness, McLuhan's history of technology is rich in surprises and reversals, as we will soon see.

There is also an important difficulty with both Heidegger and McLuhan, which I note here for its general importance, even though it cannot be a focus of this lecture. Namely, there is an unfortunate tendency by both thinkers to over-identify the figure/ground pair with conscious and unconscious, as though it were really a Gestalt *psychology* of figure and ground rather than an *ontology* of figure and ground. Consider the following point. The electric lights in this room may hum in the background without my consciously noticing it. Or I may lose interest in the speaker and turn my conscious attention directly to the lights instead. But in both cases, the light itself remains in a background that I can never exhaust. In other words, the reason the electric light is ground rather than figure is not because I happen not to be staring at it in this moment. Instead, it is background because *even when I am staring at it* I do not exhaust the reality of the light. In a number of publications I have also noted that the same is true of objects in relation to each other. The fact that I cannot exhaust the reality of the electric light either by unconsciously relying on it *or* by staring at it openly does not result from my tragic status as a poor limited human condemned never to grasp the thing-in-itself. Instead, even lights, flames, cotton balls, and cosmic rays are also cut off from access to the thing-in-itself.

How could flames and ocean waves exhaust the reality of what they strike any more than we humans can? The fire interacts with the flammability of the cotton, not its whiteness and softness; the waves strike the sand as a feeble barrier, unaware of the odors that dogs have found there. The figure/ground interplay has nothing to do with the difference between conscious and unconscious and everything to do with how things are distorted and simplified by any relation whatsoever, whether with human or nonhuman things. This is the key proposition for which I have argued in philosophy, but since it is not the focus of this lecture, we can move on to more central themes. We need only remember that the difference between figure and ground is much deeper than the difference between explicit and implicit, though both Heidegger and McLuhan share this same mistake. And just as this fact modifies Heidegger's ontology in a strange direction, it might well do the same to McLuhan's media theory.

But let's look instead at a different pair of terms that McLuhan uses for the interplay between the hidden and the visible. That pair is "enhancement" and "obsolescence." When McLuhan was asked to prepare a new version of his early classic *Understanding Media*,[140] he came up with a system of four media laws known as the "tetrad," which were supposed to hold good for all human artifacts. The first two terms of the tetrad give us the "morphology" of any artifact, any medium. Of any such entity we can first ask: "What does it enhance or intensify?" and then: "What does it render obsolete or displace?"[141] Numerous examples are given in the sample tetrads in the back of the book, and here are a few of the simplest. The washing machine enhances the speed of doing laundry and obsolesces the scrubboard and the washtub.[142] The Copernican Revolution enhances the sun and obsolesces the earth.[143] Romanticism enhances spontaneity of emotion and obsolesces eighteenth century rhetorical technique.[144] Wine enhances the occasion on which it is used while obsolescing personal inhibition.[145]

The principle is both simple and interesting, though in a certain sense the McLuhans have the terminology backwards. For whereas they hold that enhancement makes something more visible and obsolescence less so, this contradicts the claim that the medium is the message and that the background is where the action is. Consider the washing machine. By obsolescing the scrubboard and the washtub, it does not make these older devices *less* visible. Instead, it makes them more so: for even the McLuhans tell us that what is obsolesced turns into a visible cliché. A cliché is a medium that is now dead but once was living. In this sense, the visible realm is not a realm of enhancements, but of obsolete media that were yesterday's rulers. Our visible world, for McLuhan as for Heidegger, seems to be filled with petrified statues, with things that have the mere semblance of life. At the same time, it is misleading to say that the washing machine simply enhances the speed of doing laundry. What it really enhances is a laundry-machine world that is still with us and therefore cannot yet be defined, since it is not yet an accessible cliché. It is a world of idle 45-minute loungings in the basement waiting for the machine to finish its cycle, a world of laundromats in which love affairs, robberies, and murders can occur, alongside harmless daydreams and the reading of newspapers. Contrary to what the McLuhans sometimes say, what is enhanced becomes hidden in the ground, while what is obsolesced becomes visible clutter, like the previous-generation iPod rattling in your drawer, or the George W. Bush Administration.

We already saw that the McLuhans link enhancement and obsolescence with the morphology of media, their status in any given instant. But this morphology is paired with "metamorphosis," which describes how one medium transforms into another. The two terms here are "reversal" and "retrieval." Reversal occurs through what the McLuhans call the "overheating" of a medium. To overheat means to become too filled up with detail and information, until at a certain point the medium flips into its opposite. The speed and convenience of cars reverses into the hassle-filled life of traffic jams and hour-long searches for parking. The speed of the washing machine reverses into a lifestyle of continuous laundry.[146] The Copernican Revolution reverses into relativity, so that the sun is replaced by an infinite number of centers.[147] The individuality of Romanticism flips into sheer abstraction detached from any personal meaning.[148] Wine reverses into insults and hangovers.[149] Every medium contains the seeds of its own downfall, its own reversal, once it is pushed past the point of equilibrium.

The second pole of metamorphosis is "retrieval." The McLuhans hold that every medium has an older medium as its content. The Copernican Revolution retrieves the ancient sun-centered astronomy of Aristarchus.[150] Wine retrieves both the "ritual observance" and the "festive spontaneity" of an earlier period of civilization.[151] But it is interesting to ask which is cause and which is consequence. Does the older medium appear as a byproduct of some new medium? Or do we summon the new medium by re-enacting the old? While it seems like both of these scenarios must be possible, the McLuhans seem primarily interested in the second. We repeat a citation already made earlier:

> the study of ground "on its own terms" is virtually impossible; by definition it is at any moment environmental and subliminal. The only possible strategy for such study entails constructing an anti-environment: such is the normal activity of the artist, the only person in our culture whose whole business has been the retraining and updating of sensibility.[152]

The McLuhans continue:

> Once the old ground becomes content of a new situation it appears to ordinary attention as aesthetic figure. At the same time a new retrieval or nostalgia is born. The business of the artist has been to report on the current status of ground by exploring those forms of sensibility made available by each new mode of culture long before the average [person] suspects that anything has changed. [The artist] is constantly making "raids on the inarticulate." T.S. Eliot pointed this out in regard to Dante...[153]

Content, it seems, has a double role. On the one hand it is empty cliché, an obsolete medium discarded into the rag-and-bone shop of the spirit and cluttering our awareness while the real action unfolds in a hidden ground. On the other hand it is aesthetic figure retrieved from the junk heap either as a result of some new medium, or by the outright *generation* of that new medium thanks to the work of the artist.

2. The Crucial Role of Content

Already we have quietly stumbled across the central paradox of Marshall McLuhan's career. It looks at first as though content means nothing for McLuhan, just as it seems to mean nothing for Heidegger. You are wasting time with moralization if you argue over whether this or that radio program is socially valuable for children. Far more important are the explosive global forces unleashed by radio as a medium, irrespective of which programs are transmitted. Everywhere, McLuhan deplores the overemphasis on literate-visual culture (though he claims to prefer it personally) and the corresponding under-emphasis on the acoustic resonances of the global village and its socially interconnecting, de-individualizing technologies. Everything seems to boil down to a question of ground. Figure is nothing, ground is everything; content is nothing, medium is everything.

This is precisely why McLuhan is often dismissed as a "technological determinist." If everything of importance is decided by the nature of the background, if all human consciousness is the puppet of the media it inhabits, then it does start to look as if all deliberate human action is pointless. We must await the character of the next great medium, much like Heideggerians awaiting the next dispensation or epoch of Being. We become the passive shepherds of whatever sheep are delivered to us by television, radio, fax machines, cruise missiles, and other lava lamps of our era. Those who hold that intellectual life always boils down to politics thus have little use for McLuhan, who seems to leave us with no active mission, given the superficiality of our conscious words and deeds in comparison with the rumbling cryptic background that determines us always.

Yet this is hardly the picture that emerges from the second axis of the tetrad, the one called "metamorphosis." I speak here of reversal and retrieval, the only two ways specified by McLuhan in which one medium can transform into another. And what is most remarkable about reversal and retrieval is that both must occur in the realm of figure, not ground. Let's begin with the case of reversal, which occurs for McLuhan solely through overheating, through the excessive saturation of information, detail, or quantity. I'm not aware of any passage in which McLuhan considers that overheating might occur in any other way. Cars appear on the scene, as a medium of speed and personal efficiency. Within a few generations, they numerically overheat to the point that they no longer function as efficient and silent background media. Instead, they become slow-moving metallic bulks, expensive to maintain, insure, and park, locking their owners into long-term payment arrangements and killing a certain percentage of their users each year. Now, where does this overheating occur? Obviously not on the level of ground. A car is a car, and is always a car. Overheating takes place not in the essence of the car itself, but through the peripheral features of the car that are purely accidental to its sleek functionality— such as its metallic mass, or its insertion in a financial system of payments and insurers. In the case of reversal, events on the superficial level of *figure* are what trigger a reversal of the ground, a transformation of the car from a liberating techno-logical breakthrough into an obtrusive burden and cliché. In the case of reversal, while the medium may be the message, the content of the medium is able to tamper with the medium, flipping it upside-down and ending its original career.

Is this "technological determinism"? Only if you believe that overheating and the prevention of overheating is entirely outside human control. Yet this is not how political activists view the world. They behave as if we could act to reduce carbon emissions and thereby prevent any flipping of the global climate. They act as if carpooling and municipal light rail options could help end the nightmarish acceleration of car culture. In a sense, *all* political activism assumes that the forces of technology *are not* beyond our control, and that the overheating of any technological medium can be managed, controlled, or even tamed and deliberately reversed. More importantly for our current purposes, nowhere does McLuhan say that this is impossible. He does speak of the "overheating" of media, yet he never calls this inevitable. Indeed, in other places he treats media as if they had a constant temperature, referring for example (in a frequently criticized doctrine) to radio as an inherently "hot" medium and television as an inherently "cold" one. Moreover, numerous media surround us at all times, and McLuhan knows it is not the case that they are all simultaneously heating towards reversal. Overheating for McLuhan seems instead to be a special crisis condition that might occasionally slip out of control, but need not do so. It seems, then, that there is no technological determinism in the case of reversal.

We turn now to retrieval, the other metamorphic force in McLuhan's world. Here it is even clearer that figure is where the action is, not ground. Indeed, McLuhan grants the individual artistic genius a truly phenomenal power of creating antienvironments in opposition to the reigning technologies of an era. In other words, artists are not simply commenting on the technological environments of their day, but creating brand new environments. This gives artists a formidable political power according to the McLuhan view of reality. But we must take "artists" in the widest sense to refer to anyone who turns an apparently dead archaic cliché of the past into a new and living medium, as when Copernicus retrieves the sun-centered astronomy of Aristarchus with modifications for the new environment. If reversal occurs due to "overheating," we might coin a term and say that retrieval is a way of "overcooling" a dead medium so as to turn it into a living one. To cool something down, for McLuhan, means to reduce its level of information or detail or quantity, to push it towards the conditions of a medium. When Copernicus retrieves Aristarchus, when Thomas Aquinas or Averroës retrieve Aristotle, when Paul Cézanne retrieves Nicolas Poussin, they do not copy all the extraneous detail of their predecessors in antiquarian fashion. Instead, they boil them down to a nectar or essence, reduce them to a spore that can travel across time and take root in new soil under vastly different conditions. When Deleuze claims to "paint a moustache on the Mona Lisa"[154] by giving strange but plausible readings of Bergson or Spinoza, what he succeeds in doing at his best moments is "overcooling" these thinkers, retrieving them by finding a living skeleton beneath the dead flesh of their familiar written works. More like Dr. Frankenstein than the sodomites he openly praises as a model, Deleuze transplants these living skeletons into new flesh, thereby hoping to animate it, and sometimes succeeding.

Is this "technological determinism"? Only if you believe that artists in the widest sense have no freedom of choice in any given generation, that their tasks are handed to them in binding, ironclad fashion. But rather than serving up a technological determinism, McLuhan seems to be going to the other extreme, and placing almost too *much* power in the hands of individuals to counter the wider forces of history. Suddenly, rather than thinking of him as a determinist, we might start to hear that McLuhan is a genius-worshipping individualist who neglects the determinizing drift of societies and other collectives that were supposed to shape the lowly individual all along. McLuhan will thus be under attack from opposite sides simultaneously—

always a good sign for a thinker, since it suggests that both sides equally misunderstand what is really happening.

And here we find the second sense of the medium in McLuhan referred to at the beginning of this lecture. In the first and usual sense, the medium for McLuhan is a hidden background that can never be reached, as humans remain hypnotized by the various figures that dance within the medium without having any relevance to its deeper determining force. But we have seen that in a second and more paradoxical sense, it is the *content* or *figure* that is actually the medium, since only content or figure allows us to touch and control the background beyond our grasp. We can never make direct contact with the ground, but McLuhan allows us to overheat or overcool our environments, thereby allowing us to control our media environment, whether through activism or (especially) through the arts.

In short, while the usual figure/ground dualisms from Plato through Heidegger treat the visible figure as a shadow on the cave wall and as cause for despair, McLuhan retains the dualism but grants us the power to manipulate the ground from below. It's almost as if the prisoners in Plato's myth could change the perfect form of the horse by drawing wings, horns, or dragon's jaws on the *shadow* of the horse. If not unprecedented in the history of philosophy, this wonderful perversion is certainly rare.

3. Philosophical Implications

Recent philosophy has sometimes claimed that the surface is sterile and that everything dynamic happens at a deeper layer. This might have seemed to be McLuhan's slogan as well, but now we have discovered almost exactly the opposite. The hidden ground of any situation does retain the power of dominating all the figures that appear within it, reducing them to puppets of limited importance. Yet the ground has no inherent power to change or develop. It merely sits there, dominant, always being what it is. The trigger for changes in the ground can be found only on the surface of the world. Where does this idea fit in present-day philosophy?

Earlier I suggested one extreme consequence of Heidegger's ideas. What we learn from Heidegger is not just that praxis is the deeper ground of theory, since sitting in a chair is just as superficial a relation to the chair as looking at it; the chair is deeper than looking, but also deeper than sitting, its properties equally unexhausted by either act. And furthermore, the chair is not just deeper than any *human* contact with it, since fire and raindrops are no better equipped to drain the chair dry than poignant human praxis and cognition are. Instead, all things are deeper than any possible contact with each other. Recent philosophy already loves to say that "relations are external to their terms," yet it has never drawn the properly shocking consequences of this phrase. For if relations can never make full contact with that which they connect, if colliding billiard balls or two shaking hands can never fully touch one another, then we ought to ask how they can relate at all. It will not suffice to say that they make "partial" contact with each other, because parts of things are themselves things, and if I make partial contact with you by touching your hand, then I am touching your hand, not you. And the same problem occurs here again, since I will not be able to exhaust the reality of your hand by touching it any more than I have exhausted the reality of you. The reason I cannot touch another person directly is not simply because it is impractical and rude to make contact with all of their physical surfaces simultaneously, but because even total physical contact with a person or thing would not exhaust their reality. The thing is different from any touching of the thing.

The philosophy known as "occasionalism" arose for different reasons, though it addresses a similar concern. The radical school of Islamic theology known as the Ash'arites, which arose in Basra in present-day Iraq, held that not only was it blasphemous to let any being other than Allah be a creator, but blasphemous even to let any other being be a causal agent of any sort. Handshakes, arrows striking their targets, the collision of billiard balls, fire burning cotton, and even the link between an atom and its own accidents were not natural events, but showed the direct intervention of Allah. After a delay of more than seven hundred years, the idea appears in Europe when Descartes puzzled over the communication between mind and body, and again invoked God to do the job, even while preserving science from religion by denying that body-body interactions posed any problem. But Malebranche retrieved this old Arab problem and placed body-body contact back in the hands of God, with different variations on this approach found in Spinoza, Leibniz, and Berkeley.

Laugh all you please at this seemingly gratuitous theological metaphysics, but more likely than not you already believe in an upside-down version of the same theory. For what is truly characteristic of occasionalism is not the presence of God, but the granting of a causal *monopoly* to one entity at the expense of all others. And though in the so-called developed world everyone has a good laugh at the apparently benighted religious people of bygone eras, we do much the same thing as the supposedly ignorant mullahs and priests when it comes to the philosophy of causation. Instead of giving *God* the causal monopoly, we give it to the human mind. Either we treat causation in Humean fashion as the byproduct of habit or customary conjunction, as a structure of the mind rather than as a necessarily independent force outside the mind. Or, we treat causation as a category of the human understanding in Kantian fashion, once again giving the human an effective monopoly on causes.

After a century in which Alfred North Whitehead boldly embraced the occasionalist solution of God to explain how entities can prehend one another, it was his admirer Bruno Latour who took the first decisive step forward in two hundred years on the occasionalist question. Latour secularized the problem, voiding the claims of any *specific* entity (whether God or human) to have a causal monopoly. For Latour all causation is local, and all causation requires a mediator. As he demonstrates in *Pandora's Hope*, politics and neutrons had no link, but then Frédéric Joliot did a fair job of linking them, in the context of promoting a French atomic bomb project that was eventually overtaken by military events. And the same for the link between any two actors: any link needs a mediator, and results in a translation. This, I believe, will be remembered as one of Latour's greatest contributions to metaphysics— his secular version of occasionalism, the first the world has ever known.[155]

As I tried to explain in *Prince of Networks*, the remaining problem is as follows. If Joliot is needed as the link between politics and neutrons, then what enables Joliot to link up with either of these in the first place? If all actors are to be placed on equal footing (and this notion lies at core of Latour's thinking more generally) then we cannot grant magic causal powers to Joliot any more than to God or the human mind. And if we place new mediators between Joliot and politics and Joliot and neutrons, then the problem has simply been pushed back a step further. We will need mediators between mediators between mediators. No infinitesimal calculus can save us here, since we are trying to determine how any contact can occur at all, not simply *measure* the quantity of mediation. There must be some place where direct contact occurs, and obviously it cannot be due to a privileged God or privileged Frédéric Joliot being established as Lord of All Causation.

We now come to the final, summarizing thought of this lecture. What we seek is the unification of three apparently contradictory demands. First, we want to avoid all privileged causal lords; all causation must be local, not solely divine or solely human. This principle can be called the Latourian Breakthrough (and I do believe it opens the gates to many fresh things in philosophy). But second, we need direct contact to be possible somewhere; otherwise there will simply be an infinite insertion of mediators between any two points in the world. And third, given that all objects have been placed on the same footing, in what is sometimes called a "flat ontology" (it was Manuel DeLanda[156] who seems to have first used the term in this sense, rather than Roy Bhaskar's[157] opposite sense) it is hard to see how direct contact can be possible sometimes but not always, given that all entities are now playing by the same rules.

There is no choice but to sacrifice one of these three principles. As I see it, our earlier discussion of McLuhan and Heidegger gives us a hint that the *third* principle is the one that must be abandoned. There cannot be a purely flat ontology, because there are two different kinds of things in the world: figures and grounds, in the ontological rather than the psychological sense. That is to say, the ground is not just the unnoticed background of human awareness, and the figure is not just the target of conscious attention. Instead, the ground is the thing deeper than any possible human or non-human relation to it, and the figure is the thing in any sort of relation, whether theoretical, perceptual, practical, or brutally causal. The figure is the medium between two grounds, the only place where they meet and transform each other. Only by abandoning flat ontology in favor of a frank dualism of figures and grounds do we preserve both the ban on Causal Lords *and* the possibility of direct contact somewhere in the cosmos. Only by allowing grounds to emit superficial figures do we enable any retroactive transformation of those grounds. We can call this principle the McLuhan Supplement to the Latourian Breakthrough.

13. Non-Relationality for Philosophers and Architects (2012)

Following the official portion of the Brazil trip, I was invited to give a standalone lecture in Curitiba on the evening of August 10, at the beautiful Museu Oskar Niemeyer. The source of the invitation was a group of young Curitiba residents for whom I had written the preface to a book some months earlier: the sociologist Hugo Loss and the architects Pedro Duschesnes, Juliano Monteiro, and Gustavo Utrabo.[158] The crowd was large and receptive. Someone also seems to have exaggerated my degree of celebrity, since there were dozens of requests for autographs after the talk, shattering my previous record of three or four for a single event. Otherwise, my young hosts offered superb treatment throughout the visit to Curitiba, including housing me in a marvelous jazz-themed hotel near the city center.

Jacques Derrida was famously bewildered by the interest of architects in his philosophical work. He described the situation in an interview in the early 1990's:

> If someone had asked me twenty years ago whether I thought deconstruction should interest people in domains that were foreign to me, such as architecture and law, as a matter of principle my response would have been yes, it is absolutely indispensable, but at the same time I never would have believed that it could happen. Thus, when faced with this I experience a mixture of surprise and nonsurprise. Obviously, I am obliged, up to a certain point, not to transform, but rather to adjust or deform my discourse, in any case to respond, to comprehend what is happening.[159]

These words ring true, due to certain recent experiences. Although the influence of object-oriented philosophy has by no means reached the level of deconstruction, there has recently been a great deal of interest in my philosophy among artists, architects, and designers.

Like Derrida himself, I am both surprised and unsurprised by this development. In one sense I have no official training in any of these fields, and am certainly not in a position to offer advice to those who work in them. Quite the contrary: what I expect instead is retroactive inspiration for my writing when seeing how others put it to use in their own fields. But in another sense, I am not surprised at all by the growing attention. For what could be of greater interest to all fields of human inquiry than *objects*, since there are objects in every field: humanistic and scientific, fictional and non-fictional, mathematical and erotic, serious and frivolous. Recently I have warned that the scientism of Ray Brassier and the mathematism of Quentin Meillassoux would prove more difficult to export to fields outside philosophy than object-oriented thought. Aside from the inherent philosophical logic that pushed me in the direction of objects throughout the 1990's, there was also the tacit desire to create a general intellectual toolkit that might be useful to everyone working in any intellectual field. This cannot be done if philosophy is subordinated to the best brain science of 2012 (as Brassier recommends) or if human beings remain at the center of ontology out of groundless fears of "vitalism" (as is the case with Meillassoux's most recent statements of his position).

There is the further consideration that object-oriented philosophy cuts against the grain at just the right moment, as is so often true of theories that prove to be useful. Since the 1960's, avant-garde intellectual life has generally favored events over substances, dynamic flux over stasis, context over autonomy, relation over non-relation, the constructed over the independent, what something can *do* over what something *is*, and so forth. What is paradoxical about object-oriented thought is its reversal of each of these typical cutting-edge positions If forced to choose, then one hundred times out of one hundred I would choose substance over event, stasis over flux, autonomy over context, non-relation over relation, the independent over the constructed, and what something is over what it can do. This is not for perversity's sake, nor out of some deviant wish to erase half a century of purported intellectual progress. Instead, experience has led me to believe that, at least in philosophy, categories such as event, dynamism, context, relation, construction, and capacity are ideas once but no longer liberating. I will focus my remarks this evening on the concept of relationality. In most humanistic and artistic fields, there is still a widespread assumption that context and relationality are at the cutting edge, while the forces of non-relation comes from the side of tired, conservative reaction. I will give reasons why I think this is not the case in philosophy, and will suggest that it may not be the case for some other fields as well.

1. How Some Architects View Object-Oriented Philosophy

Rather than jumping headfirst into metaphysics, perhaps we can situate object-oriented philosophy in terms of what architects and architectural theorists have been saying about it. In October 2011 I was invited by the architect and designer David Ruy to contribute an article to the Spring 2012 *tarp Architecture Manual*, published at Pratt Art Institute in New York. The invitation had a somewhat casual feel, and I assumed that my long acquaintanceship with Ruy himself (we were undergraduates together at St. John's College in Annapolis in the late 1980's) was the primary reason for it. Hence I was astonished to find the entire Spring 2012 issue of *tarp* peppered with references to object-oriented approaches to architecture and design. We can begin with the first paragraph of the journal, where Erik Ghenoiu writes as follows:

Younger scholars and practitioners are raising their voices against the now twenty-year-old paradigm of an architecture based on the management of relationships of meaning, program, use, and flow... Widespread attention has returned to the inexhaustible meaning of architectural objects that always exceed the intentions, techniques, and even aesthetics that generated them. This turn is now finding common ground in the object-oriented ontology... emerging in continental philosophy and led by writers including Graham Harman and Timothy Morton.[160]

This was news to me, but let's follow Ghenoiu in more detail and see where he leads us. But first, I should add that I cannot accept that portion of the credit offered by Ghenoiu when he claims that object-oriented philosophy challenged the idea of nature lying behind "sustainability" in architecture. Bruno Latour already did this in 1991 in *We Have Never Been Modern*, and again in 1999 in *The Politics of Nature*, and I for one (Morton's case is different) cannot say that I have added anything in particular to Latour's brilliant critique of the modern conception of nature. But Ghenoiu makes a more plausible link between object-oriented thought and contemporary practice when he states as follows:

The manipulation of relations has favored the distraction technique of making the built place seem like the result of forces and considerations over which the designer had no control... [But] the object turn leaves the forces in the perceived field of relations ambiguous and sometimes contradictory, but achieves a kind of naturalized authenticity of the object through the presence of a technically-complex excess of detail. In this mode, a project that is ideologically and formally bizarre can appear as almost banal due to its concurrent and highly-orchestrated claim of (visual) normalcy.[161]

This is where Ghenoiu makes a link with my philosophy:

> In all of these trends, architecture not only creates objects in the sense of [object-oriented ontology], it also stages them. Harman, Morton and their allies posit a kind of hermetic object: hermetic not in that it is sealed away from our understanding, but in that it cannot be *entirely* understood, that some aspect (and perhaps most) of it lies outside of the part susceptible to understanding in general, and much more so to any specific understanding.[162]

This might sound like an unproblematic alliance between me, Morton, and a growing movement of younger architects. But Ghenoiu takes a balanced approach by also identifying a point of friction between the two trends:

> almost all of the architecture of the object turn relies on a privileged viewer, if not for the sake of its own formal character, then at least for the judgement that can recognize its formal procedure as distinctive, fascinating, original, or successful as architecture... This reinstatement of the subject-object relationship and the constitution of the subject through the object-world makes the object turn something of a refusal of the ideas of Morton and Harman or at least a hard limit on their appropriation, but safe for the older architectural proposition of posthumanism.[163]

Ghenoiu's views, then, can be summarized as follows. A new trend in architecture is turning away from a two-decade program of managing relationships, and towards the object as something excessive and partially hermetic. Nonetheless, this so-called object turn retains a privileged viewer, and in this way also contradicts what Morton and I and our colleagues have tried to accomplish in philosophy. I will leave it to architects to assess these recent trends, but am pleased to report that Ghenoiu gets the philosophy part right. Object-oriented philosophy does treat objects as a hermetically sealed surplus, never fully knowable and never fully expressed in their relations, and does undercut the privileged viewer insofar as all objects are to be treated equally with no priority for the human subject as a privileged finite observer.

In the same issue of *tarp*, Sarah Ruel-Bergeron deals with the topic concisely but accurately: "Object-oriented philosophy returns the object to the architect by claiming that a field of relations is no longer the main thing that makes up the world around us. As a practice interested in aesthetics, architecture [has been] finding itself constricted by a form-making process based on networks, forces, fields, swarms."[164] She also expresses skepticism as to whether processes and dynamic networks can be excluded from consideration entirely.

David Ruy sees recent shifts in architecture as hinging on the entrance of nature into architectural practice:

> Since the mid-nineties, architecture has accelerated its move away from the discourse of the architectural object towards the discourse of the architectural field. Architects today are preoccupied with considerations of architecture as a by-product of socio-cultural milieus, as a conditional component of technocratic systems and networks, or even as the provisional end calculations of measurable parameters within the literal or construed environment.[165]

Although Ruy grants the *sincerity* of this desire that architectural practice become more relevant to current events, he also maintains that "there are some profoundly problematic assumptions in theories of the architectural field from an ontological point of view."[166] These can be seen in the recent ascendance of "nature" as a force to reckon with in the discipline. According to

Ruy, "architectural practice has not had much concern for nature until recently. Besides basic pragmatic concerns for manipulating the ground, keeping the rain out, or making sure the interior has enough light and air, the practice of architecture has been more concerned with the endless logistics of the building itself."[167] But now, "faced with the impending doom of global warming and environmental collapse, architectural practice has been forced to also contend with the even more impossible logistics of the environment itself."[168] While Ruy concedes that this turn to nature is completely understandable given the dangers and pressures of our era, he also worries about architecture dissolving into ecology:

> Nature, seen through the ecological telescope, is a grand network of relations where the appearances of objects (rock, tree, frog, cloud, human, etc.) are superficial, and the network of relations is understood to be the deeper reality. The grand finale of architecture's movement from object to field may very well be the collapse of the architectural object into a field of relations that then dissolves into a general ecological field of relations that constitutes the world.[169]

While the tendency is to view nature as a holistic system thrown out of balance only by human intervention, we need not be climate change skeptics to grasp Ruy's point that "nature is not and has never been in a state of equilibrium.... If we are to take the flux of nature seriously, we would then have to understand sustainable practice as a willful act that seeks to maintain an artificially constructed equilibrium with maximum benefit for human occupation over the long term. Because nature itself is not stable, the stability would have to be forced."[170]

The holistic view of ecology has always had difficulty explaining transformation: if everything is in balance, defined by its interrelations with everything else, then why would anything ever change? Ruy correctly summarizes my position by saying that:

> If an object could be completely exhausted by a summation of its relations, there can be no way for an object to change its relations. Therefore there must always be something about the object that is in excess of its qualities and relations. There will always be some "dark nucleus of objects" (as Harman puts its) that is withdrawn from access by other objects. The being of an object is always more than its relations... The architectural object, like any object, would have that "dark nucleus" that cannot be exhausted by a list of its qualities. Going further, this object-oriented ontology would have to throw the being of any relational model into doubt. Though networks and fields may continue to be eminently useful models of understanding, they carry with them a flawed ontology... We can continue to incorporate field models for their usefulness, but should remind ourselves that they are artificial constructions.[171]

Rather than nature as a holistic web of definitive relations, individual objects within nature must be treated as mutually opaque and disruptive, as withdrawn and strange. Ruy makes another striking observation when he notes that since architects themselves must be viewed as peculiar objects rather than as privileged transcendent subjects, the door is open to a renewed respect for the specific talents of human individuals, which has long been out of fashion as well. As he puts it:

> a successful object-making event cannot be completely encapsulated by a methodology that might repeat the success... The authority of the craftsman comes from the strange individuality of the maker. There is something about the master craftsman, as object, that cannot be reduced to a set of

qualities and is irreproducible.[172]

To summarize, Ruy joins Ghenoiu in noting a shift from the architectural object to holistic or ecological fields ultimately flowing into the concept of nature and a sustainability imperative. Ruy argues more adamantly than Ghenoiu against the ontological failures of this shift and correctly cites object-oriented philosophy as providing a good counter-theory for such cases. He aims to retrieve the autonomy not only of architectural objects but of architects themselves, as skilled individual craftspeople with non-reproducible idiosyncrasies.

The final piece from *tarp* that I will discuss was written by the prominent architectural theorist Patrik Schumacher.[173] Asked by the journal editors to comment on object-oriented ontology, Schumacher parries the question with reasonable hesitations. Whereas the integration of complexity theory into architecture has a long and rich history, it is too early, Schumacher holds, to determine the usefulness or sterility of the object-oriented approach. Indeed, Schumacher views "relational ontology" as a highly productive trend within architecture, and claims that the appeal of object-oriented ontology can be explained largely due to satiation with the success of relational approaches. He concludes this opening statement by saying: "For now my attitude remains 'wait and see,' while my own intellectual investment is following a different path altogether, which I will outline below."[174]

What follows is a complicated and intricate argument, though Schumacher's commitments suddenly become clear about halfway through the piece: society consists entirely of communications, and the purpose of architecture is to frame communicative interaction.[175] Schumacher tells us explicitly that his "theory of architecture… is based on an explicitly contingent theory design decision: to theorize architecture as a system of communications."[176] This theory is also "contingent" due to

Schumacher's pragmatic view of truth, according to which a theory is to be judged solely by its results. Commenting further on his theory of communications, Schumacher adds that

> according to this (Luhmannian) ontology there is only one basic type of entity to be considered: communications. In this sense the proposed ontology is a radically flat ontology. It is, however, also a radically relational ontology. Communications only exist within systems of communications, as relational nodes in endless chains and networks of connected communications... While we might imagine the beginnings of communication as initially isolated instances in order to then think of networks or systems of communications, the analysis of our contemporary social communication leads to the opposite proposition: all communications are always already systemic.[177]

The appeal to Luhmann here is somewhat peculiar. Systems for Luhmann are always radically *cut off* from their environment, and thus seem to be a poor fit for a "radically relational" ontology of the sort that Schumacher proclaims. Even if everything is a communication that gains meaning only from its place in a system, if there are countless systems of communication sealed off from environmental intrusion, this is not much of a relational ontology. Instead, it suggests the *withdrawal* of each system from its total environment of relations, which is precisely why Levi Bryant was able to enlist Luhmann as a powerful *ally* of object-oriented ontology.[178] In any case, Schumacher makes it clear that he finds it more fruitful to view society as made up of communications than of autonomous objects.

My purpose in making these extensive citations was to mark some points where object-oriented philosophy has so far been treated by architects as having possible relevance to their discipline, a relevance I am ill-equipped to demonstrate on my own.

Having done this, I would like to explain my own philosophical motivations in developing an object-based ontology. Afterward, we can return to the question of what the implications of such an ontology might be for practices outside philosophy.

2. The Object-Oriented Approach

I have now quoted four architectural theorists responding to object-oriented philosophy and its possible significance or insignificance for architecture, and of course I will leave it to real architects to decide that question. But all four of them focus, correctly, on *non-relationality* as my central concept. I would now like to explain the importance of non-relationality for object-oriented philosophy.

The most honored ancestor of object-oriented thought is Martin Heidegger, still the most recent great philosopher the world has seen, and someone we can build on for the foreseeable future as on solid rock. I hold that the key passage in *Being and Time*, Heidegger's greatest book, is the tool-analysis. But I also hold that the tool-analysis has been read in precisely the wrong way. In 1900 Edmund Husserl published the *Logical Investigations*, the founding book of phenomenology. In this school Heidegger found his voice, and in this school he later became a dissident who took things in a completely different direction. For phenomenology, the point is to bring philosophy back to the immediate evidence on which everything else is based. The sciences cannot do this job, since they focus on hidden material entities as the causes of everything that appears to us. Phenomenology works in the reverse direction. All that is immediately evident to us is what appears in the realm of consciousness. For this reason, philosophy should suspend or "bracket" all consideration of the outside natural world and focus instead on a patient description of the phenomena that appear to consciousness. In every experience, whether it be the observation of a red apple or a daydream concerning a futuristic bugle corps, there is a multitude of subtleties that can be described and explored at length.

Heidegger earned his place in history by pointing to the basic defect of phenomenology's starting point. As a general rule, the things of the world *are not* phenomena present in consciousness. Instead, things usually remain invisible as we rely upon them in our day-to-day actions. The sidewalk beneath your feet, the oxygen in the air, the infrastructure of pipes that ensures your sanitation and drinking needs, the nervous system in your body, the banking system that stores your earnings— all these things tend to remain invisible unless they break. Insofar as they function smoothly, they tend to withdraw into a concealed background where they remain unnoticed to the human observer. Whereas phenomenology treated reality as made of phenomena present-at-hand in consciousness, Heidegger supposedly shows that this presence always emerges from a prior ready-to-hand status of invisible equipment which is assigned to some purpose that gives it meaning.

This is the famous tool-analysis, first developed in Heidegger's earliest Freiburg lecture course of 1919, but first published in *Being and Time* nearly a decade later. It is surely the most enduring thought experiment of the twentieth century. But though it is widely admired, it is badly misread in at least two different senses, one of which concerns us tonight. Namely, it is believed that the tool-analysis marks the triumph of relational over non-relational ontology. The argument runs as follows. When entities are treated as present-at-hand, they are portrayed as isolated, independent appearances in consciousness, each with its own distinct features that the phenomenologist can describe. By contrast, Heidegger's tool-analysis shows that before being split up into discrete and independent entities in consciousness, entities belong to a total system of equipment, each of them mutually assigned and gaining their reality only from mutual interaction with one another. For this reason, it is held that Heidegger's relational ontology of tools overcomes Husserl's non-relational ontology of independent phenomena in the mind.

I hold that this typical reading is the exact opposite of the truth, and that phenomenology is the relational ontology and Heidegger's the non-relational one. First of all, notice that the phenomena described by phenomenology are not independent in the least. The reason is that they exist only in relation *to me*, or some other conscious observer. Husserl is quite clear that it makes no sense to conceive of entities that could not be, in principle, the object of some consciousness. For this reason, phenomenology was always thoroughly relational from the start. By the same token, Heidegger's philosophy of tools cannot possibly be a relational ontology. The reason for this is that tools can *break*. Indeed, this is one of the main features of Heidegger's tool-analysis— the fact that tools can surprise us by shattering or undergoing some other form of breakdown. But if entities were nothing more than their current relational deployment in the world, if a hammer were nothing more than its current relational hammer-uses in this moment, it could never possibly change position or use. In order for new relations to be possible, in order for change to occur in the world, there must be some *non-relational surplus in the things*. Indeed, objects, things, or entities (I use the words interchangeably, but prefer "objects" for a number of reasons) must be nothing more than such an extra-relational surplus. Any attempt to define objects relationally must fail, since objects are that which can always enter into *new* relations, and therefore are never defined by their current ones. Or as philosophers sometimes put it: relations are external to their terms. Relations are external to objects, not internal to them; objects are never defined, never drained dry by any of the relations in which they become involved. This is the central principle of object-oriented philosophy.

Let's now look briefly at the other frequent misunderstanding of the tool-analysis, which even if it is less central to our concerns today, helps explain the full scope of the non-relationality problem. Namely, it is often believed that with the tool-analysis, Heidegger meant to show the superiority of practical over theoretical reason. All theory and all perception are grounded in an unconscious background of everyday practices from which they emerge. This interpretation is superficial. The reason is that praxis distorts the reality of things just as much as theory. If I stare at a hammer or make theories about a hammer then I have failed to exhaust the full reality of hammer-being, which is always deeper than my cognitive or perceptual relation to it. But notice that when I *use* the hammer, I also fail to exhaust it. As we have seen, the hammer does not consist solely in my current use of it, since it can always surprise me by breaking, or by opening itself to new possible uses. So, instead of a difference between "conscious" and "unconscious" relation to objects, Heidegger gives us a theory in which both conscious *and* unconscious human action is on one side of the fence and objects themselves are on the other side.

But we must go another step further than this. It is not just that objects in their full reality withdraw from human access; instead, they withdraw from each other as well. When waves pound a beach or hailstones strike a wind turbine, these objects do not fully exhaust each other's properties any more than human consciousness does. Despite the assumptions of both Heidegger and Immanuel Kant, finitude is not a uniquely human burden, a special tragic property belonging only to people (and perhaps to angels, advanced extraterrestrial aliens, and a few smart dolphins, gorillas, and crows). Instead, finitude belongs to relationality in general. It is relations in general that fail to exhaust their terms, not just *human* relations. The non-relationality of objects is not a fact about human psychology, but an ontological truth about the world.

Now, Patrik Schumacher adopts a "pragmatic" criterion for the application of philosophy to architecture.[179] Philosophies are good for architecture if they prove to be useful. To this I would say both yes and no. Schumacher is certainly right that philosophy can no longer claim to be a master discourse in the humanities, nor should it ever have made that claim— though I think Schumacher goes too far in saying that the priority has now been reversed, as if philosophy were doomed to become the handmaid of architecture, art, geography, sociology, linguistics, and everything else. But it is worth considering the following passage from Schumacher's article:

> The "truth" (pragmatic efficacy) of an ontology cannot be universally asserted, but only evaluated discipline by discipline. Further, the question of its fruitfulness within a specific discipline cannot be settled in advance. One simply has to try to work with a certain ontology. So it is prudent to adopt a "wait and see" attitude, that is philosophical tolerance rather than philosophical fundamentalism. The criteria of success are different in each discipline based on the respective discipline's social function.[180]

Though this passage seems to be aiming at a unified point, I think that it mixes good and bad things together. On the good side, the call for philosophical tolerance rather than fundamentalism is welcome, since no philosophy can ever exhaust the real. It also seems obviously true that each discipline has autonomous problems that cannot be solved with the methods of another, and true as well that trends in disciplines may be de-synchronized from one another. At the precise moment when "objects" are a fresh theme in philosophy, they might be a deadening cliché in archaeology, architecture, and computer science. Who knows? There is no historical rule stating that all fields advance in lockstep along the same paths. It is surely also true that we can never know in advance which philosophical concepts will prove fruitful for any given field.

But there are two additional claims in the passage that I consider bad. The first is the identification of truth with pragmatic efficacy, and the second is the link it draws between success and societal function. These two points make the same mistake, and it happens to be a relationist mistake. As concerns the first point, it is impossible to identify truth with pragmatic efficacy, for some fairly simple reasons. For one thing, pragmatic success often occurs on the basis of half-truths or outright false-hoods. In such cases we do not always leave our theories intact simply because they seem to be working. Quite often, we change our theories to give them wider applicability and a better capacity to handle possible surprising cases. Einstein's revolution was ratified in part by its superior resolution (compared with Newton) of anomalies in the perihelion of Mercury, a problem that was never of especially great pragmatic importance. There is no reason to assume that architecture needs to be more narrowly "practical" than physics. Architecture too might make theoretical decisions that are unnecessary in the current practical state of the art, for the simple reason that truth has a greater power, reliability, flexibility, and allure than mere practical success.

My second question is why success should be linked with societal function. What exactly does "society" mean here — humanity as a whole, society as a whole, only my own nation, or the class of people whose fate is of interest to me? And more importantly, there are cases where truth may trump societal use. For example, the narrow interests of a given society may insist that philosophers should either not exist, or should only be sitting on medical ethics panels and deferring to the successes of brain science rather than wasting their time on armchair metaphysical speculation. It does not follow that society has the *right* to assign functions to persons and disciplines in this way, nor that society itself will ultimately benefit from making such assignments. An apparently selfish refusal to go along with one's pre-defined societal function might turn out to be the heroic act par excellence.

While this might still sound like nitpicking, it touches on what is most dangerous in the relationist standpoint that Schumacher endorses, which sometimes borders on a form of "actualism" in which reality is conflated with the current actual conditions of reality. This is evident in Schumacher's attack earlier this year, in *The Architectural Review*, on the state of architectural education in Great Britain.[181] "The points of departure for the majority of [student] projects," he complains, "are improbable narratives with intended symbolic messages or poetic import." What follows resembles one of those lists of "absurd" modern artworks that are frequently denounced by traditionalists:

> the Bronze Medal... proposes to place "an acoustic lyrical mechanism" into a quarry in Bangalore. "The building is played by the wind, acoustically transforming the abrasive sounds of quarrying."... The other projects in this category that have been selected and highlighted... [include] an algae monitoring facility, a retreat for Echo from Ovid's Metamorphoses, and a storage building based on the fictional narrative that all citizens would deposit personal things into safety boxes throughout their lives in order to be later confronted by their past. Although there is rather less explanation about the other entries, the project titles (eg. Pyrolytic Power Plant, Tsunami Alert Community, Hydrodynamic Landscape, Mushroom Farm, Guild of Tanners and Butchers)... suggest a similarly idiosyncratic, unreal understanding of what constitutes a worthy design brief... The 2010 winner was a "shipwrecking yard" and the 2009 winner proposed "motorised coastal defence towers acting as a warning device to mankind with respect to climate change."[182]

While there is admittedly some comic value in Schumacher's polemical tone in this passage, I somehow find myself more interested in the list of pilloried projects than in Schumacher's complaint that they offer "little or no demonstration of how the visualised spaces organise and articulate social life processes and institutions."[183] Now, architecture is Schumacher's field, not mine, and there may be specific pedagogical shortcomings with these sorts of projects that lie beyond my scope of judgment. But what I do feel capable of judging is the assumption that pragmatism and societal usefulness should be the primary criteria of truth (a word that Schumacher himself places in quotation marks). It is easy to slam the projects above as "improbable narratives with intended symbolic message or poetic import,"[184] but a more balanced assessment might simply describe them as "counterfactual architecture," and it seems to me that the counterfactual is what must be encouraged in all fields of inquiry.

Consider the already well-established discipline of counter-factual history, which explores classic "what-if" scenarios around historical moments that seem especially contingent. What if Napoleon had not invaded Russia? What if the Mongols had not cut short their European invasion due to the funeral of a remote chieftain? What if Portugal, Genoa, Venice, or England had accepted the proposed mission of Columbus rather than Spain? What if the FBI had heeded early warnings about al-Qaeda terrorists in flight training classes? While sometimes dismissed as idle and unanswerable, these questions seem to me to be the very essence of historical work. History is not made up only of concrete events, but also of actors who happen to partic-ipate in certain events but might well have participated in others. To ignore such questions it to take an overly relational view of reality. It tacitly assumes that other lives or other events were never possible, and thus erodes any hope of precisely that "optimistic probing of our contemporary world with respect to the opportunities it offers" that Schumacher calls for.[185]

In a recent article I have even called for a counterfactual literary criticism.[186] Against the New Historicism that relationizes works by embedding them in their social conditions of production, and also against the older New Criticism that cuts literature off from those social conditions while turning the *interior* of works into sleek holistic systems, we might try counterfactual experiments to see how works of literature might differ if we modify them in different ways. Slavoj Žižek recently did this with typical humor at a lecture in Bonn, imagining various alternate endings of *Antigone* (including one with the title "Run, Antigone, Run!").[187] In similar fashion, we might easily make a science out of changing the *relational events* in any work of literature or even the visual arts in order to shed light on the possibly underutilized power of the internal elements of those works. Roy Bhaskar argues that natural science does exactly the same thing.[188] It constructs its experiments in such a way as to *counteract* the accidental relations in which chemicals and particles happen to be enmeshed at any given moment, its artificial scenarios unlocking the hidden properties of objects that are crushed or repressed under the normal circumstances of nature. And in fact, this view of science goes back at least as far as Francis Bacon in the second half of the *Novum Organum*.

As for architecture, I am in no position to say whether the contemporary world really needs more mushroom farms, tsunami alert communities, guilds of tanners and butchers, or acoustic generators for India's quarries. But just as the late Steve Jobs said that it is not the task of consumers to know what they want, this is presumably true of architectural clients as well. It seems to me that if architecture represses all sense of what is disturbing, strange, or in excess of current knowledge and social practice, it will pay the same price as any field that screens out the unknown: that of falling into an actualism that risks becoming a fatalism. Luhmann's idea that what lies outside the system is ignored by the system was meant as a description of what actually happens, not as a moral imperative that we *ought* to deliberately enclose ourselves in given systems of communication. And this is where the object-oriented approach can probably make a contribution to architecture, for the same reason that it can make contributions to many fields— by better integrating the unknown and the counterfactual into our picture of reality.

14. Interview with Erik Bryngelsson (2012)

In October 2012 I gave a series of lectures at the Universities of Gothenburg and Lund in Sweden. While in Gothenburg I also gave three interviews for periodicals devoted to the arts and (more surprisingly) international relations. The following interview, conducted in a dark Gothenburg cafe on the morning of October 13, was originally slated for a Scandinavian arts journal, which ultimately opted to publish an article rather than an interview on Speculative Realism. The interview is published here for the first time.

Erik Bryngelsson: If we disregard the influence from thinkers leading up to your original philosophical position such as Martin Heidegger, Xavier Zubíri, Bruno Latour, and Alfred North Whitehead, I'd like to ask you one simple question: why is thinking the object so essential for you?

Graham Harman: My initial philosophical training was in phenomenology, and in a sense both Husserl and Heidegger give us different aspects of the object. For Heidegger there is the fact that objects withdraw behind any presence. This is actually his critique of Husserl— the idea that the hammer is not just its appearance to our minds, but that there's something deeper than that, some subterranean reality to the hammer. And I show that this needs to be interpreted more deeply than usual: it doesn't just mean that praxis is deeper than theory. There is something deeper than both the use of the hammer and our looking at the hammer. There is the reality of the hammer itself, which is deeper than both praxis and theory. And for me this also holds true for inanimate interactions, in the sense that two things colliding also do not exhaust each other: that there's a surplus in things, a depth in things that cannot be exhausted by any relation.

And incidentally, this is *not* what Derrida teaches us. Derrida is sometimes wrongly credited with seeing "withdrawal" before object-oriented philosophy did. But in fact Derrida does not give us any depth beneath the play of signifiers; that's precisely what he doesn't do. He regards the in-itself as a form of ontotheology, a kind of presence in the sense of "self-presence" (a nonsensical concept, incidentally). I think what Heidegger actually teaches us, contrary to what many think, and even contrary to what Heidegger himself thinks, is that objects are deeper than relations. Objects vs. relations is the fundamental duality in the world.

That leaves us with Husserl, who is often dismissed by Heideggerians and also by some Speculative Realists as being just an idealist, as someone who merely focuses on describing the way things appear to us. Well yes, that's true, but it's not true in just the negative sense. Because what Husserl discovers, for the first time in the history of philosophy, is that an object is not just a bundle of qualities even *within* the realm of experience. Consider David Hume, who thinks that we never experience any objects, we simply experience qualities and when things like red, cold, hard, juicy, sweet go together often enough, we think of them together as an apple. There's not really an apple for Hume, there's simply a bundle of qualities. The qualities are directly given, the object is somehow secondary— it's a posited bundle that links those qualities together. But Husserl turns this upside-down. Husserl was the one who taught us that the object as a whole comes first, for the very simple reason that we encounter objects in our experience. We don't encounter determinate qualities, we don't encounter mere content.

Hence there are two kinds of qualities in Husserl. But more importantly for the present conversation there is a tension within experience between objects and qualities that has never been seen by any other philosopher. So we end up with two kinds of objects rather than one: the real and the sensual. Real objects exist and interact whether or not we encounter them. Sensual objects are dependent on some observer. The reason this is so important is because real objects tend to be so deep that they cannot make any contact at all. Since Heidegger's objects completely withdraw from each other, we need to ask how they can ever touch or influence each other at all, which they evidently do. We see things that influence each other in the world. Everything that happens is a result of relations, but how are these relations possible? The occasionalist tradition, starting with Islamic theology, was the first to say that there is no direct contact between entities. But they solved it in a very unsatisfying way: they solved it by saying that God, Allah, is making everything touch. I pick something up, but it's actually God who picks it up, it just looks like I am the one who picks it up.

In this way all causation is given magically to one kind of entity, God. With Hume and Kant it's the human mind that does this, so in a sense they're just repeating occasionalism in a more plausible-sounding modern idiom by saying that the human mind is the new God that correlates all causal events.

Erik Bryngelsson: Why can't real objects touch?

Graham Harman: Because they are so deep that they are deeper than any possible contact that we can have with them. There's no way to encounter a real object "partially." You can't say that there's direct but partial contact. That's the lazy solution. Because for example, let's say that you shake someone's hand. You'll admit that you're not making contact with the whole person, not making total mental or physical contact with them, but you're also not even making full contact with the hand. You're shaking a distorted version of the hand. We might say that you're touching the epidermis, but then again you're not even touching the full epidermis. And even if we become "scientific" and say that you're only touching the quarks and electrons in the hand, you can't touch the full quarks or full electrons. There never comes a point at which you make direct contact with some sub-portion of the hand as a whole.

Erik Bryngelsson: So the idea is that objects can't touch completely?

Graham Harman: More than this, in the strict sense they cannot touch at all.

Erik Bryngelsson: Because they are caricatures, and when objects meet they just meet one aspect of each other, and the object they meet is the sensual object.

Graham Harman: That's right. They are not touching part of a real object, they are touching the whole of a sensual object.

Erik Bryngelsson: And for you this would apply not only to the human-object relation, but also to the object-object relation, a sort of sensibility between the objects. Would it then be fair to characterize what you propose as a kind of "aesthetics as first philosophy," where aesthetics is not only the capacity for sensi-bility for the human mind, but this capacity is localized within objects as well?

Graham Harman: Sure. For me aesthetics is about the separation of an object from its qualities, and there are four ways this can happen. Actually, art is only one of these four ways, so aesthetics might be a broader term than art. Aesthetics is the term I use for any separation between an object and its qualities. Time and space turn out to be such a separation, so time and space are themselves aesthetic, and this links up with the original meaning of aesthetics, which is perception. And we perceive by way of time and space, and more generally by way of the separation of objects and qualities. I think what aesthetics can do that the sciences cannot is that aesthetic experiences, and the arts in particular, are under pressure to be especially aware that an object is not reducible to a bundle of qualities. An artwork is not reducible to a certain amount of paint and canvas, whereas one *might* be tempted to think that a neutron is nothing more than its properties.

Erik Bryngelsson: We've seen increased interest in the art world in Speculative Realism and object-oriented philosophy. For you is this interesting and inspiring, or is there also the risk of it being a too-hasty appropriation of a philosophical idea?

Graham Harman: I have a lot of trust in reality. I have faith that if people start reading the philosophy, then everything will work itself out and good things will happen. If nothing else, it brings me into contact with artists, which is a great sense of inspiration and joy. I have no interest in policing the supposed misunderstandings of artists or others who find something interesting in Speculative Realism for their own pursuits.

Erik Bryngelsson: You mentioned one art piece in relation to your work that particularly interested you: Joanna Malinowska placed a cassette player playing Glenn Gould doing Bach fugues, and being left there in the Arctic out of reach of any human perception.[189]

Graham Harman: I thought it was an interesting way to appropriate object-oriented philosophy, taking up the idea of objects existing apart from any contact with them. But of course I don't think that this literal method is the only way to appropriate object-oriented philosophy for the arts. Anything that distances the object from its exact qualities or its exact environmental conditions could be an object-oriented piece of art. In recent decades there has been a relationist and contextualist dogma in the arts (and in architecture) and no doubt that's why people are turning to object-oriented philosophy.

Erik Bryngelsson: You write in your recent article in *New Literary History* that after the death of the author pronounced by Foucault and Barthes, we need the death of the culture. What does that mean?[190]

Graham Harman: I was talking about the New Historicists and the fact that they want to embed literary texts excessively in their socio-political surroundings. More generally, I think it's a good time to talk about the death of context. Once again, some people will tell you that deconstruction already did that, but not really. Deconstruction just says that you can never fix one univocal context in which the thing is located, it's always slipping and sliding away horizontally from one context into limitless others. But what I'm saying instead is that objects are outside *all* context, not just any determinate context. We need to decontextualize things again. The problem with past decontextualizations of objects was that they thought we could *know* things outside of their contexts; they thought we could *know* the essence of a thing outside of how it's affected by other things. But we cannot do that. Things do exist outside their contexts, but not in a way that's knowable. There's no *direct* contact possible between me and the objects. There's always going to be a certain mystery, a certain allusiveness that presupposes a *reality* to which one can only allude.

Erik Bryngelsson: When Latour perceives the need for criticism to move beyond the divisions between nature and culture or facts and fetishes in order to get away from the supposed bare, objective reality of things, from matters of fact to matters of concern (which he conceives of as a gathering of things), what would be object-oriented philosophy's take on this contemporary artistic practice of collecting and creating constellations of things— of in a sense "curating the world"?

Graham Harman: I think there can be a certain practical value to that; it can create unexpected connections and resonances. But in metaphysical terms, I don't agree with what Latour is doing here. The reason he wants to call the thing a "gathering" is because he wants to say that there's no reality to the thing outside of the elements that are assembled to make it up. The thing *is* its alliances. I think that's absolutely wrong. For me, a thing can enter different alliances only because the thing is already there. I know that for Whitehead and for his admirers such as Latour, this amounts to a theory of "vacuous actuality." It's supposedly an outdated theory of substance— this idea that there could be a thing sitting in a vacuum outside all relations. Yet this is precisely what I defend: vacuous actuality, in the sense of vacuum-sealed and non-relational reality.

Erik Bryngelsson: In Latour's 2005 exhibition in Karlsruhe, *Making Things Public*,[191] he connects the thing (*res*) to the public (*res publica*). In fact, things only matter for him when they are visible, and hence everything should become public.

Graham Harman: I think this is the wrong way to go. On the contrary, what we need is a greater privacy of things!

Erik Bryngelsson: So if Latour can be said to intervene in the *Realpolitik* of matters of fact with his *Dingpolitik* of matters of concern, what then would be an *Objektpolitik*?

Graham Harman: *Realpolitik* in Latour's sense (which is by no means the usual sense of the term) means using our supposed access to an external reality in order to denounce other people, using one's knowledge to denounce the ignorance of others. And

I'm opposed to that as much as Latour is.

Erik Bryngelsson: That would be what you call the debunking process of criticism.

Graham Harman: Right. And I think Latour's *We Have Never Been Modern* was the most brilliant philosophical book of the 1990's, because there he shows quite effectively that debunking can occur either downwards or upwards. It can be the scientific version where you try to find the foundational components of which a thing is made. But you can also debunk by going upwards, by saying that everything is just power, everything is just language, and that there's nothing hidden behind power, language, perception, events, whatever. And Latour's answer to that is to have a flat ontology where everything is equally real but not equally strong. *Dingpolitik* has to do with how you assemble things to be stronger, how you create better alliances. And admittedly (Latour himself admits it) there is the danger of "might is right" with this standpoint, the danger of overestimating the winners.

But my bigger concern about Latour is not his overestimation of the winners, but his overidentification of people and things with their alliances. Take politics, for instance. If people were nothing more than their relations, then why would they ever revolt? Why would they ever feel oppressed? Why would the Egyptians have rebelled in Tahrir Square if the Egyptians were nothing more than their alliances with Mubarak's regime? Obviously that's not what they were. They were something more than that. There was something dignified and worthy that was held in reserve, something not adequately expressed under the Mubarak regime, and that is why a political upsurge was possible.

Erik Bryngelsson: Could object-oriented philosophy be your plea for a retrieval of all those objects, works of art, styles, or movements that have been forgotten? Would it be a sort of resurrection of dead objects through a justice to come, to play on Meillassoux's prediction in *The Divine Inexistence*?[192]

Graham Harman: It's certainly a plea to consider that some things might have been the victims of unjust forgetting. But for me unlike for Meillassoux, it's not a *universal* resurrection. It's not an archive. I'm not pleading that all things must be preserved as if in some Library of Babel. I'm simply pleading that our current idea of what the greatest things are may be incomplete or inaccurate. Justice requires constant toil when assessing the relative merits of various works in philosophy, literature, or art. But I'm not pleading for all things to be resurrected. Some things are best left behind.

15. A New Look at Identity and Sufficient Reason (2013)

This lecture was given at DePaul University in Chicago on January 11, 2013 at the invitation of Michael Naas, Chair of the Department of Philosophy. It was a pleasant return from Egypt to my doctoral institution, nearly fourteen years after the defense of my dissertation. The lecture was attended by some sixty people, said by Naas to be a record for a Friday lecture at the Department of Philosophy. Attendee Liam Heneghan later reported on Twitter that the "discussion veered towards feistiness," which matches my recollection as well. Nonetheless, the discussion generally seemed constructive even if occasionally heated. Afterward, a long table of faculty and graduate students assembled at the Thai restaurant PS Bangkok on Halsted Street, just as was always done during my own DePaul student years in the 1990's.

Today I will speak about the principle of identity and the principle of sufficient reason, which can be restated roughly as "everything is what it is," and "everything has a reason for what it is." I will try to show that these principles are central not only to classical metaphysics, but also to what is going on right now in the newest continental philosophies.

In order to get ourselves in the mood, let's review a few interesting passages concerning these two principles. The name most associated with identity and sufficient reason, of course, is that of Gottfried Wilhelm Leibniz. As he puts it in his brief 1689 work *Primary Truths*:

> The primary truths are those which assert the same thing of itself or deny the opposite of its opposite. For example, "A is A," "A is not not-A," or "if it is true that A is B, then it is false that A is not B or that A is not-B." Also "every thing is as it is," "every thing is similar or equal to itself, "nothing is greater or

less than itself," and others of this sort. Although they themselves may have their degrees of priority, nonetheless they can all be included under the name 'identities.'[193]

Another of these identities, as Leibniz puts it, is "the received axiom that nothing is without reason, or [that] there is no effect without a cause... otherwise there would be a truth which could not be proved *a priori*, that is, a truth which could not be resolved into identities, contrary to the nature of truth, which is always an explicit or implicit identity."[194] For this reason, "everything that will happen to Peter and Judas, both necessary and free, is contained in the perfect individual notion of Peter and Judas..."[195] And "every individual substance contains in its perfect notion the entire universe and everything that exists in it, past, present, and future."[196] And "no created substance exerts a metaphysical action or influx on any other thing."[197] And there is neither a vacuum nor atoms, and each particle of the universe contains an infinity of creatures and nothing can arise or perish, and all the other ideas that follow for Leibniz from the primary truth of identity.

But someone might hold the reverse— that the principle of identity follows from the principle of sufficient reason, renamed as the principle of ground. Heidegger made this suggestion in the 1950's, entertaining the possibility that since the same belongs with the same on the basis of some shared ground,

> the nature of identity cannot do without a reason. But the principle of reason deals with reasons. Thus the principle of identity could be grounded in the principle of reason. So the highest fundamental principle of all fundamental principles would not be the principle of identity, but the principle of reason.[198]

Let's turn now to contemporary philosophy. If we fast-forward to the year 2006, we find this intriguing passage from Quentin Meillassoux:

> Leibniz founded metaphysical rationality upon two principles whose scope was considered to be absolute: the principle of non-contradiction and the principle of sufficient reason. Hegel saw that the absolutization of the principle of sufficient reason (which marked the culmination of the necessity of the belief in what is) required the devaluation of the principle of non-contradiction. [Wittgenstein and Heidegger]... insisted upon de-absolutizing both the principle of reason and the principle of non-contradiction. But the principle of unreason [that is to say, Meillassoux's own fundamental principle- g.h.] teaches us that it is *because the principle of reason is absolutely false that the principle of non-contradiction is absolutely true.*[199]

Though the reading of Heidegger here is questionable, that is not our concern at the moment. What is interesting for us today is that the difference between the attitudes of Leibniz, Heidegger, and Meillassoux could hardly be more stark. Whereas Leibniz in the quoted text views sufficient reason as following directly from identity, and Heidegger at least entertains the reverse option, Meillassoux not only drives a wedge between the two principles, but actually derives the *truth* of identity from the *falsity* of sufficient reason. Contingency alone is necessary. The laws of nature can change at any moment for no reason whatsoever, and even a virtual God might emerge to resurrect the dead and inaugurate a reign of justice.[200]

But perhaps not even the principle of identity is safe. I quote now from the Australian philosopher Graham Priest, in his discussion of the closely related law of non-contradiction: "I know of no historical defense of the law of non-contradiction since Aristotle worth mentioning. Is this because Aristotle's arguments were conclusive? Hardly. Arguably, they do not work at all."[201] He adds, in even more cavalier fashion, that the law of non-contradiction is "an historical mistake."[202]

Clearly, there is some controversy surrounding these principles, both as to which has priority over the other and as to whether they are valid at all. I propose that we begin our discussion with Meillassoux, who has an ingenious if ultimately unconvincing way of addressing these problems.

1. In Defense of Sufficient Reason

Meillassoux's debut book *After Finitude* is one of the most inter-esting and controversial works of continental philosophy to have been published in our still-new century. His challenge to the continental tradition is centered in his chief polemical term, "correlationism," a term that catalyzed Speculative Realism and annoyed many critics who regarded correlationism as a pseudo-problem. But this status of "pseudo-problem" is precisely the point. In analytic philosophy, the realism/anti-realism dispute has always remained on the map, and the positions taken by analytic philosophers on realism have been at nearly *every* place on the map. But in the continental tradition, there has been a tendency since Husserl and Heidegger to treat the realism question as a false problem. In my opinion, this is the price phenomenology began to pay even in the 1890's. For Franz Brentano, the intentional object was not an object *outside* the mind at which we point, but a kind of *immanent* objectivity. The status of objects outside the mind was left vague. Brentano's Polish disciple Twardowski tackled the problem by offering a duality between "objects" outside the mind and "content" inside the mind.[203] Husserl famously wrestled with the ideas of the younger Twardowski for several years before reaching his own, very different conclusion: there cannot be a doubling between objects outside the mind and content inside the mind, because then the

Berlin of which I speak and the real Berlin would be two different things, which at first glance seems nonsensical.[204] Nothing lies beyond possible phenomenal manifestation to an observer; there is no "deep Berlin" that could not be the object of an intentional act.

Here I am reading Husserl as a very strict idealist, despite the frequent refrain that we are "always already outside ourselves" in aiming at an intentional object. As I see it, while the Berlin of which we speak may be the same thing as the real Berlin, the city Berlin insofar we perceive or cognitively access it is a Berlin-for-me that cannot step into reality and do the same work as Berlin itself. Or to use a more vivid example, the fire that I encounter in my intentional life does not burn my brain as I think or perceive it. Perfect knowledge of a horse would not itself be a horse that runs, jumps, eats, and breeds. This is one of the basic arguments made by realists, though realism was a position only rarely defended in the continental tradition before the early years of the twenty-first century. Yet the attempt to view realism as a "pseudo-problem" was not only the fault of phenomenology. It was just as true of the German Idealist tradition, with its amputation of the thing-in-itself, and can also be found in Bergson's universal theory of images in *Matter and Memory*,[205] and in William James (a sort of honorary continental philosopher) in his *Essays in Radical Empiricism*.[206] Merleau-Ponty is often praised for his supposedly innovative realist tendencies, but all he tells us is that the world looks at us just as we look at it, not that different parts of the world look at each other as well; the human always remains part of the equation, and hence the human-world correlate still stands at the center of his philosophy.[207] In *Of Grammatology*, Derrida's main target seems to be "naïve objectivism"[208] (that is to say, realism). He writes, in a spirit of praise, that "Heidegger's insistence on noting that being is produced as history only through the logos, and is nothing outside of it, the difference between being and the entity— all this clearly indicates that fundamentally nothing escapes the movement of the signifier, and that, in the last instance, the difference between signified and signifier is nothing."[209] More recently, Slavoj Žižek tells us brazenly that "the true formula of materialism is not that there is some noumenal reality beyond our distorting perception of it. The only consistent materialist position is that *the world does not exist...*"[210]

Yet despite all these claims that reality is no more than the target of an intentional act, no more than images, no more than a viscous flesh intertwining human and world, no more than signifiers, no more than the fantasy of a mad subject lost in the night, full-blown idealist positions are just as rare in continental thought as full-blown realist ones. Where is the praise for Berkeley's wildly sardonic claim that "it is indeed an opinion strangely prevailing amongst men, that houses, mountains, rivers, and in a word all sensible objects have an existence natural or real, distinct from their being perceived by the understanding"?[211] Even Žižek feels the need to reassure us that "we are not idealists,"[212] where the word "we" refers to Žižek himself. In short, almost no one in the continental tradition has wanted to own up to an explicitly realist or explicitly idealist position. For this reason, I completely fail to understand why some people dismiss Meillassoux's term correlationism as a "straw man." Indeed, probably the central ontological feature of continental philosophy has been the notion that we cannot think human without world, nor world without human, but only a primordial correlation or rapport between them.[213] Although I had already used the term "philosophies of access" in 2002 to describe roughly the same phenomenon,[214] Meillassoux's "correlationism" is much snappier and etymologically more to the point. Any philosophy that requires thought to be one ingredient of any situation is correlationist as long as it is not outright idealist.

The real question is not whether or not correlationism really exists, but whether it is really so bad. If it's not so bad, then we can stay with the human-world correlate as the center of philosophy, and Speculative Realism will prove to be an unnecessary distraction. But I happen to think that correlationism is very bad, though not for the same reason that Meillassoux thinks so. More than this, I also think that Meillassoux's own approach to correlationism is what makes him go wrong with respect to the theme of tonight's lecture: identity and sufficient reason. Let's spend a moment recalling the philosophy of Immanuel Kant, in whose shadow all of us still work. There are perhaps two basic features of Kantian philosophy; Meillassoux rejects only one of these, while I think we ought to preserve that one but reject the other. One of these is the Kantian conception of finitude, of the unreachable character of the thing-in-itself. Now, Meillassoux obviously dislikes finitude. The title of his now-famous book is of course *After Finitude*, and Meillassoux (like Badiou and Žižek, philosophers he closely resembles in many respects) shows surprisingly little interest in assimilating any of Heidegger's arguments on behalf of finitude. This remains the case even though Badiou and Žižek both concede without explanation that Heidegger was the most recent great philosopher in the West. In short, they are heirs to the German Idealist tradition of the critique of the in-itself.[215]

But there is a second major aspect to Kant's philosophy other than finitude, and that is the priority Kant grants to the human-world relation over all other relations. We can speak of the human perception of fire in terms of time, space, and the twelve categories, but we cannot speak directly of the relation between fire and cotton, since speaking means thinking, and thinking means thinking within our finitude. The human (or rather, "the rational being") must be implicitly on the scene, and therefore all relations between entities are philosophically reabsorbed into the human-world relation no matter how hard we try to escape it. My historical thesis is that German Idealism took the wrong fork in the road. Instead of trying to eliminate the thing-in-itself, the thing-in-itself should have been treated not as some tragic residue inaccessible to poignantly limited human beings, but as characteristic of relationality in general. All relations caricature, distort, or translate some reality that is untranslatable into relational terms. Instead of German Idealism, we could have had a "German Realism" that preserved finitude while denying its limitation to the human-world interaction. In other words, the surface agreement among Speculative Realists as to the harmful character of correlationism masks a deeper disagreement on what is wrong with the human-world correlate and how to address that wrong. Let's briefly review the key steps of Meillassoux's argument and see how he is led to reject the principle of sufficient reason while affirming the principle of identity.

One of the most interesting facts about Meillassoux is that despite his well-known critique of correlationism, he is deeply sympathetic to it. The reason this is often overlooked is because Meillassoux begins his book with the theme of "ancestrality," or the existence of natural phenomena prior to the emergence of any consciousness in the universe. He even gives us a list: the origin of the universe was 13.5 billion years ago, the accretion of the earth 4.56 billion years ago, and the origin of life on earth 3.5 billion years ago.[216] Meillassoux comments as follows:

> Empirical science is today capable of producing statements about events anterior to the advent of life as well as consciousness... Thus contemporary science is in a position to precisely determine —albeit in the form of revisable hypotheses— the dates of the formation of the fossils of creatures living prior to the emergence of the first hominids, the date of the accretion of the earth, the date of the formation of stars, and even the "age" of the universe itself.[217]

This might make Meillassoux sound like a straightforward defender of scientific realism, unwilling to grant any special ontological role to human thought. The ancestrality of the pre-human world might seem to let science attain unproblematic access to things-in-themselves. Against this, the correlationist would say that "event Y occurred X years before the emergence of humans— for humans...,"[218] or that "being is not anterior to givenness, [but rather] it gives itself as anterior to givenness."[219] But it needs to be realized that Meillassoux *agrees* with the correlationist here, at least at the outset. The correlational circle tells us that we cannot think the thing outside thought without turning it into a thought, and that for this reason we remain barred from any access to the thing-in-itself. And please note that Meillassoux fully affirms this point, affirms that any access to the real must pass through the correlational circle. Rather than dismissing correlationism as absurd sophistry, Meillassoux thinks we can work our way out of the circle only through a difficult and paradoxical line of proof. Anyone who doubts this only needs to read Meillassoux's portion of the Speculative Realism workshop transcript from April 2007, published in Volume III of *Collapse*.[220] There his admiration for the force of the correlationist argument is explicitly stated, while those who dismiss it out of hand are accused of an anti-rationalist attitude. Initially, we cannot think the in-itself without turning it into a thing-for-us. Hence Meillassoux is not a realist in the usual sense. His discussion of the ancestral world in the opening chapter of *After Finitude* is not intended as a proof against the correlationist, but only as an *aporia* demonstrating the difficulties faced by both sides: correlationism and scientific realism alike. His eventual access to the thing-in-itself is achieved not directly, but along a circuitous path that in my opinion never reaches its goal.

What is Meillassoux's intended path to the in-itself? In a book published in 2011, I invented the term "Meillassoux's Spectrum" to describe a continuum of possible views on the realism question.[221] Despite many possible variations, there are essentially four options that count for Meillassoux's argument. At one extreme we have straightforward realism, often called "naïve realism," which holds that there is a world outside thought and that we can gain access to this world. At the other extreme would be idealism, defined as the view that the world consists solely in being perceived. In between these two poles is correlationism, defined as the notion that both of the extremes just mentioned are wrong. This is the view that we cannot think the world without thought demanded by the realists, nor the thought without an independent world of the idealists, but only a primordial correlation or rapport between world and thought, henceforth viewed as inseparable. As Meillassoux notes, if philosophy before Kant was often a debate over who had the best model of substance, since Kant it has often been a struggle to decide who has the superior model of the thought-world correlate: "is it the thinker of the subject-object correlation, the noetico-noematic correlation, or the language-referent correlation?"[222] Here we could add the *Sein-Dasein* correlation, and many others.

But there are two distinct forms of correlationism, and it is no exaggeration to say that Meillassoux's entire philosophy hinges on this distinction. There is "weak" correlationism, and there is "strong" correlationism. Weak correlationism is best identified with the position of Kant: there are things-in-themselves, and we can think them but not know them. But strong correlationism is the view that the things-in-themselves cannot even be thought, since this would lead immediately to contradiction. We cannot think the unthought without turning it into something thought. This is the correlational circle we discussed earlier, and it should now be clear that this circle is upheld only by the strong correlationist. Weak correlationists would never say that we cannot think the unthought without turning it into a thought, because their whole point is that we *can* think it, and simply cannot know it.

And here is the difficult situation that Meillassoux faces. He definitely sympathizes with strong correlationism rather than the weak variety; he always defends the idea that we cannot think the unthought without turning it into a thought. Yet he wants to avoid slipping into idealism, the next further step along the spectrum, due to his respect for the claim of science to describe a world independent of thought. So, how can Meillassoux preserve what he takes to be the brilliant insight of the correlational circle, without slipping into full-blown idealism? He gives a rather intricate discussion of this question,[223] but the nuances are not all relevant to the current discussion, and we can safely summarize it for our purposes as follows. Both the strong correlationist and the idealist agree that we cannot think the thing-in-itself without turning it into a thought. But whereas the idealist concludes that we therefore know with certainty that there is nothing outside thought, the strong correlationist says that we cannot be sure; there still might be something outside thought. This possible world outside thought must be *absolutely* possible and not only possible relatively to us, because in the latter case the idealist would win, since there would be no remaining difference between idealism and strong correlationism. But this means that the strong correlationist is converted into a new character, whom Meillassoux terms the "speculative philosopher" (which is to say, converted into Meillassoux himself). Whereas the correlationist simply claims that we cannot know if there is a world outside thought, the speculative philosopher says that we *can* know that the world might be uncorrelated with thought and might thus have an independent existence different from how it appears to thought.

The epistemological uncertainty as to whether there is a world differing from thought is thus converted into an ontological certitude that the world might differ from thought. The fact that anything might be different means that there cannot be any necessary being, and for Meillassoux the principle of sufficient reason ultimately requires some necessary being as the ultimate ground or reason. As he puts it: "We are no longer upholding a variant of the principle of sufficient reason, according to which there is a necessary reason why everything is the way it is rather than otherwise, but rather the absolute truth of a principle of unreason. There is no reason for anything to be or to remain the way it is; everything must, without reason, to be able not to be and/or to be able to be other than it is."[224] This leads to "hyperchaos," or the idea that anything can happen at any moment for no reason at all. And since Meillassoux also employs Cantor's transfinite mathematics to show that we cannot calculate probabilities at the level of the world as a whole, it means that we should ignore probability at this level. Since all events are equally probable and improbable, we should focus instead on the most important possibilities. Some of these have already occurred, such as the sudden advent of life from matter and thought from life. The final important possibility has not yet happened and might never happen: namely, the advent of justice thanks to the virtual god who does not yet exist but might exist in the future, and the Christ-like mediator who will pave the way for this god and then abandon the status of Messiah to return to life as a normal citizen, equal to the rest of us.[225] Though some readers laugh at these consequences, they follow quite logically from Meillassoux's attack on the principle of sufficient reason.

But rather than discuss the intricacies of the Meillassouxian system, let me   give a few reasons why I don't think it works, despite its great brilliance and originality. We saw that speculative philosophy claimed to be a radicalized form of strong correlationism. The problem, as I see it, is that strong correlationism is an impossible position to begin with, since it immediately collapses into idealism. Recall that the strong correlationist is the one who accepts the correlational circle ("we cannot think the in-itself without turning it into a thought, and therefore into something correlated with us") but does not accept the idealist assumption that nothing exists outside thought. The strong correlationist is supposedly modest, and says "we cannot think an it-itself outside thought, but just because it's impossible for us to *think* it doesn't mean it's impossible that it might *exist* without our being able to think it." The problem is that strong correlationism has long since abandoned any such modesty. If in the first step you accept the correlational circle ("the thing-in-itself is thought by us, and therefore is not in-itself") you cannot come back in the second step and say "but there might be an in-itself anyway." After all, in the first step you already showed that the idea of an in-itself outside thought is *meaningless*. And it is a contradiction if you call the in-itself meaningless in order to avoid Kant's weak correlationism but then call it meaningful in order to avoid idealism. I am not setting an empty logical trap for Meillassoux here: he knows exactly what he is doing. The reason he wants to avoid idealism is to preserve scientific access to a world outside thought. And the reason he wants to avoid weak correlationism is that he hates the finitude of the Kantian position, since he wants philosophy to be able to deduce eternal truths about the world. But once you accept the correlational circle as Meillassoux does, you have to be an idealist, since the very meaningfulness of a world outside thought has been eliminated by the circle in advance.

And here again, I am not setting a logical trap for Meillassoux. When he introduces his own non-naive or speculative sense of the in-itself, what he tries to show is that the in-itself could exist outside humans in time, before the emergence of thought or after all thought has been extinguished. But this isn't a very strong sense of the in-itself, because it implies that as long as humans are alive, we *can* gain direct access to the things. Indeed, this is Meillassoux's whole purpose, since he has no love for the philosophies of finitude so prevalent in continental thought. But it leads to a big problem: if there is no in-itself beyond humans in anything but a temporal sense, then what is the difference between the things and our conceptions of them?

What is the difference between a tree and a perfect concept of a tree? The question has especial force in Meillassoux's case, given his view that the primary qualities of things are those that can be mathematized.[226] For although he tries to head off charges that he is a Pythagorean by insisting on the difference between thought and its referent,[227] he never really tells us in what this difference consists. Is the difference between a tree and a perfect mathematical model of the tree merely that the former inheres in physical matter and the latter does not? But then what is this formless physical matter in which the mathematical forms inhere? This is never explained.

But it is time to steer this discussion of Meillasoux back to today's main topic: identity and sufficient reason. There are at least four important objections that can be made to Meillassoux's view on sufficient reason.

First, he wrongly identifies sufficient reason with determinism. Meillassoux seems to assume that if everything exists for a reason, then everything must be foreordained, and either there will be a necessary being or (ultimately, and even worse) *all* beings will be necessary. This is how he defines "metaphysics," which is a pejorative term for him. If Heidegger and postmodern philosophies reject the term "metaphysics" due to its apparent connection with presence, Meillassoux rejects it due to its complicitous relationship with necessity. But the fact that everything has a reason does not entail that every reason must generate one and only one definite thing. This is intuitively clear in the human realm: we can give reasons why we ate at a certain restaurant or accepted an invitation, but this does not mean (without further argument) that we were causally determined to do so. The rise of Islam or the emergence of German Idealism after Kant can be illuminated by giving reasons, but we are not stuck with the false alternative of claiming either that these were destined to happen or that they happened suddenly for no reason at all, which is the only alternative allowed by Meillassoux. We should even be open to the possibility that the same thing is true in the inanimate realm. Reasons can be given for why a hurricane or tsunami occurred in a certain time or place, but it is not necessarily true that as soon as the reasons for a climate phenomenon are in place that the phenomenon must then automatically take place. An accidental trigger might be necessary, or (who knows?) there might be something analogous to "freedom" in the heart of nature itself. And not only do the same reasons not necessarily have to generate the same result every time: the same result does not necessarily result from the same reasons every time. The supposed supervenience of larger things on their constituent pieces does not mean that things have no autonomy from those pieces. For example, what makes Saul Kripke's *Naming and Necessity* ultimately so disappointing is that after doing so much work to show that anything designated by a name is autonomous from the features above it through which it is known (so that we can name Columbus or Einstein even if everything we think we know about them is false), he does not allow the thing any independence from the features below it by which it is generated. The essence of gold is to have 79 protons, ignoring that it is metaphysically conceivable if not chemically possible for gold to come about through alternate causes. Or, the essence of an individual human is to have been formed from two specific parents, even though it is unlikely but genetically possible for the same DNA to result from two completely different parents.

Nor is this true only for analytic philosophy and its typical scientism. Manuel DeLanda, for instance, claims that the only way to distinguish between two helium atoms is to give a historical-genetic account of how each was formed in the core of a specific star. But this assumes that everything that ever happens to an entity is somehow recorded in its heart by a sort of universal cosmic memory. In truth, most of the history of each thing is forgotten by that thing, leaving no trace on it at all.

Though each of us is shaped by personal history, we are not promiscuously shaped by every tiniest detail of that history, such as the shirt we happened to wear on April 24 last year or whether we were fifth or seventh in line on our last visit to the Department of Motor Vehicles. The fact that such accidents *can* have profound impact by leading to important chance meetings does not mean that *all* chance circumstances are recorded in the history of a given thing. Stated more simply, my point here is that we can say that things have a sufficient reason without reducing things to that reason. The same reason might generate different effects, and the same effect might arise from different reasons. To avoid utter determinism, we do not need to pay Meillassoux's shockingly high price of saying that anything can happen for no reason at all.

Second, this leads us to a very paradoxical aspect of his critique of sufficient reason, which is that it only holds for changes at the uppermost level of laws of nature. Within the framework of any given set of laws of nature, Meillassoux (ironically) seems to be the champion of a robotic form of determinism. If it is a law of nature that all masses attract one another, then they must attract one another without exception. And if it is a law of nature that water boils at 100 degrees centigrade at sea level, then this must happen in all cases, other things being equal. What Meillassoux adds to this typical determinist picture is simply that the laws of nature themselves might change at any moment for no reason whatsoever. Locally, there is determinism; globally, there is absolute contingency. What leads Meillassoux to such a paradoxical result, so paradoxical that it is hard to notice even on one's first few readings of his book? I suspect that this is a holdover from the philosophy of his teacher Alain Badiou, for whom there is a similar dualism between the "state of the situation" (normal life as usual) and rare "events" in which the situation is ruptured: revolutions, falling in love, or paradigm-shifting breakthroughs in science and the arts. Although both

Badiou's and Meillasoux's philosophies seem to be radically open to sudden change at the highest levels of the structure of the world, both paint a fairly dismal picture of everyday causal events and sub-revolutionary political action. Here there is no room for surprise, no place for novelty.

Third, Meillassoux seems to be exclusively concerned with sufficient reasons unfolding *over time*. That is to say, when he talks about the sufficient reason for the existence of a human, this would be a story about one's parents, whose sufficient reason would be one's grandparents, and so forth. But sufficient reason does not just have to do with time; it also has to do with composition, the relation between part and whole (or "mereology," as it is known in technical terms). The sufficient reason for a specific piece of gold is not just to be found in stories about a far-off supernova; the sufficient reason of gold is also its molecular and atomic structure here and now, regardless of the history of how these structures were produced by exploding stars. If pushed far enough, Meillassoux's theory of radical contingency should not just be temporal, but should also be compositional. Gold molecules would not necessarily generate gold, but might lead to the appearance of silver, a planet, or a horse, or might even lead to nothing at all.

This is not just a lacuna in Meillassoux's argument, as if he simply forgot to mention it and can deal with it in a future book within the same theoretical framework. The problem is that Meillassoux's philosophy tends to exclude composition altogether. In this philosophy, there can be no hidden reasons for things. Gold can be known exhaustively by mathematizing its primary qualities, and so can horses and trees; nothing is hidden in reserve as long as we use our reason correctly. There is no obscure connection between part and whole or ground and consequent, but everything lies at the surface of the world, present for possible mathematizing. The obvious counter-philosopher here is Heidegger. The famous critique of presence-

at-hand, which I would claim is the heart of Heidegger's philosophical advance, can be read essentially as a commitment to
sufficient reason, or to a strange form of composition.
Phenomena are not sufficient in their own right, but are
grounded in something sub-phenomenal. The broken hammer
has its ground in the hammer, something not present that is
nonetheless able to reveal itself.[228] As I have often argued
elsewhere, it is not just that theory is grounded in praxis, but that
both theory and praxis are equally grounded in a reality that
neither is able to exhaust. And not just human theory and praxis,
but even the inanimate interaction among hailstones, trees, hurri-
canes, and swamps is grounded in these things themselves,
which are never exhaustively deployed in their interactions.
Stated differently, realism is itself a theory of sufficient reason.
Realism is a commitment to autonomous reality and not, as
Meillassoux and others claim, a commitment to the view that this
reality can be directly known. Between reality and access to
reality there is a gulf that can only bridged obliquely, never
directly. My relation to a tree is a composite grounded in me and
the tree, not a legible surface of the world in which reality itself
is made present in mathematizable form. Wherever we are,
reality is always elsewhere from where we are looking. This is
what the principle of sufficient reason really means: that a thing
is deeper than its presence. And though presence is often taken,
by Heideggerians and Derrideans alike, to mean self-identity
apart from any relation, I claim that the opposite is true. For
when something is present it is present to something or someone,
and this is purely relational: the very opposite of self-identity and
autonomy. Presence is not non-relation but relation, and the real
lesson of Heidegger as I see it is that being is the purely non-
relational, that which is deeper than any relational configuration
at all. If you hold that reality is mathematizable, then you simply
cannot be a realist in the strict sense, no matter how many caveats
you offer that you are not a Pythagorean. Respect for the real

requires respect for its unmasterability by knowledge. And this is why the "finitude" side of Kant is precisely the wrong side to abandon. The price Meillassoux pays for discarding finitude and reinstating absolute knowledge is that human thought remains ontologically central. The human-world relation remains the correlationist capital city, and all other relations can be discussed only by passing through the gates of this one. The reinstatement of a basically Cartesian dualism between thought and matter creates a "taxonomical" ontology in which certain entities think and certain entities move with dull mechanical torpor. But what we really need instead is a flatter ontology which acknowledges that all things translate one another: the fire does not drain the reality of the cotton any more than my thinking of it does. Finitude is not a tragic human problem, but the consequence of relationality as such, which can never fully bring its relata into play, so that the whole is always less than its parts.

Heidegger is worth mentioning here for another reason of relevance to present-day continental philosophy. The two dominant living figures in our subfield are surely Badiou and Žižek, and Meillassoux works very much in their vicinity. One of the curious things about Badiou and Žižek is their strange relation to Heidegger.[229] What is strange is that both of them praise Heidegger in various places as the last great philosophical figure, and yet both make hardly any use of Heidegger at all. Their true philosophical background, like Meillassoux's, is to be found in German Idealism, and (at least in the case of Badiou and Žižek) in a Germanidealized version of Lacan. Neither Badiou nor Žižek (nor Meillassoux, for that matter) has any sympathy at all for the usual notion of the thing-in-itself as lying beyond all access. All of them initially accept the correlational circle: we cannot think the unthought without bringing it back into the embrace of thought. And all tend to view any claim to the contrary as a crusty philosophical archaism that has not yet learned the obvious lessons of the immediate post-Kantian period. On the other side of the fence, does Heidegger agree with this view of the thing-in-itself? Hardly, despite the widespread efforts to treat Heidegger as an anti-realist. There is not only the famous defense of the thing-in-itself at the close of *Kant and the Problem of Metaphysics* (which Lee Braver completely ignores in his anti-realist version of Heidegger).[230] There is not only the concession (though admittedly watered down with unearned scare quotes) that readiness-to-hand is the characterization of things as they are "in themselves." There is the sheer fact that Heidegger's critique of Husserl does not even work if there is no in-itself. The problem with the presence-at-hand of phenomena in consciousness is not that they are independent. The problem, instead, is that the phenomena exist only as a correlate of our intending them. The famous tool-analysis tries to demonstrate a surplus in things beyond their presence to us. But despite Heidegger's own reading of this analysis as delivering a kind of holism, with all equipment gaining its meaning from other equipment and ultimately from Dasein as the heart of any system of equipment, Heidegger is inconsistent when he draws this conclusion. For the main point of equipment is not that it is always assigned to other equipment and to Dasein. This is only true when it happens to be working. The main point of equipment, instead, is that it can break.

Stated differently, equipment is not really holistic at all, but is that which is able to disrupt all holism by generating ruptures and surprises. Not only is equipment hiding behind phenomena present in consciousness, it is hiding just as much behind the current interaction between hammers, drills, screws, rail platforms, cities, planets, paintings of circles and all poetic hymns to rivers, centaurs, and unicorns. The history of philosophy, like the history of anything, does not just precede in linear fashion by debunking the errors of our ancestors and never looking back. Just as often, and perhaps more essentially, it consists of retrievals of what was left behind before it was fully grasped (a very Heideggerian point, of course). I see no way to do justice to Heidegger if we do not read him as basically a realist committed to things-in-themselves that are deeper than phenomena but also deeper than the current interactions between people and practical gear, and even deeper than the interactions between inanimate things and other inanimate things. But this being the case, the question arises of what Badiou and Žižek see in Heidegger, given their low regard (Žižek's in particular) for any model of the thing-in-itself? My suspicion is that they have simply ignored Heidegger without incorporating him much at all, and that their praise of his greatness is simply a tacit pre-emptive strike against any claim that they are not doing him justice. And if every period of philosophy is bound in part to address the excesses of its predecessors, I suspect that the era *following* the Badiou/Žižek era of continental philosophy (two thinkers who really took off among the young over the past decade) will de-emphasize the ballooning role of the subject in the current period and re-emphasize the status of the things themselves. This is another, more contingent historical reason that I think Meillassoux's attempted mathematization of the real is on the wrong track.

The fourth point about Meillassoux's rejection of sufficient reason is less an objection on my part than a transition to the closing part of the lecture. For in a remarkable new twist on the various permutations of identity and sufficient reason in modern philosophy, Meillassoux derives the law of non-contradiction not from sufficient reason (as Heidegger toys with doing in *Der Satz vom Grund*) but from the failure of sufficient reason. Namely, if a thing were to violate the law of identity, it would have no opposite. It could not turn into anything else. Therefore it would be necessary, and since necessary beings cannot exist, contradictory beings also cannot exist. This is not the place to analyze this innovative and fascinating argument, especially since Meillassoux admits that he has not yet given a full proof of it.[231]

Instead, having defended sufficient reason, let's give a brief defense of identity, since time is running short.

2. In Defense of Identity

Technically, identity is about things and non-contradiction is about statements. But to violate non-contradiction about statements is a relatively trivial matter for realism, which even provides strong *support* for contradiction at this level. After all, one of Aristotle's best definitions of a primary substance is something that can bear opposite properties. One person can say that Socrates is happy at one moment and sad at the next, and the supposed contradiction is not very important. We could even say different things at the same moment if one person thinks Socrates looks happy and another thinks he looks sad. In short, the real issue here comes from identity, not non-contradiction. This holds for example for the so-called *dialethism* of analytic philosopher Graham Priest, who makes it clear that he thinks contradiction is present in reality itself, not just in thought.[232] In his amply researched book *Beyond the Limits of Thought*, Priest shows numerous examples of how contradictions are supposedly reached once thought reaches its limit— in the Sophists, Socrates, Cusanus, Anselm, Berkeley, Kant, Hegel, Derrida, Davidson, Quine, Heidegger, and (even more easily) the Buddhist logician Nagarjuna. But for our purposes it is enough to ask about just one of these passages: Priest's treatment of what Meillassoux calls the correlational circle. We try to think an in-itself outside thought, yet in doing so we are thinking it, an apparent performative contradiction. Priest embraces this claim as well, but not quite in the same sense as Meillassoux. For Meillassoux, the attempt to think the in-itself in the usual sense simply *fails*; we cannot leap outside the circle in the name of a naïve realism. No contradiction is identified, here or elsewhere; Meillassoux remains committed to identity, since anything contradictory would be necessary, and this is forbidden by his philosophy of contingency. But for Priest, there is a real contradiction here, and he is prepared to celebrate it. We are unable to think the in-itself, yet at the same time *we really are* able to think it. Here, as in all the various paradoxes of self-reference and those connected with infinity and related matters, we reach a true contradiction at the limit of thought.

But however successful Priest's other examples of contradiction might be, his treatment of the correlational circle is no more successful than Meillassoux's. For there is no real contradiction in saying that I can talk about a thing outside my thinking it, even though I must think of it while doing so. The realist claim is not that we can *think* of a thing without thinking of it, but that it can *exist* without our thinking of it. To claim otherwise is an instance of the fallacy that has become known as "Stove's Gem," after the Australian analytic philosopher David Stove, who gave the correlational circle a prize for the worst argument in the history of philosophy.[233] Namely, the fact that we cannot think a thing without thinking it is merely a tautology that no one can or would deny. But to conclude that therefore a thing cannot *exist* without our thinking it is to derive a non-tautologous conclusion from a tautologous premise, which cannot be done. In fact, to claim that we cannot think the in-itself outside thought is actually a variant of Meno's Paradox. When Meno repeats the Sophists' claim that we cannot search for something because either we already have it and hence don't need to look for it, or else we don't have it but therefore cannot recognize it when we find it, Socrates answers with a defense of the theory of recollection. Yet we need not literally accept the Platonic theory of recollection in order to accept *philosophia*, the notion that we both have and do not have what we seek, and not in a "contradictory" sense (even if in an ambivalent one). Despite Priest's explicit denial of the fact,[234] there are indirect ways to get at reality, even though direct ones remain impossible. There is no evident contradiction in saying that the enthymeme in rhetoric says something without saying it, that metaphor speaks indirectly in a way that cannot be cashed out in literal terms (Black and Ortega y Gasset both show this nicely[235]), that jokes communicate information in ways that are ruined if these jokes are explained, and so forth. The commitment to thinking the in-itself without thinking it is neither impossible (as per Meillassoux) nor a true contradiction (as per Priest). Instead, it is simply the commitment to *philosophia*, loving something without having it and without ever being able to have it. How exactly this happens is sometimes difficult to determine, but we cannot address the difficulty either by locking ourselves inside the correlational circle and escaping by artificial and idealistic mathematical means, or by claiming that reality itself is contradictory. Instead, we need to return to the apparently discredited gap between the saying and the said, as seen for example in Aristotle's point that we cannot define a substance, since substances are individuals and definitions are made of universals.[236] Individuals are the root of all contradiction, but are not themselves contradictory. The reason Socrates can be both happy and sad is not because Socrates is *both* happy and sad, but because he is *neither*. The contradiction is grounded in something deeper and non-contradictory.

3. Further Conclusions

Let's move to a conclusion. One of the most satisfying chestnuts among old philosophical sayings is that no one can refute solipsism. What makes this principle so satisfying is that it marks a limit to the claim (already incorrect, in my view) that all philosophy is simply a matter of argument and proof. Whitehead is the great contrarian here. Not only does he point out that systems of philosophy are never refuted but only abandoned, he also noted better than anyone else that the method of philosophy is descriptive generalization, not geometrical deduction from unshakeable first principles.[237] There is in fact much to be said for abandoning the correlational circle simply because it is unfruitful, despite Meillassoux's low regard for appeals to the "rich elsewhere" that are unable to refute correlationism logically.[238]

But what is interesting for us here is that the claim that no one can refute solipsism is essentially equivalent to the claim that no one can prove the principle of sufficient reason. Solipsism holds that there is nothing behind what we encounter, that existence consists solely in its being perceived or thought by me. But sufficient reason makes the opposite claim that there is a reason for everything, including what is perceived or thought; perceptions and thoughts cannot be the exhaustive specimens of reality. To reject sufficient reason, to say that everything is contingent, that perceptions —like the roses of Angelus Silesius— have no why, but bloom because they bloom,[239] is identical with the solipsistic gesture. Of course, we need to add the caveat that Meillassoux only rejects sufficient reason at the level of the world as a whole. He is in perfect agreement that a vase falls form the table for a reason: the law of universal gravitation. He simply denies that this law has any necessary existence, and for him that is enough to say that the vase falling from the table has no sufficient reason. And yet it does: there is in fact a grounding relation between the law of gravitation and the vase falling from the table.

Thus, if we could prove the principle of sufficient reason, we could in fact refute solipsism and thereby dispose of the old chestnut that no one can refute solipsism except by a practical decision to regard it as useless. Though we cannot attempt this in the remaining time today, we can show that Meillassoux already does make one concession to sufficient reason, and it is one foreshadowed by a philosopher who is not among his favorites: Edmund Husserl. Count me among those who view Husserl as very clearly a full-blown idealist. The fact that we are always already outside ourselves intending objects does not change the fact that intentionality means *immanent* objectivity (objectivity that falls within the scope of experience rather than transcending it), and also does not change Husserl's claim that it is meaningless to imagine something that might not be the correlate of some intentional act. This is clearly not a realist position. Nonetheless, Husserl *feels* like a realist, and phenomenology in general *feels* like realism in a way that is not even true of Kant and certainly not true of Hegel. Why is this so? Why do we feel like we're adrift in carnal reality whenever we read Husserl's accounts of mailboxes and blackbirds, Levinas on bread, orphans, or smoke, and Merleau-Ponty's even juicier descriptions of black ink, burning houses, and the sudden appearance of the devil? The reason is that while the intentional objects of phenomenology do not lie outside experience and hence are not the ground of experience, the objects of phenomenology *are* the ground for the *appearances* of the object. This can be explained quite briefly.

The empiricist tradition always had a low regard for the notion of objects as unified independent things. The tendency was always to view objects as "bundles of properties," just as souls were reduced to "bundles of perceptions." If Husserl made a single greatest contribution to philosophy, I think it was the reversal of this notion of a bundle of properties. Instead, for phenomenology, the object *precedes* its properties. We may see the blackbird flying from many different angles, seeing first its head and later its tail. We may see it at various distances. But never do we think: "these are closely related appearances that I am bundling together arbitrarily into one." Instead, the unity of the blackbird is what allows me to unify all its different appearances. In more Husserlian terms, the intentional object is always deeper than its adumbrations. The intentional object "blackbird" (which is not a real one, since I could easily be hallucinating) is the ground or reason for all the different "adumbrations" of the blackbird viewed in some specific position and at a particular distance. And not only is that the case, but there is even a hierarchical grounding structure *within* the various features of phenomena. After all, the blackbird needs to retain certain features constantly in order for us to keep considering it as a blackbird rather than a blue jay or a distant airplane. The intentional object not only has intentional or sensual qualities, but also has real qualities as well— the ones it really needs in order to continue being itself, as if the classical notion of essence were projected for the first time in the history of philosophy onto the *surface* of the world rather than brooding in its depths. These real qualities, Husserl tells us, cannot be given to the senses. They are achieved through free variation and eidetic reduction, and are accessible only to the intellect— though for Heideggerian reasons, I would not agree that the intellect can directly access them any better than the senses can; I would say that they are real but not accessible except in oblique fashion.

So, the intentional object is the ground of its adumbrations, and in a sense the real qualities are the elusive ground of the intentional object itself, since it needs them in order to exist. This does not yet disprove solipsism, but it does show that even in the extreme case that "everything is just a dream," a minimal sense of the principle of sufficient reason must be at work. Moving from Husserl to Meillassoux, we find a similar minimal sense of sufficient reason at work in Meillassoux as well. After all, he wants to hierarchize the qualities of things into primary and secondary, and wants to say that the primary are the ground of the secondary, and that the primary qualities are the ones that can be mathematized. He then also wants to say that these primary qualities exist even after all humans are extinct and before all humans exist, though of course the secondary qualities will vanish in such a case. The same would hold even for those laws of nature that can change suddenly for no reason at all. For here too, we would need to distinguish between the primary qualities of those laws and the secondary qualities of the laws as they appear in the minds of various human beings. In short, to distinguish between primary and secondary qualities is to concede a hierarchy of levels that already takes us beyond the prison of the correlational circle and its marked solipsistic tendencies.

To say that "no one can refute solipsism" can thus be restated as "no one can prove the autonomy of things beyond their appearance to me." Husserl gives us a first foothold for objecting to this claim, and I would argue that Heidegger's tool-analysis gives us an even better one. But let's look at a related claim that people do not make as frequently as "no one can refute solipsism." Namely, what if someone were to say "no one can refute *holism*"? What this would mean is that nothing has any reality independent from the networks in which it is involved. Bruno Latour, my favorite living philosopher, says as much when he claims that entities are nothing more than whatever they transform, modify, perturb, or create. If we can begin to refute solipsism by defending the principle of sufficient reason, we can begin to refute holism by defending the principle of identity. This principle says simply that a thing is what it is, that it has some real internal constitution not generated by its interactions with anything else. If we do not adopt this principle, if we settle instead on a holism in which everything is interconnected with everything else, then it should be clear that nothing could ever change. Everything would already be what it is, exhaustively deployed in its interactions with everything else. Heidegger's tools would be a perfect system and could never break, since they would hold no surplus in reserve behind their current state. Latour's actor-networks could never change and the world would never move, since actors would already be defined by their current modifications, transformations, perturbations, and creations of other entities. There would simply be nothing more to them than this. Indeed, Latour seems to recognize this problems in recent years, and that is why he is positing a formless "plasma" lying beneath all definite things but responsible for changes in all things, much like the pre-Socratic *apeiron*. The only way out of this predicament is to accept the identity of individuals outside their relations, not to dream up some formless lump or to finesse the situation with some impossible model of a "pre-individual" realm that is both one and many at the same time.[240] We must return to substance, even while ridding this concept of its worst historical baggage— the privileging of the natural, the simple, and the eternal even though the artificial, the composite, and the transient are often can be just as real as the tinier, more natural, and simpler things.

This suggests that the principles of identity and sufficient reason are both true, and that neither is derivable from the other. Both principles have to do with a depth behind the given, whether a givenness to perception or a givenness of inanimate things to each other in causal interaction. Both principles require an adamant realism, but one in which the real can never be made directly present. Identity means that the thing is deeper than its relations and effects; sufficient reason means that every time we reach a depth, there is a deeper depth below it serving as its condition, leading to a *good* infinite regress of things with no final term. Despite the recent tendencies to celebrate relation, flux, and non-identity, the more challenging position may be to champion non-relation, durability, and identity in a manner that even knowledge cannot master. The future of Speculative Realism, and possibly other things as well, hinges on this point. Do we attempt an impossible radicalization of Strong Correlationism, by claiming in contradictory fashion that we cannot think the in-itself yet the in-itself might exist anyway? Or do we pursue the more promising radicalization of Weak Correlationism, by claiming that Kant's real limitation was in restricting finitude to rational beings, rather than seeing that finitude is characteristic of relationality as a whole, even in the interaction between spiders, oil drums, comets, strawberries, atoms, and tar. This would provide the basis for the never-attempted German Realism, even if it happened in Canada, Turkey, or New Zealand instead. The real is so real that knowledge cannot master it. We should not move to an era after finitude, but to one after the twofold ontology of human and world. *This*, and not finitude, is our most burdensome philosophical inheritance.

16. Heidegger on Being and Causation

Exactly one week after my appearance at DePaul, I gave the following lecture at St. John's College in Santa Fe, New Mexico on January 18, 2013, which provides a good final summary of ideas developed in the earlier chapters of this book. It was another homecoming occasion, since I had spent my freshman year (1986-1987) at St. John's in Santa Fe before transferring to its sister campus in Annapolis, Maryland (1987-1990). St. John's is well known in the United States for its rigorous liberal arts curriculum, including its exclusive use of the classic texts of Western civilization and exclusion of normal textbooks and examinations. Another part of the curriculum is the traditional Friday night lecture. As a St. John's alumnus, it was one of the great honors of my career to be invited to give one of the Friday lectures, as determined several years in advance. It remained an honor even when the traditional evening atmosphere of these lectures gave way to an experimental afternoon starting time. The Great Hall was full, and the question period was lively. The visit generally went well. Along with longtime friend Topi Heikkerö, I enjoyed the dinnertime company of John Cornell and Eric Poppele, who had been the instructor and assistant in my freshman lab class. Throughout my brief stay in Santa Fe, I was lodged in the former home of deceased faculty member Robert Bart. Although close to the St. John's campus, it had a wild and isolated feel, with coyotes heard nearby in the dead of night.

Martin Heidegger's *Being and Time* has a reputation as one of the most difficult classics of philosophy. I hold that this reputation is undeserved, that the central claims of the book turn out to be rather simple even if rather deep. This will be one aspect of my lecture today: the remarkable simplicity of *Being and Time*. But there are some paradoxes involved as well, since *Being and Time* pushes us in a direction that deviates not only from most of the book's commentators, but from Heidegger's self-interpretation as well. An unorthodox interpretation is necessary, since we end the book in a place that the philosopher himself did not imagine: a place where he cannot help us, and not just because he has been dead for thirty-seven years.

Consider the following passage from page 1 of *Being and Time*, where Heidegger summarizes the mission of the book: "Our aim in the following treatise is to work out the question of the meaning of *Being*, and to do so concretely. Our provisional aim is the Interpretation of *time* as the possible horizon for any under-standing whatsoever of Being."[241] Today I will claim, among other things, that *Being and Time* tells us nothing about time at all. There are better places than Heidegger to find a *bona fide* philosophy of time. We can find one explicitly in the philosophy of Henri Bergson, and even in Aristotle's *Physics*, where we encounter time as a continuum that cannot be sliced up into a discrete set of points. By contrast, I will explain why Heidegger's analysis of temporality would hold perfectly good even for a world that *was* composed of atomic nows. For this reason Heidegger resembles Bergson less than Alfred North Whitehead and the older Arab and French occasionalist tradition of continuous creation, in which time is made up of individual nows that perish rather than endure and become. In fact, what Heidegger calls "time" is really just a ubiquitous threefold structure that has more to do with *space*, so that *Being and Space* would have been a more suitable title for his major work.

But if Heidegger has nothing to tell us about time in the usual sense, he does address the topic of being, though half of his treatment of being is possibly irrelevant. For there is a dual meaning to the term "being" in Heidegger, as reflected in the ambiguity of his term "ontological difference." In one sense the difference between being and beings is a difference between that which withdraws and that which is present. This is the *good* sense of the term, and remains Heidegger's major breakthrough beyond the phenomenological school in which he came of age.

But in a second sense, the differenc[...] [...]ing and beings
refers to an opposition between the [...]
the diversity of beings in the p[...]
between the one and the many. I [...]
sense of being, since there is no es[...]
plurality of entities, or "objects" [...] p[...]

Throughout Heidegger's work, we find this forked-tongue
approach to being: sometimes as that which is deeper than all
possible presence, at other times as that which is deeper than any
specific entity. Yet the notion of a single unified being fails for the
same reason as the pre-Socratic *apeiron*: there can be no "pre-
individual" realm. There is no way to proceed from the one to
the many unless being is already pre-inscribed with individuality, in such a way that the one becomes superfluous. Stated
differently, holism is a lie. Not everything is connected; connections between things must be earned with hard work. It is
actually quite a difficult problem to know how things can link
up, not an obvious phenomenon to be assumed in advance.

And that will lead us to our final theme for today, as
announced in the title itself: *causation*. It looks at first as though
Heidegger thinks of entities as having no independent reality, as
existing only through their interconnectedness in a system, with
each referring to the others and gaining its meaning from them.
Against this frequent view, I will claim that entities are interconnected only if we take them to be exhaustively deployed in each
moment. But one of the most important themes of Heidegger's
tool-analysis is that tools can *break*, and they could not possibly
break if they were exhausted by their current functions. In order
for hammers to shatter, trains to arrive late at the platform,
friendships to collapse, and fissures to open in the earth, entities
must hold something in reserve behind their current relations.

Yet the point is not just that entities can surprise *humans*.
Heidegger works very much in the shadow of Immanuel Kant
(as does most of contemporary philosophy), and in this respect it

is not surprising that we find something like the Kantian thing-in-itself in the shape of Heidegger's being that withdraws from all access. But there is a second and less fortunate aspect to Kant alongside the thing-in-itself: namely, the fact that the human-world relation is granted priority over all others. For Kant, we cannot speak of the collision of two rocks in the same way that we speak of the human observation of this collision, since all talk of anything is mediated by the uniquely human finitude of time, space, and the twelve categories. Thus for Kant, the thing-in-itself becomes a souvenir of tragic and poignant *human* limitations, one that German Idealism tried to remedy by disqualifying the in-itself and converting human finitude into a speculative infinity in which nothing is ultimately concealed. But we should note that there was another way that Kant could have been challenged. Instead of attacking the thing-in-itself as his successors did, they could have attacked the other pillar of Kantian philosophy: by preserving the thing-in-itself while denying that it was merely something haunting human awareness. Instead, even inanimate things would be things-in-themselves to each other. Fire would not burn cotton but only a caricature or distortion of cotton, due to the inability of fire to make contact with the full depths of that which it burns. Bacteria, lizards, and bricks would be characterized by finitude no less than human beings are.

But if this is the case —and I think it is Heidegger who inadvertently leads us to such a position— then such a "German Realism" (as opposed to German Idealism) would still have a problem explaining the causal interaction between things. For if fire cannot make full contact with the reality of cotton, then it is unclear how fire could burn cotton at all. Stated differently, if fire only makes contact with a *finite image* of cotton, then how can it ever burn the real cotton lying behind the image? In this way, a familiar and wrongfully mocked epistemological question about how humans can go outside and make contact with the real becomes a question even in the realm of physical nature. How can one thing ever touch, caress, destroy, or interfere with another? While this topic may seem far removed from Heidegger's *Being and Time*, I will try to show that it lies at the very heart of the book, however unsuspected by its author. So much for preliminary remarks. Let's move to *Being and Time*, by way of phenomenology.

1. From Being to Time

Though phenomenology has a number of precursors, it began in full-fledged form in Edmund Husserl's *Logical Investigations* in 1900-01, roughly the same time as Freud's *On the Interpretation of Dreams*. Phenomenology is aptly named. Its central principle is that we should focus on things solely as they give themselves to us. We must suspend all theories and hypotheses about the world outside consciousness. Instead of scientific theories of vision involving rods, cones, and optic nerves, we must describe all the subtleties of how a mailbox or a wolf appear to us. Instead of psychoanalytic theories of human motivation, we must describe the varying shades of psychic experience precisely as they seem. As everyone familiar with Husserl knows, the external world is "bracketed" or placed in parentheses, and internal experience becomes the center of philosophy. Yet not only is the external world bracketed, it tends to disappear altogether. Husserl asserts that it would be meaningless to imagine something that might not be the correlate of a possible mental act. The world is essentially knowable, or at least presentable to the mind; there is no noumenal in-itself that would haunt all human experience as an indigestible remainder. Heidegger's step forward comes from his noticing that for the most part, we do not encounter the world as present in consciousness. In fact, conscious awareness makes up only a tiny portion of our dealings with the world, as shown in his famous tool-analysis. If Husserl is a textbook case of an idealist,

Heidegger takes things in a realist direction, even though both thinkers view the distinction between realism and idealism with unjustified scorn. For Heidegger, whatever is consciously accessible is just one form of what he calls *Vorhandenheit* or presence-at-hand.

But let's leave this aside for a moment to discuss what Heidegger *missed* in Husserl. I find Heidegger's critique of phenomenology basically convincing; there is no reason to begin philosophy with what is given directly to consciousness. Nonetheless, Husserl does something unusual and perhaps unprecedented in his treatment of conscious presence. In the empiricist tradition, objects were treated as groundless fictions. An apple, for instance, is really just a bundle of qualities: cold, hard, red, sweet, and juicy, which go together so often that we form the habit of treating them as a unit: namely, as an apple. Only the qualities are real, and "apple" is really just an abbreviation or nickname for the customary conjunction of all these separate traits. I would say that Husserl's central philosophical advance was to challenge this empiricist tradition. Instead of only qualities being accessible to the mind, and their underlying objects being either purely fictional or hidden away in some unknown depth of "I know not what," Husserl created a genuine tension between objects and their qualities *within* the experienced world. What comes first is the apple, not its qualities. I can turn the apple in my mind, watch its temperature rise and fall, take bites from the apple, and view it from various distances in both euphoric and depressive moods. Never do I think that "this apple viewed despondently in shadow at 4 PM has a close family resemblance with the one I viewed happily in bright light at 10 AM, and therefore I will arbitrarily call them 'the same' apple despite their many differences." This is not what happens; it is a theory that falsifies experience. Instead, I immediately think: "this is the same apple, even though its qualities are shifting hour by hour." How do we know we are right in this assumption? It does not matter, because here we are talking about inner experience, not about facts in the outside world about which we might be wrong. Though Husserl is an idealist, he always *feels* like a realist, due to his constant descriptions of how blackbirds, centaurs, and friends on the sidewalk remain constant and identical despite the numerous shifting profiles or adumbrations through which they are seen. Phenomenology may be an idealism, but it's an object-oriented idealism nonetheless, one which holds that we encounter unified objects rather than disembodied qualities. Husserl's reversal of empiricism is to my knowledge unique in the history of philosophy. It will return later in this talk to complicate Heidegger's model of the world.

The heart of that model, as I see it, is the famous tool-analysis, a thought experiment rich enough to sustain interpretations very different from Heidegger's own. Though the tool-analysis was first published in *Being and Time* in 1927, it is already fully available in his Freiburg Lecture Course of 1919, delivered when Heidegger was merely twenty-nine years old. Whereas Husserl treats the world as phenomenally accessible to consciousness, for Heidegger what is conscious is not what is primary. As you consciously listen to this talk, you silently rely on many other things that serve as an obscure and implicit background: the solid floor beneath your feet, the chair on which you sit, the oxygen you breathe, the heart and liver and kidneys that keep you alive without difficulty, your easy mastery of English grammar, and so forth. All *Vorhandenheit* or presence-at-hand emerges from a previous quiet background of *Zuhandenheit* or readiness-to-hand. Please note that this is not some sort of taxonomy of different *kinds* of entities. Heidegger is not teaching us that the world is made up of two kinds of things: with hammers, screwdrivers, jigsaws, and pickup trucks on one side, and colors, shapes, and mathematical diagrams on the other. Instead, *every* entity has two faces: the one deep and hidden from us and the other directly accessible in consciousness — as if every object were like the moon, with its dark side and bright side. Nor can human beings (or *Dasein*) be excluded from this duality. Granted, Heidegger openly asserts that the present-at-hand and the ready-to-hand are categories that pertain only to non-human or "intraworldly" entities, and that Dasein needs to be treated by completely different categories. But this is clearly just a residue of the assumption, found throughout most of modern philosophy, that the undeniable differences between humans and everything else must be built into an *ontological rift* between humans and everything else. Descartes' distinction between *res cogitans* and *res extensa* is just one prominent example of this tendency, with which *Being and Time* is also saturated. But while special human features such as language and advanced cognition are something for us to be proud of, there is no reason to assume that these gifts are any more amazing than events such as the birth of stars, the creation of all elements heavier than iron in supernova explosions, the breakup of Pangaea and the beginning of continental drift, the emergence of primitive life from puddles of acid struck by lightning, or even the appearance of vertebrate creatures or sexual dimorphism. All of these things are marvelous. And even if we think the appearance of human Dasein is more amazing than any of them, we are not justified in creating a philosophy in which human vs. non-human is a radical difference in ontological kind. Notice that Dasein too is both present-at-hand and ready-to-hand. If I describe you by means of personality traits and a physical description, then I have turned you into something present-at-hand. When you as a person stubbornly withdraw from these imperfect descriptions, holding surprises in store for me, then you are ready-to-hand: not because I am using you like a hammer for my own devious purposes, but because you can surprise me just as a hammer does when it fails.

And that brings us to our next important theme: broken tools. For the most part, tools withdraw into a silent background and come to our notice only when they fail in some way. The hammer draws the carpenter's attention when it is too heavy, or when it shatters in the hand. The bus is noticed when it fails to arrive on time. But equipment does not need to "break" in order to become present-at-hand. This also happens if I simply turn my attention to equipment that is working perfectly well: we can stare at the washer and dryer, making them present in the mind even though they are not failing in the least. We can make theories about tools, which also brings them to presence in the mind. And even if we merely conceive of the washer and dryer as physically present in the world according to geometrical co-ordinates, they are also present-at-hand even when they do not break. We can use the phrase "broken tools" as a synonym for present-at-hand entities, as long as we do not literally believe that only failed metallic or wooden hardware counts as a broken tool.

Two other important points need to be made about tools and broken tools in Heidegger. The first is that the flip to brokenness is never complete. The fact that a hammer shatters in your hand does not mean that the reality of the hammer is now utterly transparent to your mind. Likewise, the fact that we now have a good theory of electricity does not mean that electricity has no more surprises in store for the human race, nor (obviously) does it mean that there is no difference between our knowledge of electricity and electricity itself. And finally, the presence of an object in a well-defined place does not mean that the object's reality is fully expressed in that place. The "breaking" of equipment is always only partial. The second point is that Heidegger misleadingly describes tools as if they formed a holistic system of equipment and could not exist in isolation. For example, the hammer refers to the iron resistance of a nail, the sharpness of a nail to the toughness of leather, and the water-proof character of leather to the need for human Dasein to keep its feet dry despite all changes of weather. For Heidegger, all tools fit together into a global system ultimately defined by Dasein's own potentiality for being. Any individual character of specific tool-pieces seems to be derivative of the prior, global, systematic whole. On this basis, it would appear that *Zuhandenheit* or readiness-to-hand means holistic interdependence while *Vorhandenheit* or presence-at-hand means the false independence or autonomy of beings ripped away from their natural contextual reality.

But as I have said, this second point concerning the supposed holistic system of equipment is false even on Heidegger's own terms. Tools are actually not holistically interconnected at all. Despite the obvious way in which tool-beings refer to each other's properties and capacities (such as hammer, nail, shoe, and human), the most important fact about equipment is not that it refers to other equipment. Instead, the most important fact is that equipment can *break*. And this automatically takes us beyond any form of holism. Why? Because if the hammer were nothing more than its current reference to the hardness of nails and the softness of my hand, then the hammer could never break. In order to break, in order to surprise us either with its failure or with its new possible uses, the hammer must exist as a surplus beyond its current uses. The hammer can be used by me and even by the nail, but cannot be *used up* by us or by anything else. In short, the hammer is not exhaustively deployed by the things it does, but only partly so. Things are an excess beyond their current use, and even beyond all possible uses. But this requires that we reverse Heidegger's own notion that present-at-hand means independence and ready-to-hand means holistically dependent. For in the first place, we have seen that the ready-to-hand (also known as "tools" in the widest possible sense) means that which is *deeper* than any possible relational system. To be a tool is to be autonomous, independent, deep, withdrawn from any access. It means to be a thing-in-itself— and even Heidegger says that readiness-to-hand is the characteristic of things as they are "in themselves." And though he tries to hedge his bets by using scare quotes, we should almost always ignore scare quotes and hold authors accountable for the words contained inside them. Meanwhile, what could be more bizarre than the idea that entities present-at-hand before the mind are *independent*? After all, they exist purely as correlates of my encountering them. For this reason, we need to reverse the frequent notion that Heidegger disdains independent substances and replaces them with a cryptic relational network hidden from the conscious mind. Instead, both the objects present in the mind and the objects acting in tool-networks are guilty of the same vice: namely, both are overdetermined by their relations, whether their relations to the human thinker or to each other. What Heidegger really gives us with the question of being is the point of entry into a radically *non-relational* ontology. Being is what withdraws behind all presence, meaning all relation of any sort, always capable of disrupting these relations.

To summarize so far, Heidegger speaks of being not in many ways, but in exactly *two*. In one sense, being is that which is incommensurable with any form of presence. Being is that which withdraws: always absent, always irreducible to any perception or conceptualization of it, so that we can only have indirect or oblique access to it. This point is vintage Heidegger. Many of his other most famous thoughts follow directly from this one, such as his alarm over the enframing of technology that reduces the world to a calculable stockpile, and his infamous claim that "science does not think." But in a second sense Heidegger uses "being" in opposition to "beings" not because of their presence, but because of their plurality and specificity. Here, being is held to be great because it is a boundless reservoir, not carved up into trivial specific districts such as trees, telephones, armies, and nations. This second claim is embodied in Heidegger's tendency to treat the system of equipment as a single primordial whole, but as suggested earlier, tools are deeper than any tool-system for the simple reason that they can break. When the hammer malfunctions, what breaks is a hammer, not being as a whole. *At most*, being as a whole can break in the experience of Angst (or anxiety), but even Heidegger treats this as a very special case, and the case could be made that Heideggerian Angst does not even exist, though this is not the right time to argue the point.

In any case, Heidegger's discussion of the reversal between ready-to-hand and presence-at-hand is not a limited description of chisels and hacksaws, but is pertinent to everything that exists. All entities can become present, yet in all cases this presence is derivative of a dark subterranean background that makes up the inexhaustible and not fully presentable *being* of every object. And this being always takes the form of "time," though this word turns out to be extremely misleading. Human Dasein does not choose its environment, but in each instant finds itself *thrown* into a specific world. This is analogous to what we usually call the "past," since it is always already there for us without our being able to control it. Simultaneously, we "project" our possibilities onto the situation into which we are thrown. This same event today in the Great Hall means vastly different things for the speaker, the tutors, the students, to those who are intensely interested in Heidegger, and those who are barely interested at all. This is analogous to what we usually call the "future," since it has to do with what we make of the current situation and how we view it as helpful or harmful or interesting or pointless for our human Dasein. These two structures always go together, which is why Heidegger speaks of human existence as "thrown projection." The two moments together form his new and ambiguous concept of the "present," since the present is a combination of a pre-given world and our interpretation of that world at any given moment. All the various recurring threefold structures in *Being and Time* simply reflect this basic triad, such as the otherwise astoundingly subtle description of how every question has three parts: that which is interrogated, that which the question is about, and that which is to be found out by the questioning (or in the more economical German version: *das*

Befragte, das Gefragte, and *das Erfragte).*

Unfortunately, though Heidegger uses the word "time" to refer to this ubiquitous threefold structure in his philosophy, it has nothing to do with time at all. I have not been able to persuade many scholars of this point, though I think it is not difficult to show. Indeed, we can prove it with a simple thought experiment. Imagine that all time suddenly comes to a halt. Change and becoming suddenly cease, and everything is frozen in its current state (there is nothing in Heidegger's philosophy to prevent such a thought experiment). This threefold structure of so-called "temporality" still works perfectly in this situation. As I sit frozen at my desk, the environment of the room is already there for me (that's the "past"), that environment means something very specific for me compared to what it means for others who are pressured by different deadlines and whose lives are guided by vastly different aspirations (that's the "future"), and these two together form the ambiguous present. How different the case would be for a philosopher such as Bergson. For Bergson, unlike for Heidegger, the thought experiment just described would be impossible from the start. Time for Bergson cannot possibly be broken up into isolated cinematic frames; the unity of becoming is primary, and the cinematic standpoint on time is a derivative abstraction not relevant to how the world really is. By contrast, Heidegger is nothing if not a brilliant analyst of the unified instant, showing the dark fissures and crevices found even in a single moment. Admittedly, Heidegger says that time is not a sequence of now-points. But only for Bergson is it a problem to divide time up into "nows." For Heidegger, the problem is actually the *sequence*, since it implies that no individual moment has anything interesting going on internally to it. Throughout the history of philosophy, we find thinkers who start from a primal dynamism and try to account for instants of time as derivative of the dynamism, and we find others who start from the individual instants and try to construct the flow of time as derivative of the instants. Heidegger belongs squarely in the latter group, along with the occasionalists and their theory of "continuous creation." But Bergson belongs in the former. Whitehead belongs with Heidegger as a theorist of instants or occasions, and Deleuze belongs with Bergson as a theorist of becoming. For this reason, it is somewhat comical when present-day authors try to link Whitehead with Deleuze as "process philosophers," given that the word "process" has utterly different meanings in the two cases. At any rate, Heidegger himself is no thinker of dynamic becoming, but a theorist of the ambiguous complexities internal to any instant; Emmanuel Levinas is right that Heidegger's so-called "future" is merely a future of the present, not the constant unrolling of novelty that we find in Bergson. Though the claim has been controversial, I insist once again that there is no bridge between Heidegger's conception of temporality and what we normally mean when we speak about "time."

But let's return to the tool-analysis, where we have unfinished business that is strange business once again. An easy way to interpret the tool-analysis would be to say something like this: "Heidegger shows that all theory emerges from unconscious background practice. He gives us a priority of practical over theoretical reason." One might even add in the manner of Richard Rorty that "therefore Heidegger tells us nothing that John Dewey hadn't already seen thirty years earlier." One of the commentators who disagrees with this view is Hubert Dreyfus, probably the most widely read interpreter of Heidegger, whose book *Being-in-the-World* has been cited more than 1,800 times— a staggering number for a secondary source in philosophy.[242] While many readers of Heidegger assert that he is telling us that praxis comes before theory, Dreyfus disagrees for the following reason. Whereas an author such as John Searle ends up treating both theory and praxis as forms of mental content, Dreyfus holds that our use of equipment shows nothing mental at all, not even in some tacit background sense. Dreyfus describes our dealings with equipment as "background coping," and his terminology has become highly influential. However, it seems to me that this distinction is hairsplitting, and worse yet, it is the sort of hairsplitting that leads Dreyfus down the wrong path. For what makes Dreyfus think that background coping is different from John Searle's theory of praxis as an obscure sort of mental content? First, to call praxis "mental content" is to imply that there is also an objective world outside the subject's mental content, and Dreyfus thinks that Heidegger breaks down the subject/objet dualism. And second, to call praxis mental content is to make it something individual, whereas for Dreyfus what is key for Heidegger is that *social* reality precedes individual reality. In fact, Dreyfus pushes this claim awfully far. Along with his numerous stock examples of cultural relativism (such as the different ways in which American and Japanese babies are raised, the different options available in the two cultures when someone fails to complete a school assignment on time, and so forth) Dreyfus goes so far as to hold that a newborn baby is not Dasein. Instead, one must be acculturated into some specific group in order to be Dasein. But this looks like a clear case of cart-before-the-horse. Although social phenomena are clearly important for Heidegger, there are no grounds for *defining* Dasein as if it meant belonging to a given social group. To support this strange interpretation, Dreyfus is forced to suppress a number of passages in Heidegger that suggest precisely the opposite, and is forced to overidentify Dasein with *das Man* (or "the they"), which he even retranslates from the German to support his own bias.

But these are simply points of detail. What Dreyfus gets right is that the difference between theoretical content in the mind and practical content in the mind is not such a great difference, and cannot be the central point of the tool-analysis. Heidegger is not just telling us that first we do things unconsciously and only later do we become conscious of them. Yet the Dreyfus solution is hardly any better, since Heidegger is also not telling us that first we are American or Japanese and only later do we use tools and make theories about things. Heidegger is doing fundamental ontology, not transcendental sociology. The point is not praxis over theory, but the point is also not the priority of the social over *both* praxis and theory. The real point is that theory, praxis, and society all distort things to an equal degree. When we as botanists invent theories about trees, inevitably we turn the tree into an oversimplified version, into a caricature. The same is true when we merely perceive the tree, noticing only those things that we as humans are capable of registering, while utterly failing to grasp those tree-features that are accessible to seagulls, dogs, and honeybees. But praxis is no less guilty of such distortion or translation. If we use the tree for shade, or for intense fruit cultivation, we do not exhaust the being of the tree any more than when theorizing about it or looking at it. In other words, theory and praxis are on exactly the same level, both of them failing to do justice to the tree in its dark subterranean being that withdraws from all human contact. But neither does Dreyfus' sociological interpretation get us off the hook. Whether I have an American interpretation of trees as a lumber field, a Japanese interpretation of trees as aesthetic apparitions, or an animist interpretation of trees as dead human ancestors, in all these cases the tree itself is something deeper than any of them. A cultural interpretation is no more the bedrock of reality than are practical handling or theoretical observing. *No* human relation to trees, whether individual or social, will be able to come into direct contact with their being.

If we were to force the issue in conversation with Heidegger himself, he would quite likely be brought to agree with this point: praxis is no closer to being than theory and perception are, and —if he were to read the commentary of Dreyfus— he would surely agree that American, Japanese, or even German society do not make direct contact with being itself (despite a number of alarming claims about Germany's special status during the period of Heidegger's Rectorate). But we also need to push the argument one step further than Heidegger himself would have been willing to go. Namely, not only are objects deeper than any human theoretical, practical, or social interaction with them, they are even deeper than their interactions with each other. It is not the limitations of human cognition or perception that makes things withdraw from presence, but the simple fact that this is a *relation*, since relations can never exhaust or replace their terms. When one billiard ball smacks another on a green felt table, the first ball does not make contact with the whole of the other ball's reality, but only with a caricatured, translated, or distorted version of it. The same is true when fire burns cotton or raindrops strike asphalt. Inanimate things fail to grasp each other fully, just as we fail to grasp them in turn. Contra the German Idealist tradition, the mistake of Kant was not to cling naively to a thing-in-itself beyond human access, but to limit the thing-in-itself to a special poignant burden of human finitude when it is actually characteristic of relationality in general. This is what I meant earlier when suggesting that the history of philosophy could have generated a "German Realism," perhaps based on Leibnizian influence, rather than the German Idealism that actually took hold, and which is resurgent today in the widely influential philosophies of Alain Badiou and Slavoj Žižek, which mix Hegel with Lacanian psychoanalysis in a way that pushes objects away from the center of philosophy where they belong.

And now we encounter the theme of causation, referred to in the title of today's talk. For if objects cannot make contact with one another directly, it is unclear how they can make contact at all. That is to say, if I never have access to anything other than a distorted tree-image, it is unclear how my contact with this image can ever have a retroactive effect on the tree itself, or how one thing can have causal effects on another more generally. And here we find that Heidegger leads us for a second time towards the school of philosophy known as occasionalism. The occasionalists not only thought of each temporal instant as momentary and perishable, so that continuous creation would be necessary to keep the world going; even more importantly, they saw all causal relations as being mediated by God. Occasionalism has roots in the early Islamic theology of southern Iraq, in the so-called Ash'arite school. A particular passage in the *Qu'ran* was interpreted to mean that nothing happens at all without God's direct intervention. Only after a long delay did this theory catch on in Cartesian France, where the duality of substances between extension and thought seemed to require a God to correlate the two; Malebranche soon restored the body-body problem as well, so that even inanimate causation seemed to require the

intervention of God. This might seem quaint today, and it is easy to mock a philosophy that requires God to help me even to scratch my head or pick up a bottle of juice. But what is really important about occasionalism is not that *God* is treated as the sole causal agent, but that there is a sole privileged causal agent at all. If the occasionalists are widely mocked in undergraduate philosophy classes today, the same is not true of Hume and Kant, who seem very contemporary even now and whose positions are widely viewed as respectable. Of course, neither Hume nor Kant claims that God is the locus of all causation. But notice that they do make an analogous claim for the causal monopoly of human thought. For Hume, causal relations as far as we know are nothing more than a habitual link or customary conjunction, so that human habit is what links fire with deadly heat or bread with nourishment. For Kant, causation is more explicitly a category of the human understanding, whatever one might think about his contradictory claim that the noumena "cause" the phenomena. In this way Hume and Kant, who continue to dominate contemporary philosophy at a distance, give us an inverted or upside-down form of occasionalism, in which human thought rather than God monopolizes the causal realm. A single privileged agent is allowed to break the rule of no direct influence. In the philosophy of Whitehead, who is always so bold in challenging the legacy of Kant, we see a bold return to the divine form of occasionalism. All relation, all prehension of one entity by another, is mediated through the eternal objects contained in God. Of Whitehead's present-day admirers, perhaps the most original is the French philosopher Bruno Latour, who despite being even more religious in person than Whitehead himself, aims to *secularize* occasional causation. For Latour, any two entities require a third in between as a mediator. In his famous example from the book *Pandora's Hope*, there was no link between politics and neutrons in France until that link was established by Frédéric Joliot in his failed early effort to argue for a French atomic bomb program. Yet Latour does this in an impossible manner, since it is unclear how Joliot can make contact with either politics or neutrons if these themselves cannot make contact with each other. We would have to keep inserting new entities in between these, and additional mediators between the new mediators, and so on in a bad form of infinite regress, since nothing will ever make direct contact with anything at all. It is disappointing that Latour tries to solve this problem with a watery pragmatic solution: namely, we can keep on analyzing mediators between mediators until it becomes *boring*, and then we can simply stop. While this may be a useful solution for doing field research, it solves nothing at all in metaphysical terms.

Finally, there is the strange position of my colleague Levi R. Bryant. What makes Bryant's position so strange is that he denies that direct relations between objects are problematic even though he *accepts* that objects can only translate each other. That is to say, Bryant agrees that my perception of an apple is merely a caricature of the apple itself, yet he sees no problem with my making contact with the apple in the first place. What Bryant overlooks is that translation is not just a result, but also a starting point. It is not just that humans make direct contact with apples and then (God knows why) distort those apples into perceptual form despite having made perfect direct contact with them beforehand. Instead, the problem is that we only make contact with caricatures of apples in the first place. Although Bryant never says so explicitly, I suspect that he is under the sway of those who claim that contact between entities is "direct but partial." That is to say, fire may not make contact with the whole of the cotton when burning it, but perhaps makes contact with 74% of the cotton's features and failing to make contact with the other 26%. But this view is not helpful. For if the fire makes direct contact with 74% of the cotton's features, it would still have to be shown how this 74% makes contact with the cotton as a whole—every object is unified, not a bundle of features. In short, Heidegger leads us to the doorstep of the problem of how we can have indirect rather than direct causation. Another possible name for this problem is "vicarious" causation. In other words, how does contact between real fire and the translated image of a cotton ball ever lead to influence between the real fire and the real cotton ball it destroys?

2. Objects in the History of Philosophy

But since we are defending the status of objects here, let's turn to the more general theme of objects in the history of philosophy. I would argue that objects are the *central* theme of the history of philosophy, even if in a majority of cases this is for the purely negative reason that objects are what everyone wishes to annihilate or at least avoid.

Consider the pre-Socratics, at the dawn of Western philosophy and science. As Aristotle already noted, the pre-Socratics fall nearly into two groups, neither of them friendly to everyday objects such as tables, horses, and trees. With the first group we can say that the first principle of everything is water, like Thales; or air, like Anaximenes; or air, earth, fire and water mixed by love and hate, as for Empedocles; or atoms, as for Democritus. Whichever of these positions one might adopt, individual objects above the tiniest scale will be pulverized, reduced downward to some tiny underlying physical element. It is hardly different for the second group of pre-Socratics, which views even ultimate physical elements as already too specific to serve as the foundation of reality. And here we have the great theme of the boundless *apeiron*, with the argument being merely over whether the *apeiron* will exist in the future through the work of justice (as for Anaximander), in the present though the senses and opinion trick us into believing otherwise (as for Parmenides, who calls it *being*), or in the past before it was destroyed by some decisive rupture (through the *apeiron* inhaling void, as Pythagoras sees it; or the *apeiron* rotating quickly and shattering into parts through the work of *nous*, according to Anaxagoras). Whatever their differences, all these positions *undermine* the status of most objects, reducing them to some ultimate basis which alone is granted genuine reality. Modern-day scientific materialism clearly descends from this strand of ancient philosophy, as does a surprising amount of recent French thought: such as the so-called "pre-individual" realm of Gilbert Simondon, the real but indeterminate "whatever" of Jean-Luc Nancy, or the anonymous *il y a* or "there is" (revealed in insomnia) as discussed by the young Levinas. The problem with all such undermining theories is that, first, they fail to explain adequately why an unarticulated One would ever break into pieces (despite the lovely creation myths of Pythagoras and Anaxagoras), and second, they fail to account for what is now usually called "emergence." For it is by no means evident that one's own body changes with the replacement of various atoms or cells, or that St. John's College is no longer the same place as during my long-ago freshman year despite significant turnover in faculty and (one hopes) *complete* turnover in students during the twenty-six years since then. Entities are something over and above their constituent parts: unable to exist without them, but not entirely dependent on their exact configuration.

But the modern tendency is to reduce in the opposite direction: upward. For this I have coined the term "overmining," by obvious analogy with undermining (this cannot be done in all languages, of course). If the pre-Socratic and scientific underminers say that macro-sized objects are too shallow to be the truth, overminers say that they are too *deep* to be the truth. An extreme case would be Berkeley, for whom there is no reason to posit a ghostly substance beneath what is directly perceived, but empiricism more generally is suspicious of objects. Equally good examples can be found in more recent philosophy: in the notion that everything is just a social construction, or a language game, or a verb-like event rather than a noun-like object, or a network of things that are reducible upward to their effects on other things, as in Latour's claim that entities are nothing more than whatever they transform, modify, perturb, or create. Or that things are really just phenomena in consciousness that can be subtly analyzed without recourse to their real underpinnings outside the mind. Or that we can only count as things whatever makes a difference of some sort, as the pragmatists among others have claimed. Or that objects are nothing more than their actual state here and now, as the Megarians said according to Aristotle. Or that man is the measure of all things, of those that are that they are, and of those that are not that they are not. In all of these cases, autonomous objects are treated as the figments of "naive realism," as fruitlessly posited substrata that any rigorous and innovative thinker will quickly abandon. Objects are not too shallow to be the truth, but too deep. We have already seen when discussing Heidegger's tool-analysis, why such overmining approaches cannot work: namely, they cannot explain change. If things are nothing more than their current revealedness, their current action, their current stance in the world, then there is no reason why they would ever find themselves transformed into a different state.

Most often, we don't find undermining and overmining in isolation from each other, even if one of these strategies tends to predominate in each anti-object-oriented thinker. Instead, we find them in a mutually parasitical relationship, drawing on each other's energies in a silent conspiracy to ensure that at least objects will not win, even if the opposite strategy does. To define this co-dependency between the lowest and highest levels of the world, I have borrowed the term "duomining," which is admittedly unpleasant, but at least has the virtue of already existing in the data sciences. One example would be scientific materialism. In claiming to reduce the world to the tiniest components from which all else is built (undermining), it also makes these components completely transparent to mathematical modeling (overmining). The same happens in reverse. Consider Latour, who reduces things upward to their effects on those other things with which they interact in a network. But in recent years, as if realizing that this network-based approach cannot explain the change we experience in the world, Latour has posited a hidden underlying source called the "plasma," which he holds responsible for everything from the unexpected breakup of the Soviet Union, to the dissolution of human relationships, to the sudden composition of a brilliant symphony by a previously mediocre academic musician. He even estimates for us the size of the plasma: if all the networks of objects are the size of the London Underground, then the plasma is the size of London as a whole. But the plasma is supposedly an inarticulate mass, much like the pre-Socratic *apeiron*, and it is difficult to see how such a uniform mass could have different effects in different places: why it would manifest as Soviet collapse in one place and as a brilliant symphony in another. Ultimately, even Kant's position can be seen as a clear case of duomining, since he undermines all appearances with the inaccessible things-in-themselves, while also overmining those things by turning our attention to the truly accessible categorial structures as well as space and time that shape the finite experience of human beings.

But these anti-object voices are not the only ones to be heard in the history of philosophy. There are at least two separate alternative currents in which individual things are the heroes of philosophy, one more obvious than another. The obvious one is the Aristotelian tradition, visible in Leibnizian philosophy and other theories of substantial forms, in which we reach a macro- rather than micro-layer of things that cannot be predicated of anything else: which can be happy and said at different times, and which unlike qualities have no opposite. I mean *substances*, of course. The other, more surprisingly, is the phenomenological tradition. This claim may seem paradoxical due to the markedly idealist flavor of phenomenology. But as discussed earlier, Husserl is in some ways the Aristotle of the phenomenal sphere — finding relatively durable intentional objects that can withstand numerous changes in angle and distance of viewpoint, in lighting conditions, and in the mood or elevation of the viewer.

During my graduate student years, the least popular great philosopher was Plato. Everyone had to reverse Plato, turn him upside down, escape the "vulgarized Platonism" of Christianity, and other such formulae. For reasons still unclear to me, that tendency eventually vanished, and Plato became an acceptable figure to the avant-garde once more. But perhaps it is no accident that Plato has been replaced as an outcast by Aristotle and Husserl, now the two least popular of the great thinkers in the continental philosophy circles in which I travel. Aristotle is blamed for everything from Western imperialism to the holocaust, while Husserl is treated as a dull technician long since eclipsed by Heidegger and his French heirs. What Aristotle and Husserl have in common (along with their shared and under-rated weird sense of humor) is their attention to objects or substances as the key philosophical personae.

What we most need in philosophy today is not some new form of undermining or overmining methods, or even a fruitless mixture of the two. Instead, we need a theory of objects in their irreducibility to relations. This is admittedly difficult, because such a theory by definition cannot make objects directly present, which would simply be a form of overmining— a claim that an object could be exhaustively accounted for by a theoretical model of it. This is one of Heidegger's chief lessons in his discussion of the withdrawal of being from presence, and arguably even one of Aristotle's lessons since he tells us in the *Metaphysics* that a primary substance cannot be defined, given that a substance is always particular while definitions are made of universals. Since phenomenology, for all its merits, has a built-in idealist bias, we really need something more like a "noumenology." It is not a contradiction to speak about that which is outside speech, any more than it is contradictory to love wisdom without being able to have it (and in fact, I find that many of today's arguments against the thing-in-itself unconsciously repeat Meno's paradox). Let me also add that Heidegger's discoveries have very little to do with Derrida's improvisations on them. If Heidegger attacks presence by pointing to the thing outside all context, Derrida attacks presence with the diametrically opposed method of showing that nothing is outside any context, while simply adding the proviso that no context is ever fixed. Stated differently, if Heidegger challenges presence by invoking a spirit of depth, Derrida condemns all claims to depth in favor of a constant horizontal gliding across the surface of signification. When Derrida praises Heidegger in *Of Grammatology* for holding that there is no being apart from its various historical manifestations to Dasein, he praises Heidegger for something that exists only in Derrida's own mind. This is equally true when Derrida attacks both the "transcendental signified" and "naive realism," attacks that Heidegger would never make in precisely this form, since Heidegger's critique of phenomenology requires a fairly strict form of realism (even if not all commentators accept this point). Stated differently, Derrida is what I have called an "overminer," as is Michel Foucault, as are the more recent stars of continental philosophy: Badiou and Žižek and their rising younger ally Quentin Meillassoux. For all of these authors, the human subject remains at the center of philosophy, and this is just an upside-down form of occasionalism in which human beings replace God as the causal anchor of the universe, in however subtly disguised a form.

3. A Positive Program

Let's move toward a conclusion, by quickly summarizing the lecture so far and then adding one new theme with which some of you are familiar (or so I am told) due to recent Heidegger reading groups on campus. Under the interpretation I have given, being means withdrawal behind any form of presence. While I think Heidegger is right to say this, I do not believe he is also right to think of being as one over against the many of particular beings. Being itself is already articulated into multiple zones and districts, indeed into multiple withdrawn entities. Temporality simply refers to the simultaneously concealed (or "past") character of entities and their revealed (or "future") aspect combining into a single ambiguous present. However, this temporality is one that can be found even in a single instant, and thus has nothing at all to do with "time" in the usual sense; time in philosophy must be found in other authors. As for causation, any direct form of causation turns out to be impossible, given that inanimate entities withdraw from each other in the same way that they are veiled from human access. Given that real entities cannot make contact so as to influence each other, and given that we cannot invoke God or the human mind as privileged causal agents responsible for all communication between things, we are left with just one alternative. The link between real objects is mediated by the objects of the mind described by Husserl: which he calls "intentional" objects but which I call "sensual" objects instead. Just as magnets repel when the same poles touch, but can be made into chains of infinite length when opposite poles are brought together, we find that real objects make contact only by way of sensual objects, and vice versa. Stated more provocatively, causation does not occur between bodies, but only on the interior of human, animal, vegetable, or inanimate minds: in the sphere of primitive mental experience where all objects are encountered only as images by other objects. How exactly this happens is an important and fascinating philosophical problem with a tinge of the weird about it, and is best left for another occasion. So much by way of a quick summary. Let's now add a final Heideggerian theme to the mix.

I have heard that some members of the St. John's community have recently held a reading group on Heidegger's *Bremen and Freiburg Lectures*. The Bremen lecture cycle "Insight Into What It Is" is among Heidegger's most important works. This is true for biographical reasons, since it was his first public appearance following denazification. But it is also true for purely conceptual reasons, since it is the first explicit introduction of his concept of the *Geviert* or "fourfold" of earth, sky, gods, and mortals, a concept that dominates his more famous late works of the 1950's. Until quite recently, the fourfold has been treated as an embarrassment to Heidegger studies, and few serious attempts have been made to interpret it. Isn't the talk of earth, sky, gods, and mortals just a vague poetic appeal to the hymns of Hölderlin, in an effort to avoid rigorous philosophical scrutiny? I think not. I happen to think that the fourfold is the crowning achievement of Heidegger's thinking during the three decades from 1919 through 1949.

Let's give a quick interpretation of the fourfold at the close of this lecture. In the first place, it seems obvious that Heidegger's fourfold cannot be a taxonomy of four distinct *kinds* of entities. Earth is not meant as a category including dirt, worms, caverns, melons and potatoes buried underground. Sky does not mean planets, comets, and black holes way up high above us. Gods does not refer to Wotan, Zeus, and Yahweh. And mortals does not mean Herodotus, Pico della Mirandola, Queen Victoria, and the rest of us. Not only would such a philosophy of four *types* of things be innately childish and arbitrary, it is also completely foreign to Heidegger's working methods to give *taxonomies* of entities in the world.

Then what is the fourfold? We recall that there are many fourfold structures in the history of philosophy, none of them exactly alike. There is the air, earth, fire, water of Empedocles; there is Plato's divided line; Aristotle's four causes; John Scotus Eriugena's fourfold permutation of creation and created; Francis Bacon's four idols; Kant's four groups of categories; the semiotic square of Algurdas Greimas; and Marshall McLuhan's media tetrads, which are more serious than people realize. What all such theories have in common, despite their vast differences, is that they result from the intersection of two basic dualisms. What are the two dualisms in Heidegger's case?

One of them is basic Heidegger, already discussed frequently this afternoon: the concealed realm of being vs. the revealed realm of presence-at-hand, where science and technology now hold sway (unthinkingly, in Heidegger's view). Heidegger's second axis is also not difficult to find, since it is the one I have already criticized: the idea that "being" means one and "beings" means many. We can find this assumption already inscribed in Heidegger's fourfold of earth, sky, gods, and mortals. On the concealed side of withdrawal and absence, we find the nourishing juices of the earth and the hinting of the gods who do not communicate directly. Earth and gods thus belong together as quadrants of obscurity. Meanwhile, the sky refers not just to stellar and planetary bodies but to all visible things, while mortals is described as the moment of death "as" death— being-towards death as what makes the whole explicitly visible rather than tacit and absent. Mortals and sky thus belong together as quadrants of explicit presence. As for the other axis of division, Heidegger makes this surprisingly easy for us. Earth is not plural, but is identified with the supposed *unity* of being. Mortals, we have already seen, refers not to specific individual entities, but to the world as a whole. Earth and mortals thus belong together insofar as both refer to the non-articulated unity of the world. Meanwhile, gods and sky, as is clear from murkier but still compelling textual evidence, belong together as reflecting the numerous specific things of the world, both concealed (gods) and revealed (sky). This fourfold structure is not some senile quirk of the post-denazification Heidegger, but is already sketched in his earliest critique of his teacher Husserl as far back as 1919. A similar structure is visible even if the terms earth, sky, gods, and mortals are never uttered in Heidegger's terminologically more academic youth.

But it seems to me that Heidegger took the wrong path here. There were no grounds for including the world as a whole as two terms of the fourfold, since the world a whole is already a relational illusion: the tool-system, for instance, is only a whole insofar as it functions, though the tools themselves are anything but holistic. A better version of the fourfold would incorporate Husserl's most important insight, completely ignored by Heidegger: the tension between unified *individual* objects and their plurality of traits. To give a concrete example, Heidegger's fourfold would describe an apple as a tension or mirror-play between the real world in its own right, the real world as revealed to Dasein in Angst, the apple as a real unit in the world, and the apple as a present-at-hand bundle of qualities before the mind. But by adding Husserl we transform the picture of the fourfold so that the real unified apple and its numerous qualities are in fourfold tension with the apple present in consciousness with all its sparkling plurality of qualities. By driving wedges between the two kinds of objects and their two kinds of qualities, we have an interesting method for ontology. Perhaps earth, sky, gods, and mortals have a future that is more than laughable. Perhaps they are the provisional answer to the interrelated questions of being and time.

Endnotes

1. Graham Harman, *Towards Speculative Realism: Essays and Lectures*. (Winchester, UK: Zero Books, 2010.)

2. Graham Harman, *Quentin Meillassoux: Philosophy in the Making*. (Edinburgh: Edinburgh University Press, 2011.)

3. Originally a July 23, 2010 blog post that can be found at the following address: http://doctorzamalek2.wordpress.com/?s=brief+sr%2Fooo+tutorial

4. http://doctorzamalek2.wordpress.com/

5. For a history of the Speculative Realism movement, see pp. 77-80 of Graham Harman, *Quentin Meillassoux: Philosophy in the Making*. For a lightly edited transcript of the April 2007 Speculative Realism event at Goldsmiths College, University of London, see Ray Brassier, et al., "Speculative Realism," *Collapse* III (2007), pp. 306-449.

6. For Meillassoux's ambivalent acceptance and rejection of German Idealism, see my interview with him on pp. 159-174 of Harman, *Quentin Meillassoux: Philosophy in the Making*.

7. For my full assessment of Latour's philosophy, see Graham Harman, *Prince of Networks: Bruno Latour and Metaphysics*. (Melbourne : re.press, 2009.)

8. See Emmanuel Levinas, *Totality and Infinity: An Essay on Exteriority*, trans. A. Lingis. (Dordrecht, The Netherlands: Kluwer Academic, 1991.)

9. See Martin Heidegger, *Being and Time*, trans. J. Macquarrie & E.Robinson. (New York: Harper, 2008.)

10. See Jacques Derrida, *Of Grammatology*, trans. G.C. Spivak. (Baltimore: The Johns Hopkins University Press, 1976.) Nonetheless, Derrida's critique of ontologies of presence has a bluntly anti-realist flavor that I hold to be foreign to Heidegger's own tendencies. For some thoughts on how

Heidegger and Derrida differ on this point, see pp. 195-199 of Graham Harman, "The Well-Wrought Broken Hammer: Object-Oriented Literary Criticism," *New Literary History*, Spring 2012, Vol. 43, No. 2.

11. See especially the first hundred or so pages of Martin Heidegger, *History of the Concept of Time: Prolegomena*, trans. T. Kisiel. (Bloomington, IN: 2009.)

12. Lee Braver, *A Thing of this World: A History of Continental Anti-Realism*. (Evanston, IL: Northwestern University Press, 2007.)

13. One example can be found in John D. Caputo, "For Love of Things Themselves: Derrida's Hyper-Realism," *Social Semiotics*, Vol. 11, No. 1 (2001). A more recent and extended version of this claim is the centerpiece of Michael Marder's hard-to-read book *The Event of the Thing: Derrida's Deconstructive Realism*. (Toronto: University of Toronto Press, 2009.)

14. Jacques Derrida, "White Mythology: Metaphor in the Text of Philosophy," in *Margins of Philosophy*, trans. A. Bass. (Chicago: University of Chicago Press, 1982.)

15. For my full critique of Derrida's misreading of Aristotle on metaphor, see pp. 110-116 of Graham Harman, *Guerrilla Metaphysics: Phenomenology and the Carpentry of Things*. (Chicago: Open Court, 2005.)

16. As far as I can determine, the first unabashed defenses of realism in continental philosophy can be found in two books published in 2002, one of them written by me: Manuel DeLanda, *Intensive Science and Virtual Philosophy*. (London : Continuum, 2002); Graham Harman, *Tool-Being*. (Chicago: Open Court, 2002.)

17. See for example Ray Brassier, "Concepts and Objects," pp. 47-65 in Levi Bryant et al. (eds.), *The Speculative Turn: Continental Materialism and Realism*. (Melbourne: re.press, 2011.)

18. For my critique of this monopoly, see Graham Harman, "I am also of the opinion that materialism must be destroyed," *Society and Space*, Vol. 28, No. 5, Octoer 2010, pp. 772-790.

19. Quentin Meillassoux, *After Finitude: Essay on the Necessity of Contingency*, trans. R. Brassier. (London : Continuum, 2008.)

20. Meillassoux, *After Finitude*, p. 32.

21. For my critique of this inconsistency, see pp. 141-145 of Harman, *Quentin Meillassoux: Philosophy in the Making*.

22. Heidegger's explicit critique of Husserl by way of the tool-analysis was presented to his students in the 1919 War Emergency Semester, almost a decade before the publication of *Being and Time*. The 1919 course is available as *Towards the Definition of Philosophy*, trans T. Sadler. (London: Athlone Press, 2000.)

23. See especially Harman, *Tool-Being*.

24. See Graham Harman, *Prince of Networks: Bruno Latour and Metaphysics*. (Melbourne : re.press, 2009.)

25. Henri Bergson, *Matter and Memory*, trans. N.M. Paul & W.S. Palmer. (New York: Zone Books, 1991.)

26. See Quentin Meillassoux, "Subtraction and Contraction," *Collapse* III (2007), pp. 63-107.

27. See Daniel Dennett, "Real Patterns," *Journal of Philosophy* 88 (1991), pp. 27-51.

28. Emmanuel Levinas, *Existence and Existents*, trans. A. Lingis. (Pittsburgh, PA : Duquesne University Press, 2001.)

29. Gilbert Simondon, *L'individuation à la lumière des notions de forme et d'information*. (Grenoble, France: 2005.)

30. For my critique of Merleau-Ponty's supposed escape from idealism, see pp. 45-58 of Harman, *Guerrilla Metaphysics*.

31. Translated as Franz Brentano, *Psychology from an Empirical Standpoint*, trans. A. Rancurello, D. Terrell, and L. McAlister. (New York : Routledge, 1995.)

32. Kazimir Twardowski, *On the Content and Object of Presentations*, trans. R. Grossmann. (The Hague : Martinus

Nijhoff, 1977.)

33. Edmund Husserl, "Intentional Objects," in *Early Writings in the Philosophy of Logic and Mathematics*, ed. D. Willard. (Dordrecht, The Netherlands: Kluwer Academic, 2010.) Pages 345-387.

34. For a discussion of the term "sensual" see Graham Harman, *The Quadruple Object*. (Winchester, UK : Zero Books, 2011.)

35. Levinas, *Existence and Existents*.

36. G.W. Leibniz, "Monadology," in *Philosophical Essays*, trans. R. Ariew & D. Garber. (Indianapolis: Hackett, 1989.)

37. See G.W. Leibniz and Samuel Clarke, *Correspondence*, trans. R. Ariew. (Indianapolis: Hackett, 2000.)

38. Blog post made on August 2, 2011 and available at http://doctorzamalek2.wordpress.com/2011/08/02/possibly-the-4-most-typical-objections-to-ooo/

39. See Harman, *Tool-Being*.

40. The first use of the pair "overmining" and "undermining" was in my Bristol lecture of April 2009. See Graham Harman, "On the Undermining of Objects: Grant, Bruno, and Radical Philosophy," in Bryant et al. (eds.),*The Speculative Turn*, pp. 21-40.

41. For my critique of Ladyman and Ross see Graham Harman, "I Am Also of the Opinion That Materialism Must Be Destroyed," *Environment and Planning D: Society and Space*, Vol. 28, No. 5 (2010). Pages 772-790.

42. Shakespeare, *Othello*. Act 1, Scene 1.

43. Aristotle, *Metaphysics*, trans. J. Sachs. (Santa Fe, NM: Green Lion Press, 2002.)

44. See Levi R. Bryant, *The Democracy of Objects*. (Ann Arbor, MI: Open Humanities Press, 2011.)

45. Graham Harman, "Filozofia zwrócona ku przedmiotom contra radykalny empiryzm," trans. K. Rosiński & M. Wiśniewski, *Kronos* 1 (20)/2012, pp. 48-61.

46. See above all David Lapoujade, *William James: Empirisme et*

pragmatisme. (Paris: Empecheurs de penser en rond, 2007.)

47. William James, "Pragmatism," in *William James: Writings 1902-1910*. (New York: Library of America, 1988.)

48. William James, *Essays in Radical Empiricism*. (New York: Longmans, Green and Co., 1958).

49. Twardowski, *On the Content and Object of Presentations*.

50. The simplest summary of the object-oriented model so far can be found in Harman, *The Quadruple Object*. The book was originally published in French as *L'Objet quadruple*, trans. O. Dubouclez (Paris: Presses universitaires de France, 2010.)

51. In what follows, all page numbers in parentheses refer to William James, *Essays in Radical Empiricism*. (New York: Longmans, Green and Co., 1958).

52. In the French: "*Je crois que la conscience, telle qu'on se la représente communément, soit come entité, soit comme activité pure, mais en tout cas comme fluide, inétendue, diaphane, vide de tout contenu proper... je crois, dis-je, que cette conscience est une pure chimère...*"

53. In the French: "*n'est... qu'une suite d'expériences intermédiaires parfaitement susceptibles d'être décrites en termes concrets.*"

54. In the French: "*...sont faites d'une même étoffe... que l'on peut nommer, si on veut, l'étoffe de l'expérience en general.*"

55. In the French: "*n'est... qu'une suite d'expériences intermédiaires parfaitement susceptibles d'être décrites en termes concrets.*"

56. Graham Harman, "The Third Table," in *The Book of Books*, ed. C. Christov Bakargiev. (Ostfildern, Germany: Hatje Cantz Verlag, 2012.) Pages 540-542.

57. A.S. Eddington, *The Nature of the Physical World*. (New York: MacMillan, 1929.)

58. "Simulation" henceforth replaces the term "confrontation" as introduced in Harman, *The Quadruple Object*, p. 111.

59. Martin Heidegger, "The Origin of the Work of Art." In *Off the Beaten Track*, trans. J. Young & K. Haynes. A(Cambridge, UK: Cambridge University Press, 2002.) pages 1-56.
60. The ATMOC website an be found at www.atmoc.fr/
61. Morelle's own lecture has already been published in English. See Louis Morelle, "Speculative Realism: After finitude, and beyond?", trans. L. Orth et al., *Speculations* III (2012), pp. 241-272.
62. http://www.atmoc.fr/files/archive-jan-2012.html
63. Tristan Garcia, *Form and Object: A Treatise on Things*, trans. M.A. Ohm & J. Cogburn. (Edinburgh: Edinburgh University Press, forthcoming 2014.)
64. Morelle, "Speculative Realism," p. 242.
65. Meillassoux, *After Finitude*, p. 5.
66. Morelle, "Speculative Realism," p. 248.
67. Morelle, "Speculative Realism," pp. 244-245.
68. Morelle, "Speculative Realism," p. 246.
69. See Tristan Garcia, *Forme et objet: Un traité des choses*. (Paris: Presses universitaires de France, 2011.)
70. See Dubouclez's choice of terminology in his translation of Harman, *L'Objet quadruple*.
71. Morelle, "Speculative Realism," p. 253.
72. Morelle, "Speculative Realism," p. 251.
73. Martin Heidegger, "The Thing," in *Poetry, Language, Thought*, trans. J.G. Gray. (New York: HarperCollins, 1971.) Pages 161-184.
74. Morelle, "Speculative Realism," p. 254.
75. Morelle, "Speculative Realism," p. 253.
76. Brassier, "Concepts and Objects."
77. Morelle, "Speculative Realism," p. 255.
78. Recall William James's failed attempt to answer this question as descibed in Chapter 4 above.
79. Serbian version of "Speculative Realism" conference (R. Brassier, I.H. Grant, G. Harman, & Q. Meillassoux)

broadcast as radio drama with voice actors on Radio Belgrade 3, on January 20, 2012. See the website at http://www.rts.rs/page/radio/sr/story/1466/Radio+Beograd +3/1027814/Spekulativni+realizam.html

80. Bruno Latour, "Irreductions," p. 162, in The Pasteurization of France, trans. A. Sheridan & J. Law. (Cambridge, MA: Harvard University Press, 1988.)

81. The term was first coined by Ian Bogost, "Alien Phenomenology: Toward a Pragmatic Speculative Realism." Plenary address at the annual conference of the Society for Literature, Science, and the Arts. Atlanta, GA, November 5-7, 2009. Bogost has also written an amusing web-based "Latour Litanizer" that randomly selects Wikipedia article topics to create Latour Litanies on demand. See http://www.bogost.com/blog/latour_litanizer. shtml

82. Latour, The Pasteurization of France, p. 163.

83. Brassier, "Concepts and Objects," p. 52.

84. See Bruno Latour, Aramis or the Love of Technology, trans. C. Porter. (Cambridge, MA: Harvard University Press, 1996.)

85. Manuel DeLanda, A New Philosophy of Society: Assemblage Theory and Social Complexity. (London: Continuum, 2006.)

86. Bruno Latour, We Have Never Been Modern, trans. C. Porter. (Cambridge, MA : Harvard University Press, 1993.)

87. Bruno Latour, Pandora's Hope: Essays on the Reality of Science Studies. (Cambridge, MA : Harvard University Press, 1999.) Page 122.

88. See Graham Harman, "On Interface: Nancy's Weights and Masses" in Jean-Luc Nancy and Plural Thinking: Expositions of World, Politics, Art, and Sense^, ed. P. Gratton and M.-È. Morin. (Albany: SUNY Press, 2012.) Pages 95-108.

89. Ludwig Wittgenstein, Tractatus Logico-Philosophicus, trans. C.K. Ogden. (New York: Cismo, 2009.) Page 29.

90. Alfred North Whitehead, Process and Reality. (New York:

Free Press, 1978.) Page 29.

91. James Ladyman & Don Ross, *Every Thing Must Go: Metaphysics Naturalized.* (Oxford : Oxford University Press, 2007.)

92. Dennett, "Real Patterns."

93. Peter van Inwagen, *Material Beings.* (Ithaca, NY: Cornell University Press, 1990.)

94. David Chalmers, *The Conscious Mind: In Search of a Fundamental Theory.* (Oxford: Oxford University Press, 1996.)

95. Given that mid-sized objects are eliminated from Chalmers's ontology, it is also unclear why consciousness should be associated with mid-sized objects such as thermostats, animal bodies, or anything else. On his view, only physical simples (whatever those might be) should have consciousness.

96. For Latour's lengthiest defense of the plasma, see pages 243-244 of Bruno Latour, *Reassembling the Social: An Introduction to Actor-Network*-Theory. (Oxford: Oxford University Press, 2005.) For my critique of this notion, see Harman, *Prince of Network.*

97. Garcia, *Forme et objet.*

98. Michael Pollan, *In Defense of Food: An Eater's Manifesto.* (London: Penguin, 2008.)

99. These ideas were developed in Harman, "The Well-Wrought Broken Hammer."

100. See the opening sections of Whitehead, *Process and Reality.*

101. This idea was later developed in Harman, "The Third Table."

102. Theodor Nelson, *Computer Lib/Dream Machines.* (Self-published, 1974.)

103. Marshall McLuhan, "Playboy Interview: 'Marshall McLuhan— A Candid Conversation with the High Priest of Popcult and Metaphysician of Media," in *Essential McLuhan,*

E. McLuhan & F. Zingrone (eds.). (Concord: House of Anansi Press, 1995.) Page 238.

104. Marshall & Eric McLuhan, *Laws of Media: The New Science.* (Toronto: University of Toronto Press, 1988.)

105. Edgar Allan Poe, "The Purloined Letter," in *Poetry and Tales.* (New York: Library of America, 1984.) Page 412.

106. See for example Ladyman & Ross, *Every Thing Must Go.* The authors try to pre-empt the polemical use of the term "scientism" by sneering in advance against those who might use it. But their very use of the term to define their own position also amounts to authorizing others to use it.

107. See especially Harman, *Tool-Being.*

108. See Marshall McLuhan & Wilfrid Watson, *From Cliché to Archetype.* (Berkeley, CA: Gingko Press, 2011.)

109. Clement Greenberg, *Late Writings.* (Minneapolis: University of Minnesota Press, 2007.) Page 28. Emphasis added.

110. Percy Bysshe Shelley, from the poem "To Jane: The Keen Stars Were Twinkling."

111. Saul Kripke, *Naming and Necessity.* (Cambridge, MA : Harvard University Press, 1980.)

112. Harman, *Guerrilla Metaphysics.*

113. Latour, *We Have Never Been Modern.*

114. Imre Lakatos, *The Methodology of Scientific Research Programs.* (Cambridge, UK : Cambridge University Press, 1980.) In the lecture itself I referred to Thomas Kuhn, whom I now replace in this printed version with the even clearer case of Lakatos, who notes the *vast* number of anomalies in the Newtonian theory prior to Einstein.

115. See Graeme Wood, "Re-Engineering the Earth," *Atlantic Magazine*, July/August 2009. http://www.theatlantic.com/magazine/archive/2009/07/re-engineering-the-earth/307552/

116. See Chapter 8 of the present book, "Everything is Not Connected."

117. Graham Harman, "The Problem with Metzinger," *Cosmos and History*, Vol. 7, No. 1, 2011, pp. 7-36.
118. Harman, "I Am Also of the Opinion That Materialism Must Be Destroyed."
119. Ladyman & Ross, *Every Thing Must Go*, p. 9.
120. Carlo Rovelli, "Halfway Through the Woods," in J. Earman & J. Norton (eds.), *The Cosmos of Science: Essays of Exploration*. (Pittsburgh: University of Pittsburgh Press, 1997.) Page 182.
121. While I am unable to locate the exact source of this quotation, the words are almost surely my own, given their style and content.
122. Tristan Garcia, *La meilleure part des hommes*. (Paris: Gallimard, 2008.) Available in English translation as *Hate: A Romance*, trans. M. Duvert & L. Stein. (New York: Faber & Faber, 2010.)
123. DeLanda, *Intensive Science and Virtual Philosophy*.
124. Professor Jon Cogburn of Louisiana State University is leading the effort to establish the English mirror site at http://atmoc.wordpress.com/introduction-to-the-workshop/
125. English translations from *Forme et objet* are drawn from the Mark Allan Ohm/Jon Cogburn draft translation of the early portions of Garcia's book. Translations from Garcia's Meinong lecture are my own.
126. Tristan Garcia, "Aprés Meinong: Une autre théorie de l'objet." Both the text and a recording of Garcia's lecture are available as Séance 23 on the ATMOC website, http://www.atmoc.fr/seances/
127. Markus Gabriel & Slavoj Žižek, *Mythology, Madness, and Laughter: Subjectivity in German Idealism*. (London: Continuum, 2009.) Page 5.
128. For Žižek's praise of Metzinger see *The Parallax View*. (Cambridge, MA: MIT Press, 2006.) For my critique of him see Harman, "The Problem with Metzinger."

129. Slavoj Žižek, *Tarrying with the Negative: Kant, Hegel, and the Critiaue of Ideology.* (Durham, NC: Duke University Press, 1993.)

130. Levi R. Bryant, "Actants, Ontology, and Epistemology." blog post of February 19, 2010. http://larvalsubjects. wordpress.com/2010/02/19/actants-ontology-and-epistemology/

131. This was indeed the title of the current chapter when it was presented as a lecture in Russia.

132. See Levi R. Bryant, "The Ontic Principle: Outlines of an Object-Oriented Ontology," in L.R. Bryant et al. (eds.), *The Speculative* Turn, pp. 261-278.

133. For a discussion of Latour's masterful use of Joliot as an example of causal mediation, see Harman, *Prince of Networks.* Latour's discussion of the problem is covered on pp. 73-79, and my critique of Latour's solution can be found on pp. 144-147.

134. An early version of these thoughts were posted on my blog on May 30, 2012 in a post entitled "on Bryant's philosophy." See http://doctorzamalek2.wordpress.com/2012/05/30/on-bryants-philosophy/

135. For a biological analogy to this claim, see Lynn Margulis, *Symbiotic Planet : A New Look at Evolution.* (New York : Basic Books, 1998.)

136. N. Eldredge & S. J. Gould, "Punctuated equilibria: An alternative to phyletic gradualism," in *Models in Paleobiology,* ed. T. Schopf. (San Francisco: Freeman Cooper & Co., 1972).

137. Graham Harman, "Greenberg and Duchamp," *Speculations* V, forthcoming 2013.

138. Marshall & Eric McLuhan, *Laws of Media: The New Science.* (Toronto : University of Toronto Press, 1988.) Page 5.

139. Marshall & Eric McLuhan, *Laws of Media,* p. 5.

140. Marshall McLuhan, *Understanding Media: The Extensions of Man.* (Cambridge, MA : MIT Press, 1994.)

141. Marshall & Eric McLuhan, *Laws of Media*, p. 7.

142. Marshall & Eric McLuhan, *Laws of Media*, pp. 190-191.

143. Marshall & Eric McLuhan, *Laws of Media*, pp. 184-185.

144. Marshall & Eric McLuhan, *Laws of Media*, pp. 198-199.

145. Marshall & Eric McLuhan, *Laws of Media*, p. 206.

146. Marshall & Eric McLuhan, *Laws of Media*, pp. 190-191.

147. Marshall & Eric McLuhan, *Laws of Media*, pp. 184-185.

148. Marshall & Eric McLuhan, *Laws of Media*, pp. 198-199.

149. Marshall & Eric McLuhan, *Laws of Media*, p. 206.

150. Marshall & Eric McLuhan, *Laws of Media*, pp. 184-185.

151. Marshall & Eric McLuhan, *Laws of Media*, p. 206.

152. Marshall & Eric McLuhan, *Laws of Media*, p. 5.

153. Marshall & Eric McLuhan, *Laws of Media*, p. 5.

154. Gilles Deleuze, "Letter to a Harsh Critic," in *Negotiations: 1972-1990*, trans. M. Joughin. (New York: Columbia University Press, 1995.)

155. See Latour, *Pandora's Hope.* 80-92. For my previously published summary of the metaphysical problems with Latour's interpretation of Joliot as a causal mediator, see Harman, *Prince of Networks*, pp. 146-147.

156. DeLanda, *Intensive Science and Virtual Philosophy.*

157. Bhaskar, *A Realist Theory of Science.*

158. Graham Harman, "Prefácio/Preface," in *Approach*, ed. G. Utrabo et al. Portuguese version translated by Hugo Loss. (Curitiba, Brazil: Edicão independente, 2012.) Pages 12-25.

159. Jacques Derrida, "The Spatial Arts: An Interview with Jacques Derrida," in *Deconstruction and the Visual Arts: Art, Media, Architecture*, ed. P. Brunette & D. Wills. (Cambridge, UK: Cambridge University Press, 1994.) Page 11.

160. Erik Ghenoiu, "The World is Not Enough," *tarp Architecture Manual*, Spring 2012, p. 4.

161. Ghenoiu, "The World is Not Enough," p. 6.

162. Ghenoiu, "The World is Not Enough," p. 7.

163. Ghenoiu, "The World is Not Enough," p. 7.

164. Sarah Ruel-Bergeron, "Cheat Sheet," *tarp Architecture Manual*, Spring 2012, p. 9.

165. David Ruy, "Returning to (Strange) Objects," *tarp Architecture Manual*, Spring 2012, p. 38.

166. Ruy, "Returning to (Strange) Objects," p. 38.

167. Ruy, "Returning to (Strange) Objects," p. 39.

168. Ruy, "Returning to (Strange) Objects," p. 39.

169. Ruy, "Returning to (Strange) Objects," p. 39.

170. Ruy, "Returning to (Strange) Objects," p. 40.

171. Ruy, "Returning to (Strange) Objects," pp. 40-41.

172. Ruy, "Returning to (Strange) Objects," p. 42.

173. Patrik Schumacher, "Architecture's Next Ontological Innovation," *tarp Architecture Manual*, Spring 2012, pp. 100-107.

174. Schumacher, "Architecture's Next Ontological Innovation," p. 100.

175. Schumacher, "Architecture's Next Ontological Innovation," p. 102.

176. Schumacher, "Architecture's Next Ontological Innovation," p. 103.

177. Schumacher, "Architecture's Next Ontological Innovation," p. 103.

178. See the remarkable Chapter 4 of Levi R. Bryant, *The Democracy of Objects*. (Ann Arbor, MI: Open Humanities Press, 2011.)

179. Schumacher, "Architecture's Next Ontological Innovation," p. 101.

180. Schumacher, "Architecture's Next Ontological Innovation," p. 101.

181. Patrick Schumacher, "Schumacher Slams British Architectural Education," January 31, 2012, http://www.architectural-review.com/view/overview/schumacher-slams-british-architectural-education/8625659.article

182. Schumacher, "Schumacher Slams British Architectural

Education."
183. Schumacher, "Schumacher Slams British Architectural Education."
184. Schumacher, "Schumacher Slams British Architectural Education."
185. Schumacher, "Schumacher Slams British Architectural Education."
186. Graham Harman, "The Well-Wrought Broken Hammer."
187. Žižek and I were both faculty members at the Third International Summer School in German Philosophy, with the theme "The Ontological Turn in Contemporary Philosophy," held at Bonn University from July 2-13, 2012. Prof. Markus Gabriel was the organizer of this excellent gathering.
188. Bhaskar, *A Realist Theory of Science.*
189. David Coggins, "Secret Powers: An Interview with Joanna Malinowska," *ArtNet Magazine,* http://www.artnet.com/magazineus/features/coggins/joanna-malinowska1-15-10.asp#
190. Harman, "The Well-Wrought Broken Hammer."
191. See the exhibition catalog, Bruno Latour & Peter Weibel, *Making Things Public: Atmospheres of Democracy.* (Cambirdge, MA : MIT Press, 2005.)
192. Excerpts in English from the unpublished French thesis by Quentin Meillassoux, *The Divine Inexistence,* can be found in the Appendix to Harman, *Quentin Meillassoux: Philosophy in the Making,* pp. 175-238.
193. G.W. Leibniz, "Primary Truths," pp. 30-31, in G.W. Leibniz, *Philosophical Essays,* trans. R. Ariew & D. Garber. (Indianapolis: Hackett, 1989.)
194. Leibniz, "Primary Truths," p. 31.
195. Leibniz, "Primary Truths," p. 32.
196. Leibniz, "Primary Truths," p. 32. Italics modified.
197. Leibniz, "Primary Truths," p. 33. Italics modified.

198. Martin Heidegger, *The Principle of Reason*, trans. R. Lilly. (Bloomington, IN : Indiana University Press, 1991.) Page 8.

199. Quentin Meillassoux, *After* Finitude, p. 71.

200. See the excerpts from Meillassoux's unpublished *The Divine Inexistence* in Graham Harman, *Quentin Meillassoux: Philosophy in the Making.*

201. Graham Priest, *Beyond the Limits of Thought.* (Oxford : Oxford University Press, 2002.) Page 5.

202. Priest, *Beyond the Limits of Thought*, p. 248.

203. Twardowski, *On the Content and Object of Presentations.*

204. Husserl, "Intentional Objects."

205. Henri Bergson, *Matter and Memory*, trans. N. M. Paul & W. S. Palmer. (New York: Dover, 2004.)

206. For a discussion of the metaphysics of James, see Chapter 4 of the present book.

207. See my discussion of Merleau-Ponty in Chapter 4 of Harman, *Guerrilla Metaphysics.*

208. Derrida, *Of Grammatology*, p. 61.

209. Derrida, *Of Grammatology*, pp. 22-23. Emphasis removed.

210. Slavoj Žižek & Glyn Daly, *Conversations with Žižek.* (Cambridge, UK: Polity Press, 2004.) Page 97. Emphasis added.

211. George Berkeley, *A Treatise Concerning the Principles of Human Knowledge*, §4. (Indianapolis: Hackett Publishing, 1982.)

212. Slavoj Žižek, *The Ticklish Subject: The Absent Center of Political Ontology*, p. 36. (London: Verso, 1999.)

213. See also Braver, *A Thing of This World.*

214. See Harman, *Tool-Being.*

215. For a critical assessment of Badiou's relation to Heidegger, see Graham Harman, "Badiou's Relation to Heidegger in *Theory of the Subject*," in *Badiou and Philosophy*, ed. S. Bowden & S. Duffy. (Edinburgh: Edinburgh University Press, 2012.) Pages 225-243.

216. Meillassoux, *After Finitude*, p. 9.

217. Meillassoux, *After Finitude*, p. 9.

218. Meillassoux, *After Finitude*, p. 13.

219. Meillassoux, *After Finitude*, p. 14.

220. Meillassoux's remarks can be found in Ray Brassier et al., "Speculative Realism," *Collapse* III (2007), pp. 306–449.

221. Harman, *Quentin Meillassoux: Philosophy in the Making*.

222. Meillassoux, *After Finitude*, p. 6.

223. Meillassoux, *After Finitude*, pp. 54-59.

224. Meillassoux, *After Finitude*, p. 60.

225. See the excerpts from Quentin Meillassoux, *The Divine Inexistence*, on pp. 175-238 of Harman, *Quentin Meillassoux: Philosophy in the Making*.

226. Meillassoux, *After Finitude*, p. 3.

227. Meillassoux, *After Finitude*, p. 12.

228. See Harman, *Tool-Being*.

229. See also Harman, "Badiou's Relation to Heidegger in *Theory of the Subject*."

230. Martin Heidegger, *Kant and the Problem of Metaphysics*, trans. R. Taft. (Bloomington, IN : Indiana University Press, 1997); Braver, *A Thing of This World*.

231. See "Interview with Quentin Meillassoux (August 2010)," trans. G. Harman, in Harman, *Quentin Meillassoux: Philosophy in the Making*, pp. 159-174.

232. See Priest's reading of Hegel in Priest, *Beyond the Limits of Thought*, pp. 102-109.

233. David Stove, *The Plato Cult and Other Philosophical Follies*. (Oxford : Blackwell, 1991.)

234. Priest, *Beyond the Limits of Thought*, p. 246.

235. See Max Black, "Metaphor," in *Models and Metaphors*. (Ithaca, NY: Cornell University Press, 1962); Jose Ortega y Gasset, "Essay in Esthetics by Way of a Preface," in *Phenomenology and Art*. trans. P. Silver. (New York: Norton, 1975.)

236. Aristotle, *Metaphysics*, trans. J. Sachs. (Santa Fe, NM : Green Lion Press, 2002.) Page 145. For a fuller treatment of Aristotle in this connection, see Graham Harman, "Aristotle With a Twist," in *Speculative Medievalisms: Discography*, ed. E.A. Joy et al. (Brooklyn, NY: punctum books, 2013.) Pages 227-253.

237. Whitehead, *Process and Reality*, p. 6.

238. For Meillassoux's views on the "rich elsewhere," see his remarks beginning on page 423 of Ray Brassier et al., "Speculative Realism," *Collapse* III (2007), pp. 306-449.

239. Quoted from Heidegger, *The Principle of Reason*, pp. 35 ff.

240. The most celebrated recent defense of the "pre-individual" can be found in Simondon, *L'individuation à la lumière des notions de forme et d'information*.

241. Heidegger, *Being and Time*, p. 1.

242. Hubert Dreyfus, *Being in the World: A Commentary on Heidgger's* Being and Time, *Division One*. (Cambridge, MA: MIT Press, 1991.)

Contemporary culture has eliminated both the concept of the public and the figure of the intellectual. Former public spaces – both physical and cultural – are now either derelict or colonized by advertising. A cretinous anti-intellectualism presides, cheerled by expensively educated hacks in the pay of multinational corporations who reassure their bored readers that there is no need to rouse themselves from their interpassive stupor. The informal censorship internalized and propagated by the cultural workers of late capitalism generates a banal conformity that the propaganda chiefs of Stalinism could only ever have dreamt of imposing. Zer0 Books knows that another kind of discourse – intellectual without being academic, popular without being populist – is not only possible: it is already flourishing, in the regions beyond the striplit malls of so-called mass media and the neurotically bureaucratic halls of the academy. Zer0 is committed to the idea of publishing as a making public of the intellectual. It is convinced that in the unthinking, blandly consensual culture in which we live, critical and engaged theoretical reflection is more important than ever before.